SPEAK LOUDLY

AND CARRY A LITTLE STICK

SPEAK LOUDLY

AND CARRY A LITTLE STICK

A Conductor's Chronicles

JOHN R. GIORDANO

TCU Press
Fort Worth, Texas

Library of Congress Cataloging-in-Publication Data

Names: Giordano, John, 1937- author.
Title: Speak loudly and carry a little stick : a conductor's chronicles / John R. Giordano.
Description: Fort Worth, Texas : TCU Press, [2020] | Includes index. | Summary: "In 1965, John Giordano auditioned for Ezra Rachlin, the music director for the Fort Worth and Austin Symphony Orchestras, by playing a concerto with each. As a result of the audition, Rachlin engaged Giordano to perform with both orchestras and offered him the assistant conductor position with the Fort Worth Youth Orchestra. The results of that serendipitous audition proved to be the impetus for Giordano's grand career in symphonic orchestral conducting and led to his long-term relationship with both the Fort Worth Symphony Orchestra and the Van Cliburn International Piano Competition. Speak Loudly and Carry a Little Stick: A Conductor's Chronicles tells the story of the development of the FWSO and the Cliburn competition as the internationally renowned conductor John Giordano knew them. These humorous and often enlightening chronicles give readers insight into the expansion of the FWSO and the Cliburn during Giordano's tenure. Giordano's musical career and adventures carried him all over the world, from China and Russia to Amsterdam and Mexico, and gave him an opportunity to play with musical greats such as Ella Fitzgerald and Tony Bennett. Through friendships with these talented artists and international figures and through his relationship with music, Giordano proves how critically important music is to our society and how music can positively impact a community. -- JOHN GIORDANO is a conductor, performer, composer, arranger, and teacher. He was music director of the Fort Worth Symphony Orchestra from 1972 until 2000, founder of the Fort Worth Chamber Orchestra, jury chairman of the Van Cliburn International Piano Competition from 1973 until 2013, and music director of the Corpus Christi Symphony for twelve seasons. He is currently music director emeritus of the Fort Worth Youth Orchestra and a retired distinguished fellow in music at TCU"-- Provided by publisher.
Identifiers: LCCN 2020026919 | ISBN 9780875657608 (cloth)
Subjects: LCSH: Giordano, John, 1937- | Fort Worth Symphony Orchestra--History. | Van Cliburn International Piano Competition--History. | Conductors (Music)--Texas--Fort Worth--Biography. | LCGFT: Autobiographies.
Classification: LCC ML422.G49 A3 2020 | DDC 784.2092 [B]--dc23
LC record available at https://lccn.loc.gov/2020026919

Design by FUSION29

TCU Press

TCU Box 298300
Fort Worth, Texas 76129
www.prs.tcu.edu
To order books: 1.800.826.8911

To Mary Alice, with all my love

INTRODUCTION

For someone who would later in life interact and perform with luminaries such as Van Cliburn, Itzhak Perlman, and Mstislav Rostropovich and become friends with many more of the world's greatest artists, I had humble beginnings. I grew up in Upstate New York and Erie, Pennsylvania, and I never imagined that I would have a career in classical music. I was actually interested in electrical engineering. As fate would have it though, I was destined to become a symphony orchestra conductor and be a part of one of the most prestigious international piano competitions and travel the world.

In 1973, my young family had only been living in Fort Worth for a few days; we moved from Denton, where I had been teaching at the University of North Texas for seven years. My contract as music director of the Fort Worth Symphony had been renewed after my one-year trial contract in 1972, and we just were settling into our new life. It had been a mild summer, but little did I know, my career was about to heat up.

On September 16, my friend Catherine Russell, manager of the Van Cliburn International Piano Competition, called me. Catherine was the daughter of Grace Ward Lankford, one of the founders of the competition.

"John, we have an emergency with the Van Cliburn Competition and desperately need your help," she said. "The competition begins tomorrow and Howard Hanson, the chairman of the jury, has suddenly become ill. We need a replacement for him. Could you please help us out?"

Thus my careers with the Fort Worth Symphony Orchestra and the Van Cliburn International Piano Competition took off and soared.

ONE

My Music Education

My Introduction to Music

My early musical training began in Erie, Pennsylvania, at twelve years old when I enrolled in the instrumental music program in the public schools there. After studying the fundamentals of playing the saxophone, I learned to play by ear, coached by my father.

My father, who was from Fredonia, New York, graduated from the University of Rochester with a degree in art. He was a talented portrait and still-life artist. In 1947, he was commissioned to paint murals for several exhibits in the Buffalo, New York, zoo. Some remain to this day.

My mother, Mildred Letersky Giordano, was of Polish and Lithuanian descent and was reared in Dunkirk, New York. After the family moved to Fort Worth in 1953, she served as credit manager of the Haltom City State Bank for thirty years.

I have a sister, Carol Giordano Maid, who received her bachelor's degree from TCU. She is seven years younger than I and was eight when we moved to Texas.

From an early age, I gleaned important musical insights from my father and godfather, Dominic Guzzetta, that later influenced me as a performer and conductor. Dom was a saxophonist and clarinetist who worked his way through his entire education playing jazz in various ensembles. He served as president of the University of Akron for thirteen years. I emulated Dom as much as possible and studied clarinet and saxophone.

My father's hobby was playing guitar, primarily playing popular music of the day, and he influenced my early musical development. He could play any song after he heard it once and had a terrific sense of harmony and rhythm. He accompanied me on his guitar and taught me to play the popular songs of the day by ear. He insisted I sing the song's melody, learn its harmony, and memorize the lyrics. The most perfect instrument is the human voice, and the credit for my understanding that goes to my father. I always tried to emulate the voice as a performer and conductor.

"Johnny, it's impossible to play a song properly if you don't know the words and the chords. You should sing the tune in your head while you are playing," he would say to me.

He insisted that I sing the melody and harmonize with him, but I never have been able to sing well. That frustrated him, and he frequently became upset when I sang out of tune (which was most of the time).

"Johnny, what's the matter with you? Don't

you know you are singing the same notes I am? You're supposed to be harmonizing!"

My singing never improved much. In spite of that, in rehearsals for the Fort Worth Symphony Orchestra I often attempted to sing the phrasing I wanted the group to play. During one such rehearsal when I was singing phrases, the composer and trombonist Lew Gillis raised his hand and said, "Please don't sing, John, just tell us what you want!" Even that incident hasn't deterred me from my singing attempts.

LEFT
My father, John C. Giordano.
Author Collection.

LEFT
My mother, Mildred.
Author Collection.

My Formal Music Education

I began my musical trajectory as a high school band student.

When I entered Millcreek High School (now McDowell High School) in Erie, Pennsylvania, I learned that every band member was required to play in the marching band.

Weather in Erie during winter months is extremely cold and brings an inordinate amount of snow and ice. The football team played and the band marched during the halftime regardless of the weather. Sometimes our reeds were almost frozen. We had to wear gloves, and the yard markers were completely obscured—but still, we marched on!

After a painful, frostbitten freshman year of high school, I decided the marching band was not for me. I complained to one of my close friends who played viola in the school orchestra.

"Why don't you play in the orchestra, Johnny?" my friend suggested. "The rehearsal schedule conflicts with marching band. That gives you an out."

"What would I play? There are no saxes in the orchestra."

"You could learn viola. We desperately need more violists. The viola parts are the easiest of any in the string section, especially in the music we play."

ABOVE
Dominic Guzzetta, my cousin and godfather. Author Collection.

RIGHT
In 2018 my sister Carol Giordano Maid and I traveled to Valledolmo, Sicily, the family's village of origin, to research our ancestry. Author collection.

"Great idea, except there is one tiny problem: I don't have a viola and can't play it."

"The school has some. You can check one out for the summer, and I'll teach you."

It turned out to be a good solution; I could play viola in the orchestra and saxophone and/or clarinet in the concert band. I didn't realize it at the time, but learning viola proved to be invaluable for composing and conducting. In addition to becoming familiar with a string instrument's technique, I learned alto clef. (Viola plays in alto clef most of the time. Every other instrument's basic clef is treble or bass.) I could play the easier viola parts acceptably well enough by the time school started. My friend coached me after school a few times every week during the school year.

When I was growing up, unlike now, that era's popular music contained melodies and interesting harmony that changed frequently. Today's pop songs have a simple harmony that changes infrequently. "Big bands" of the time performed songs of that era. Musicians like Harry James, Tommy Dorsey, Les Brown, and Stan Kenton toured throughout the United States playing in ballrooms and concert venues.

My musician friends and I formed a band and called it Johnny Roberts and the Dance Kings. (I was Johnny and another member was, not surprisingly, Robert.) We had three trumpets, one trombone, four saxes, a piano, bass, and drums, and we played weekly for dances in the YMCA gym and the local Methodist church.

High School in Texas

After my sophomore year at Millcreek High School, my father announced that we were moving to Texas because it meant a promotion for him with Bell Helicopter as head of its Technical Publications Department. He explained that the position also afforded him the opportunity to make better use of his artistic talent. But I was devastated.

The news depressed me because I imagined Texas to be an unbearably hot, remote, and undeveloped desert where only cowboys and livestock lived. A member of our band who had recently visited Texas corroborated my perception:

"It's an awful place—an ugly, unbearably hot barren desert. Man, I really feel sorry for you. It's like hell on earth."

That statement was the final blow. It convinced me that I was going to spend my last two years of high school in hell. Luckily, it turned out, he had exaggerated quite a bit.

We left our home in Erie and drove in our non-air-conditioned car to Fort Worth during the summer of 1953. As we drove through the streets of Fort Worth, we were accompanied by the sound of thousands of crickets being crunched under the tires.

Our home was in Birdville, a suburb of Fort Worth. It was a small three-bedroom frame house in a new development that was formerly a cow pasture. There wasn't a tree in sight. The entire pasture hadn't been developed yet, and cattle still grazed on the other side of our backyard link fence. Everything confirmed my negative perception of Texas. My mother was the most upset of us all, especially when she opened the back door and saw a cow peering over the fence.

ABOVE
Pennsylvania All State Band. Author Collection.

"My God John, where have you taken us? I left my family, my friends, my lovely house, my garden, my beautiful trees for this hot, depressing hell hole?"

"Don't worry Millie, this house is temporary," my father said. "I bought it because it is new, less expensive than renting, and will give us some return on our money. I promise that we will have a much nicer home very soon."

I enrolled in Birdville High School and immediately sought a way to continue playing my instruments. I tried to sign up for band and orchestra, but there was no orchestra. I was forced to play in the marching band, as well as the concert band, and give up the viola (which was not necessarily a bad thing for those who had heard me play!).

Marching in the hundred-degree Texas heat on a dusty scorched football field replaced marching in Erie's ice and snow. Marching band is important in Texas, a state that has become famous for having some of the finest wind and percussion programs in the country, and everyone took it very seriously.

I developed a favorable perception of Texas public school music during my first rehearsal. The band director, Bill Bohannon, was a good musician, and the band performed well.

By the end of the fall semester I was appointed student assistant band director. I asked Mr. Bohannon to start a school jazz ensemble. He said that he was not qualified to direct a big band jazz ensemble and asked me to organize and lead it.

The band developed into a good ensemble and performed concerts for various functions in the community. The level of the ensemble reached an apex when it was named the top stage band in our division at the UIL Competition in Brownwood. I was presented an award as the most outstanding musician of the festival, an honor I still cherish.

The chairman of the jury that awarded the prize was Leon Breeden, a nationally acclaimed jazz clarinetist and saxophonist. He agreed to be my private teacher. He was a demanding and superb musician, a kind, sympathetic, and dedicated teacher to whom I attribute much of my early technical and artistic development. He demanded beautiful sound production, accurate intonation, and precise technique.

* * * * * *

I soon met Ronnie Martin, an outstanding high school trumpeter who attended Paschal High School in Fort Worth. He asked me to join his jazz quintet consisting of trumpet, saxophone, piano, bass, and drums.

We played for the weekly Pat Boone show on Channel 5, the local NBC television affiliate—a tremendous opportunity. In addition to backing up Pat, we accompanied his guests, who performed every style of music from country western to rhythm and blues and current pop songs. We had one brief rehearsal prior to the show and either played from the act's written arrangements or improvised an accompaniment.

Zanzibar Café and Night Club

My jazz experience was enriched even further when I began to play in jam sessions at the Zanzibar Café and Night Club, a Fort Worth after-hours club on East Rosedale Avenue in the older part of the city. It had been converted from a Baptist church to a jazz nightclub. The Zanzibar was well known in jazz circles as a place where some of the finest African American jazz musicians in the United States gathered after hours to play in informal jam sessions. Jazz greats such as Lionel Hampton, James Clay, David "Fathead" Newman, and Red Conner played regularly at the Zanzibar. The club offered me a unique opportunity to learn jazz by playing extemporaneously with musicians of an extremely high caliber. They were patient, helpful, and encouraging. I also met Ornette Coleman at the Zanzibar.

Ornette was older than I, and he was trying

to stretch the boundaries of traditional be-bop harmony and melody. Several years later he was recognized as one of the leaders of avant-garde jazz. Ornette explained to me that his odd arrangements weren't because he didn't understand the proper harmony or form of the songs, rather he wanted to experiment with extending their harmony and form. He eventually wrote his own songs in which this technique worked well. He called his theory "Harmolodics."

I developed a friendship with Ornette and found him to be very pleasant, intelligent, creative, quiet, soft spoken, and serious. He rarely smiled or laughed. He also loved opera.

Eventually I realized that, while I could improvise acceptably well, I was not on the same level with the finest jazz musicians. Playing jazz is an inspired gift and a skill that must be developed over years of diligent practice. I later had to make a choice between pursuing a career as a classical artist or honing my jazz skills. I chose the former.

The musicians at the Zanzibar suggested I learn to play the piano because it was the best way to understand and learn "changes." ("Changes" is a term that jazz musicians use to identify the harmonic structure of a song.) My parents bought a spinet piano on which I could practice. Practicing saxophone and clarinet in addition to my schoolwork left me little time to practice the piano. I took private lessons, but it was much too late to develop a proper technique. However, even with my limited ability, the piano proved to be invaluable when I began to arrange, compose, and study scores of classical works as a conductor.

My Professional Career Begins

Ted Weems Dance Band

In 1955, two weeks after graduating from high school, I auditioned for the Ted Weems Dance Band. The audition went well, and I was invited to join the band at the Midland Country Club. I played lead alto and doubled on clarinet and flute. From there we played at the Pleasure Pier in Galveston for a week. I was excited to learn that our next gig was The Blue Room of the Roosevelt Hotel in New Orleans. I had never been to New Orleans, but I had heard a lot about the city and knew that it was one of the jazz centers of the world. I played with well-known musicians there like Al Hirt, Ellis Marsalis, and Pete Fountain at the jam sessions.

Before one of our shows, I facetiously imitated Louis Armstrong, and Ted overheard me. He thought it would be an entertaining way to open the shows. He had Billy Gannon arrange "On the Sunny Side of the Street" and "I Met That Man from the South," featuring me singing in my Louis Armstrong imitation voice. He gave me the stage name of Johnny Jordan. It was bizarre to see "Johnny Jordan" on marques along with stars such as Ella Fitzgerald, Tony Bennett, The Four Freshmen, and Mel Tormé.

After the Roosevelt, our dance band toured throughout the US from coast to coast playing in Vegas, hotel ballrooms, and country clubs.

Jim Mitchell/Cannonball Adderly

When I was playing in Ted's band, I still harbored hope of becoming a top-flight jazz improviser. After a gig in St. Louis, my good friend Jim Mitchell, who was an accomplished jazz clarinetist and saxophonist, and I went to a late-night jam session at a nightclub in East St. Louis. We were greeted by the leader of the band, an African American saxophonist dressed in a white Arabian robe.

"Would you like to sit in?" he asked.

Jim told him we would.

"What would you like to play?"

Jim told him it didn't matter.

"How about 'Tea for Two'?" the leader of the band suggested.

We thought he was insulting us because jazz musicians consider "Tea for Two" to be a corny song.

We asked simply, "What key?"

"How about A flat?"

ABOVE
Ted Weems's big band, Blue Room of the Roosevelt Hotel, New Orleans.
Author Collection.

LEFT
Ted with the recording of "Big Man from the South."
Author Collection.

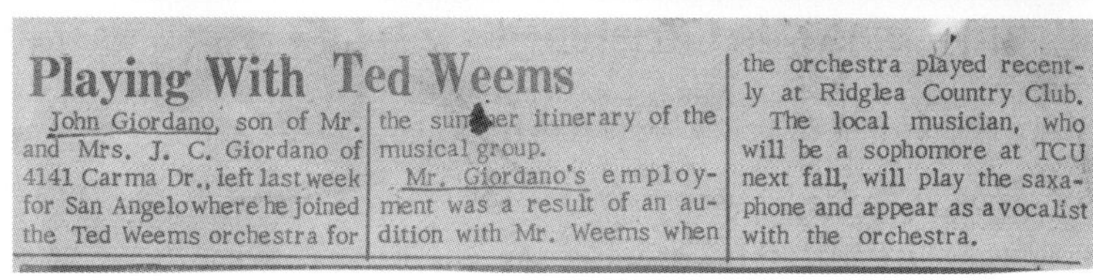

Playing With Ted Weems

John Giordano, son of Mr. and Mrs. J. C. Giordano of 4141 Carma Dr., left last week for San Angelo where he joined the Ted Weems orchestra for the summer itinerary of the musical group.

Mr. Giordano's employment was a result of an audition with Mr. Weems when the orchestra played recently at Ridglea Country Club.

The local musician, who will be a sophomore at TCU next fall, will play the saxaphone and appear as a vocalist with the orchestra.

ABOVE
Article that appeared in the Fort Worth Star-Telegram *regarding my joining the Ted Weems Band.*
© Fort Worth Star-Telegram, 1955.

A flat is the standard key for "Tea for Two." It is an awkward key in which to improvise for saxophone, but we didn't want to acknowledge that we had any weaknesses.

"That's fine, it doesn't matter," Jim responded.

He kicked off the song at a breakneck tempo and played the first solo. It was imaginative, technically flawless, exciting, and intimidating. After listening to him for a few minutes, I put my sax in its case and sat at our table. Hearing him improvise made me realize that this is a level of jazz musicianship I never will reach. At the next break he introduced himself.

"I'm Cannonball Adderley," he said as he approached our table. "Why didn't you play?"

"I'm John Giordano," I responded. "I have many of your records. It's an honor to meet you; I've admired your playing for a long time!"

"So why didn't you play?" he asked me.

"There is no way I can play after hearing you. I just want to sit here and enjoy listening to you," I responded.

Cannonball was a classically trained musician who taught school in Florida before becoming internationally recognized as one of the most prominent jazz saxophonists. We became close friends and stayed in touch. Several years later he gave a workshop for my students at the University of North Texas.

An Undergrad at TCU

After my summer of touring, I wanted to go to college, but I didn't know what major to pursue. I loved music, especially performing, but my cousin Dom—the saxophonist and clarinetist—encouraged me to pursue a different discipline and play music for enjoyment only.

"You can't make a living in music, Johnny," he said. "Just have fun with it and do something else to make money."

That struck a chord. In addition to music, I enjoyed science and mathematics. During my sophomore year of high school in Erie, I entered a Penn State science competition. My project, a robot, won in the electronics division, and I was awarded a scholarship to Penn State. I had seriously considered pursuing a career in electrical engineering at that time.

The move to Texas influenced me in a major way. I became more and more involved with music, both jazz and symphonic. My family had 78 rpm records of all the Brahms and Beethoven symphonies, as well as many other works that I listened to in addition to my jazz records. When we lived in Erie we attended Erie Philharmonic concerts and occasionally went to Cleveland to hear the Cleveland Orchestra. I was fascinated by the thrilling sounds of a symphony orchestra.

In the end, music won me over. I enrolled in TCU during the fall of 1955 and majored in music education, per a suggestion by a TCU counselor who said I should have something to fall back on in case I wasn't successful as a performer.

Hal McIntyre

In 1958, I decided to take a break from school and pursue more music adventures. Since Ted Weems retired after New Orleans and the band disbanded, Burr Linton, who played lead trombone with Ted, recommended me to Hal McIntyre to fill an opening in the sax section. Mac's band was much more jazz oriented than Ted's, and he was well known for having hired many of the best jazz musicians in the country, such as Carl Fontana, Barney Kessel, Larry Muhoberac, Phil Kelly, Mike Longo, and Eddie Safranski. His library was written by the finest arrangers.

Mac played lead alto with the original Glenn Miller Orchestra and was a musically demanding leader. It angered him when we didn't sight-read an arrangement perfectly.

We toured in almost every state east of the Mississippi River and many on the West Coast. We had the most difficult schedule imaginable: one day we would be in Memphis, the next in Norfolk, Virginia, and the next in Mobile, Alabama. We were convinced that our New York management threw darts at a map of the US

ABOVE
The TCU Horned Frog Band, 1960, Director Jim Jacobsen.
Courtesy of TCU Yearbooks. Special Collections, Mary Couts Burnett Library, Texas Christian University.

ABOVE
TCU Band fraternity Kappa Kappa Psi, 1957. Bottom Row (from left to right): Mr. Jim Jacobsen, sponsor; Hames Brezik, Bill Morgan, Ken Lawrence, James McDonough, Bobby Poer, Reuben Fechner. Top Row (from left to right): John Suddath, Barry White, John Carson, John Giordano, Paul Gray, J. O. Heath, Roger Martin, Wayne Fox, Don Filgo, Mackie Hines, Jerre Williams.
Courtesy of TCU Yearbooks. Special Collections, Mary Couts Burnett Library, Texas Christian University.

RIGHT
Joined Hal McIntyre Orchestra.
Author Collection.

once a week to make our schedule.

We spent one week in an engagement in the lounge at the Las Vegas Sands Hotel. What a week! We accompanied acclaimed artists such as Ella Fitzgerald, Tony Bennett, and Mel Tormé, and what a great learning experience that was. I developed a friendship with those artists, and those contacts proved to be important later in helping me to develop the Pops series of the Fort Worth Symphony Orchestra.

We also performed a State Department European tour, which was the first time I traveled abroad, and it was an extraordinary experience. We played in London, Paris, Munich, Frankfurt, Zurich, and several other smaller cities. It was only ten years after World War II, many places still were recovering, and Europe was unspoiled by American tourists. There were no American fast-food restaurants, few people spoke English, and the charm of the various cultures was still intact.

Upon returning to the US that summer, Mac told us we were going to record an album in Los Angeles. He added a few LA studio musicians. One was the legendary Conrad Gozzo, who was a great lead trumpet player. It was rumored that artists like Frank Sinatra scheduled their performances and recordings around his. The album was titled *It Seems Like Only Yesterday*. The album was tainted with tragedy, however. In 1959, an apartment fire broke out where Mac was staying in Los Angeles. Tragically, he died at the hospital a few days later. The album we recorded with Mac was released posthumously in 1959.

After we recorded the album that summer of 1958, I hung around LA for a while. Though my parents were supportive of my decision to leave school and perform, I had too much pride to ask them for monetary help, so I secured a job extrapolating music from orchestral scores at a music copying service located on Hollywood Boulevard and played occasional gigs on the weekends. (During that time there were no computers, and music was copied by hand with a special nib pen that had to be dipped in an inkwell.) I intended to stay in Los Angeles long enough to establish the residence requirements for the local union. While there, I became good friends with Bud Shank, a well-known jazz saxophonist and flutist who helped me out by recommending me for several jobs including substituting for him in recording sessions. Bud and I met at the LA Union, where they used to have big band sessions on Sundays. It was a great place to network, and we got to play music by stars like Quincy Jones. Studio musicians and arrangers/composers often did this for personal enjoyment, since playing commercial music and film scores could quickly become boring. I also became acquainted with jazz luminaries like Doc Severinsen, Bobby (Butter) Burgess, Stan Getz, Art Pepper, and John Williams. Those contacts, especially with Doc Severinsen and John Williams, later proved to be extremely helpful when I was music director of the Fort Worth Symphony Orchestra.

ABOVE
Playing with Stan Kenton.
Author Collection.

RIGHT
TCU Jazz Quartet concert review. © Fort Worth Star-Telegram, 1958.

12/2/58

'Musical' Jazz Skillfully Played

The musical scene witnessed something new Monday night in Ed Landreth Auditorium when the TCU Jazz Quartet presented a formal concert.

The players were John Giordano, flute, clarinet and alto saxophone; Charles Pearson, guitar; Ernest Repass, string bass, and Harold Dean, percussion. All the members are present or past students at TCU.

This is a flexible combination, completely self-contained without piano, trumpet or trombone, and with interchangeable woodwinds capable of many tonal colors.

This is something entirely surpassing, in instrumental and musical finish, the common, irresponsible jam session. These men are professionals in their field, some of them with national playing experience.

This is not jazz in the abominable Dixieland cacophony; this is musical. While the essence and the challenge of it is improvisation, it is by no means unorganized or uncalculated. Many of the most telling effects are studied. But each player in turn takes a variation, and thereupon does improvise, and therein lies the difference between the musician and the hepcat. What these men do makes sense, to the ear and the mind.

There are certain technical observations to be made. The players are not confined to one or two keys, but explore a number of tonalities, not neglecting the minor mode, which poses a new challenge, nearly approaching the old ecclesiastical modes.

Most of the program had local reference, in that the numbers were either arranged or composed by members of the group or other local players. One of the most atmospheric numbers was "Theme for a Dream" by James Ecker, local pianist. In "Journey," composed and arranged by Giordano, "Voodoo" arranged by Pearson, and "Two Degrees East," arranged by Repass, there was strikingly clever and authentic contrapuntal usage.

To this observer the most impressive numbers were the slow, mood pieces, so transparent that there was no chance for merely irresponsible faking. "Voodoo" and "Moonlight Becomes You," another Giordano arrangement, were such items.

To the attentive listener there was much more here than rhythm, urgent and complex as it was.

The audience was so large that programs ran out, and they remained to the end. Let these people show their sportsmanship by attending the next concert of formal music. It was observed that many music faculty members were present. They do not belittle this effort, when it is this resourceful.

—E. CLYDE WHITLOCK.

My Return to TCU

It was difficult to make ends meet in LA, even with the copying job and the occasional gigs on weekends. While I was at one of my occasional music gigs making little money, I finally decided that I needed to return to TCU to complete my undergraduate degree—and also to avoid the draft.

During an engagement in Fort Worth, I met Charlie Pearson, a student at Poly High School, a talented guitarist who played as well as most seasoned professionals. We became close friends and formed a jazz quartet consisting of guitar, bass, drums, and me. I played saxophone, clarinet, and flute. TCU did not have a jazz program at the time. Very few colleges, other than UNT, offered jazz studies. Charlie and I wrote most of the arrangements and original compositions for the group.

The quartet presented the first small ensemble jazz recital in TCU history. It was difficult to convince the music department director and my musicology professor, Dr. Michael Winesanker, to grant us permission to present the concert. Dr. Winesanker was a superb musician and a well-known musicologist who, as many classical musicians did then, believed that jazz was an art form that didn't belong in a music school. He eventually gave us permission but was certain that the concert would fail hopelessly.

He told us: "Don't be disappointed if the concert is not successful. We do not even attract large audiences for classical music. I seriously doubt that anyone will be interested in attending a jazz concert. Also, it cannot be sanctioned by the music department."

He was wrong; the university's performance hall, Ed Landreth Auditorium, which seats about 1,200, was completely sold out. The concert was successful from every aspect: it received great reviews and has been credited by the recent director of jazz studies at TCU, Curtis Wilson, with being instrumental in the acceptance of jazz at TCU and his development of the current nationally prominent jazz studies program.

My professional goals of becoming a studio musician and a composer/arranger were becoming more defined, and I focused on my formal studies, especially in courses relating to composition and performance. They later also proved to be invaluable in the development of my conducting skills.

* * * * * *

There were many musicians who influenced my artistic and personal development. The professional musicians with whom I worked were superb and didn't take themselves too seri-

The T. C. U. Jazz Quartet

John Giordano ----- Flute, Clarinet, Alto Saxophone
Charles Pearson--- Guitar
Ernest Repass----- Bass Violin
Harold Dean------- Percussion

The T. C. U. Jazz Quartet has been in existence less than a year, and actually came into being somewhat by accident. Originally, there was no intention of forming an organized quartet. Rather, the group has evolved as the result of informal sessions brought about by a common interest in jazz. Through experimentation at these sessions the possibilities of this combination of instruments began to present themselves. Interest in the group began to grow, and its members began writing and soliciting compositions and arrangements.

The instrumentation of the Quartet lends itself to a variety of tonal colors through the combination of guitar with the various woodwinds. The absence of a keyboard instrument in a jazz group is uncommon. Its role here is assumed by both the bass and guitar. When the guitar is used as a solo voice, the bass alone is responsible for outlining the basic harmonic structure. It is interesting to note that the bass and drums are often used melodically as well as rhythmically.

The Quartet stresses creativity. The arrangements are written with this in mind, and simply provide a framework within which the soloists can improvise with a minimum of restriction.

John Giordano

TCU's Symphonic Band Has One of Its Finest Concerts

BY WILLIAM J. MARSH.

Sunday afternoon in Ed Landreth Auditorium, the TCU Symphonic Band played one of its very finest concerts under the direction of James A. Jacobsen, who every year produces and trains better and better forces.

WILLIAM J. MARSH.

The program was chosen from newer and better material, projected with a flow of enthusiasm and sincerity quite intoxicating.

Paul Creston's "Celebration Overture Opus 61" was the first item, stressing unusual patterns, crisp and striking, with opportunities for fine shading, the whole being well developed. "Inglesina" Symphonic March by Delle Cese was another fresh number, given with clean precise effects.

From Frank Erickson's "Second Symphony for Band" came two movements rather similar in style but containing much finely written music in which the tone quality was beautifully handled.

An "American Overture for Band" by Joseph Jenkins was conducted by John Giordano in vigorous fashion and with complete control of his players.

The prelude and rondo from "Suite for Band,'" Opus 26, by Burnet Tuthill, lightly tripping in character, was followed by a richly harmonized transcription by Percy Grainger of the "Irish Tune From County Derry" known as the Londonderry Air. This delightfully melodious sketch received an almost reverent performance with the trombones alternating with woodwind section.

The most exciting moments however were during Rimsky-Korsakov's Cortege from "Mlada." Here were brilliance, technical display and swagger, depicting the procession of nobles in all its majesty and pomp.

Osterling's "Totem Pole Concert March" played with excellent intonation brought the old warhorse "Stars and Stripes For Ever" ending the concert in a blaze of glory with magnificent crescendo passages that would have made Sousa proud of his great march.

ously. If you didn't play up to a high standard, it was very simple: you weren't hired again. You were expected to be prompt, dress appropriately, sight-read the music accurately, play in tune with a good sound, blend with the ensemble, and be cordial.

TCU gave me the opportunity to play in the band, orchestra, and chamber music ensembles. The band director, Professor James Jacobsen, known affectionately as "Prof," chose me to be his student assistant director and gave me many opportunities to conduct the concert band. He also asked me to organize and direct a jazz big band.

Lew Gillis, a former TCU band director, was one of the most respected musicians in the Dallas/Fort Worth area. He often hired me for jobs, and through his recommendations I became acquainted with the best jazz musicians in the metroplex. I subsequently played with most of the big bands in the area such as Curly Broyles, Bill White, Sandy Sandifer, Don Thomas, and the legendary Harvey Anderson.

ABOVE
Review of a TCU band concert, my first conducting the band in a concert. © Fort Worth Star-Telegram, 1960.

ABOVE LEFT
TCU Jazz Quartet concert program. Author Collection.

RIGHT
First big band of the Jacobsen era at TCU, caption by Leon Breeden. Author Collection.

ABOVE
Mary Alice, my wife.
Author Collection.

Mary Alice

During my senior year at TCU, I met a young woman who proved to be the most influential and important person in my life, Mary Alice Dammann.

Mary Alice is extraordinarily talented. She could have majored in piano, voice, or art. She graduated with a degree in music education with an emphasis in vocal performance. Mary Alice has an exceptional mezzo soprano voice, and during her tenure at TCU she sang several leading roles in university-produced operas and musical comedies, in addition to roles with the Fort Worth Opera and Casa Mañana.

We met on a concert band recruiting tour during my senior year, in the spring of 1960. Prof Jacobsen, director of bands, asked the vocal faculty to recommend a female singer to feature on the tour. They recommended Mary Alice, and Prof asked her to sing "Bewitched, Bothered and Bewildered." She was the highlight of the tour, and it was a great opportunity to develop our friendship. We became engaged at the end of the spring semester and married on September 3, 1960.

Mary Alice has been my confidant, adviser, and best friend throughout my life. She has stood by my side through many difficult times—musical problems, career challenges, and health issues—and has contributed immeasurably to any success I have enjoyed.

RIGHT
Mary Alice Dammann, TCU graduation, 1960.
Courtesy of TCU Yearbooks. Special Collections, Mary Couts Burnett Library, Texas Christian University.

Graduate School, 1961–63

Because of my ROTC involvement, I had a required six months of active duty in the army and seven and a half years in the reserves.

After my active duty stint, Mary Alice and I returned to Fort Worth, and I enrolled in graduate school at TCU to pursue a major in composition. Mary Alice accepted a teaching position in a Fort Worth public school. She taught elementary music and every other imaginable course they assigned to her, including history and physical education. Her annual salary was $3,500 and was supplemented by her summer job as a singer in the Casa Mañana cast as well as by my professional engagements.

I accepted a position at TCU as the graduate assistant band director under Prof Jacobsen. The stipend covered my tuition and afforded me an opportunity to acquire invaluable conducting, composition, arranging, and organizational experience. I also was extremely fortunate to have had Dr. Ralph Guenther as my major professor. Dr. Guenther was a flutist, published composer, and highly regarded teacher who conducted the University Symphony Orchestra.

Prof Jacobsen was nationally recognized as a leading innovator of marching band drills. He and I decided to collaborate and create "Concerto for Marching Band." I composed a complicated seven-minute piece in a contemporary style that had intricate counterpoint and difficult mixed meter. Prof created a complex marching drill consisting of geometric patterns set to my music.

The result of our collaboration was poor entertainment for a football game halftime show. It was ridiculous to think that a modern sounding, esoteric piece of music accompanying an intricate marching drill would entertain thousands of football fans. It might have worked at a high school marching band contest exhibition for an audience of high school band students and their directors but not at a collegiate sports game.

LEFT
TCU ROTC Band Staff, 1959. From left to right: Frank W. Fox, drum major; Peggy Whatley, sponsor; Warrant Officer John R. Giordano, director. Courtesy of TCU Yearbooks. Special Collections, Mary Couts Burnett Library, Texas Christian University.

LEFT
TCU Band Director Jim "Prof" Jacobsen, 1959. Courtesy of TCU Yearbooks. Special Collections, Mary Couts Burnett Library, Texas Christian University.

Page 6 THE SKIFF Friday, September 29, 1961

Giordano Is First Assistant Director In History of Horned Frog Marchers

BY SUE MORTON

For the first time in its history the Horned Frog Band has an assistant director.

He is John Giordano, a 1960 graduate. This fall Giordano is working toward his masters degree in theory and composition while working as "laboratory assistant in band" in a half-time faculty position.

After receiving his Bachelor of Music Education in 1960 he was commissioned a second lieutenant in the Army in June, 1960, and served at Ft. Knox.

Giordano toured Europe while playing saxophone with the Hal McIntyre Orchestra. He also played with the Ted Weems' band in 1956. Asked about his tour of Europe four years ago, Giordano said that he was most impressed by the jazz bands. "The French had outstanding jazz musicians, but it seemed that many lacked the intangible feel of swing that the better American bands have. Germany and England also had very outstanding bands. We had several jam sessions with some of the musicians from Ted Heath's Band.

Appreciate More

"For the most part the European Jazz musician seems to approach his art much more seriously than the average American dance band musician," he commented.

"The impression that I received about most Europeans was that they seemed to appreciate more what jazz artists are doing than the average American does. They were more receptive to American jazz than were many of the American audiences here in the States," said Giordano.

Hal McIntyre, who formed this band, played lead saxophone with the original Glenn Miller Band and the original Benny Goodman Band. In the late 1940s the band had a big name. It was featured in several movies during this period. "One thing that many people don't know is that McIntyre sold more records of 'Sentimental Journey' than Les Brown. 'Glow Worm,' featuring the Mills Brothers, and 'Swanee River' were other big hits of the band."

Aug. 15, Giordano was selected to make a record album with Don Jacoby, the internationally famous trumpet player, and an All-Star Inter-Collegiate Band.

One student from each of sixteen colleges and universities throughout the United States made up the band. The record will be released sometime in October on the MGM label, according to Giordano.

Revives Program

With all this jazz experience Giordano has been placed in charge of re-activating the stage band program at TCU, which is a lab band designed to inspire young arrangers and composers.

"We hope to give students experience in this field, so that they would be qualified to perform in professional organizations in the future. It will also help give them a well-rounded musical education. We are trying to impress upon young musicians the need for learning to perform 'classical' music in conjunction with jazz," Giordano said.

As for the band prospects, Giordano says, "this year the band is capable of achieving a musical and marching quality that far surpasses that of recent years. We have a depth of quality performers in each section, which reaches to even the inner parts. This coupled with the high spirit the band has displayed so far this year will amalgamate to form an outstanding musical organization of which we can all be proud."

John Giordano, a 1960 graduate of the University, has returned to campus as assistant director of the Horned Frog Band. Giordano, who has toured Europe, has played in several orchestras.

ABOVE
Assistant director of the TCU band, clipping from the Skiff. Author Collection.

RIGHT
Review of the first classical saxophone recital at TCU. © Fort Worth Star-Telegram, 1961.

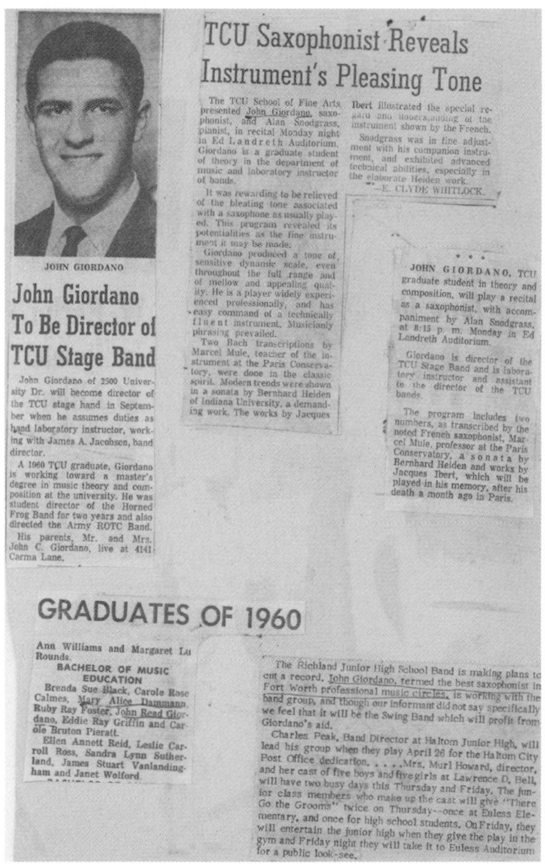

JOHN GIORDANO

John Giordano To Be Director of TCU Stage Band

John Giordano of 2500 University Dr. will become director of the TCU stage band in September when he assumes duties as band laboratory instructor, working with James A. Jacobsen, band director.

A 1960 TCU graduate, Giordano is working toward a master's degree in music theory and composition at the university. He was student director of the Horned Frog Band for two years and also directed the Army ROTC Band.

His parents, Mr. and Mrs. John C. Giordano, live at 4141 Carma Lane.

TCU Saxophonist Reveals Instrument's Pleasing Tone

The TCU School of Fine Arts presented John Giordano, saxophonist, and Alan Snodgrass, pianist, in recital Monday night in Ed Landreth Auditorium. Giordano is a graduate student of theory in the department of music and laboratory instructor of bands.

It was rewarding to be relieved of the bleating tone associated with a saxophone as usually played. This program revealed its potentialities as the fine instrument it may be made.

Giordano produced a tone of sensitive dynamic scale, even throughout the full range and of mellow and appealing quality. He is a player widely experienced professionally, and has easy command of a technically fluent instrument. Musicianly phrasing prevailed.

Two Bach transcriptions by Marcel Mule, teacher of the instrument at the Paris Conservatory, were done in the classic spirit. Modern trends were shown in a sonata by Bernhard Heiden of Indiana University, a demanding work. The works by Jacques Ibert illustrated the special regard and understanding of the instrument shown by the French.

Snodgrass was in fine adjustment with his companion instrument, and exhibited advanced technical abilities, especially in the elaborate Heiden work.

—E. CLYDE WHITLOCK.

* * *

JOHN GIORDANO, TCU graduate student in theory and composition, will play a recital as a saxophonist, with accompaniment by Alan Snodgrass, at 8:15 p. m. Monday in Ed Landreth Auditorium.

Giordano is director of the TCU Stage Band and is laboratory instructor and assistant to the director of the TCU bands.

The program includes two numbers, as transcribed by the noted French saxophonist, Marcel Mule, professor at the Paris Conservatory, a sonata by Bernhard Heiden and works by Jacques Ibert, which will be played in his memory, after his death a month ago in Paris.

GRADUATES OF 1960

Ann Williams and Margaret Lu Rounds.

BACHELOR OF MUSIC EDUCATION

Brenda Sue Black, Carole Rose Calmes, Mary Alice Dammann, Ruby Ray Foster, John Read Giordano, Eddie Ray Griffin and Carole Bruton Pieratt.

Ellen Annett Reid, Leslie Carroll Ross, Sandra Lynn Sutherland, James Stuart Vanlandingham and Janet Wolford.

The Richland Junior High School Band is making plans to cut a record. John Giordano, termed the best saxophonist in Fort Worth professional music circles, is working with the band group, and though our informant did not say specifically we feel that it will be the Swing Band which will profit from Giordano's aid.

Charles Peak, Band Director at Haltom Junior High, will lead his group when they play April 26 for the Haltom City Post Office dedication. . . . .Mrs. Murl Howard, director, and her cast of five boys and five girls at Lawrence D. Bell, will have two busy days this Thursday and Friday. The junior class members who make up the cast will give "There Go the Grooms" twice on Thursday--once at Euless Elementary, and once for high school students. On Friday, they will entertain the junior high when they give the play in the gym and Friday night they will take it to Euless Auditorium for a public look-see.

On the Monday after the game, a high school band director phoned Prof.

The band director said: "What the hell were you doing out there Saturday? I don't think another person besides me out of thirty thousand had a clue as to what was going on! It was weird. I loved it, but I think I was the only one in the stadium who did!"

So much for trying to be artistic on a football game halftime show.

USC, 1962

I became increasingly dedicated to composition, and I had a keen interest in composing music for films. So after my first year of graduate school at TCU, I decided to search for some way to further my studies in composition during my summer break.

The University of Southern California had an exceptional faculty at that time, especially in film music. That period at USC's School of Music is referred to as its "golden age." Jascha Heifetz, Gregor Piatigorsky, Miklós Rózsa, Halsey Stevens, Ruby Raksin, and Igor Stravinsky were on the faculty. I enrolled at USC during the summer of 1962 and was accepted into Halsey Stevens's class. The Mathematics for Motion Picture Music Synchronization course taught by Raksin was particularly enlightening on how to construct music for film using mathematical formulae. He explained and demonstrated how to apply mathematical formulas to enable the composer to synchronize music to the film. There were no computers, electronic keyboards, or digital applications at the time. Film ran at frames per second. Music tempos, phrasing, and style, along with dialogue and sound effects, had to be synchronized with the film using mathematical formulas.

The Los Angeles Philharmonic with Igor Stravinsky and his assistant, Robert Craft, were in residence during that summer. What a rare opportunity! It was fascinating to attend master classes conducted by one of the greatest

composers in history. It was an extraordinary opportunity to observe Stravinsky conduct and critique performances of his masterpieces such as "The Rite of Spring," "The Firebird," "Petrushka," "Pulcinella," and "Symphony in C" performed by the LA Philharmonic.

Stravinsky would conduct and speak to the class for some works and, for others, have Craft conduct while he commented. During a section when Robert Craft was conducting "Petrushka," Stravinsky interrupted the rehearsal:

"No, no, no! Why did you make a big rubato? When I want rubato, I write rubato. When I want legato, I write legato. I take great care to write every phrase the way I want you to play—do not do that."

(In direct contrast to Stravinsky's insisting that his music be played precisely as he wrote it, Samuel Barber encouraged performers to inject their personality into his works. I gleaned that during the 1977 Cliburn Competition when he explained to the jury that he wanted artists to have the freedom to express themselves.)

My study at USC furthered my desire to become a film composer/conductor and studio musician.

LEFT
Recital with pianist Alan Snodgrass. Author Collection.

First Teaching Position

Tarleton State University, 1963 – 1964

After my summer stint at USC and my final year in graduate school at TCU, I accepted a job as band director and director of instrumental music at Tarleton State University in Stephenville, Texas. It was a one-year appointment to fill the position of director of the instrumental department with the understanding that it would probably be for a longer tenure. My predecessor was pursuing a doctorate and confided in me that he had a job offer upon completion of the degree and did not plan to return. Don Morton, director of the music department, was aware of the situation and explained that my appointment would probably be for a longer period.

During registration, I was sitting between Louis Woodward, director of vocal studies, and Don Morton. Louis turned to me and said, "What are you doing here? You are wasting your time—you should go to Europe to study, absorb the culture, and receive a different viewpoint of music and life in general."

"Louis, we can't afford to live in Europe without having a job there. It would take us years to accumulate enough money."

"Apply for a scholarship. I'm certain your grades are good enough."

Don was eavesdropping. I'm sure he was puzzled that his new faculty member was plotting on how to leave even before his first day of teaching.

Louis helped me decide that a Fulbright scholarship would be the most logical one for which to apply. So before I even taught my first class or conducted the first note with the band, I applied for a Fulbright Scholarship. It was a long and tedious process, more complicated than if I had applied while still in school. There were no computers in 1963, so deleting, cutting, and pasting were not an option.

I selected Belgium as my country of choice for three reasons: (1) The saxophone professor at the Royal Conservatory of Music in Brussels was my favorite classical saxophonist. (2) There was an outstanding composition department at the conservatory headed by Marcel Poot, an internationally acclaimed composition teacher. And (3) I had studied German for several years and could use it for the language requirement because Belgium has three official languages, French, Flemish, and German. My French was limited, and I did not understand Flemish at all. I took private French lessons the summer before Mary Alice and I left for Belgium.

Because I applied after graduation and most positions had been filled, neither Mary Alice nor I had very high hopes that I would receive the grant. Surprisingly, I did, and Louis was correct that first day at registration when he said that living and studying in Europe would influence our lives more than we could imagine. Since I had only been at Tarleton for a year, it was not difficult to make the decision to leave. Mary Alice and I were elated to have the opportunity to live in, study in, and travel around Europe. Don Morton was extremely gracious about and proud of my receiving the Fulbright.

Fulbright Experience

Brussels 1964 – 1965

Our European experience took place during a unique period. Europe had not yet embraced the American culture; there were no fast-food places; prices were reasonable. The book *Europe on $5 a Day* was a realistic guide. Europeans tolerated most Americans, and few Europeans spoke English. Each country maintained its independent culture, food in the markets was fresh, and classical music was appreciated more than it was in the US.

We rented an apartment within walking distance of the conservatory. In our neighborhood, few had television sets, so local bars and cafes provided families with a place to watch TV. One evening we were watching a concert on TV featuring the Belgian National Radio and Television Symphony Orchestra. I commented to the man sitting next to me, "C'est un orchestre merveilleux et le musique est magnifique." (This is a great orchestra and the music is wonderful.)

He replied, "Oui, cest vrais, mais je prefere le premier cor dans le Monet. Je pense il est beaucoup mellieur." (Yes, that's true, but I prefer the first hornist in the Monet Opera Orchestra. I think he is much better.)

I doubt that many bars in the US have classical music concerts on their TVs or that many of their patrons can discern the quality of an orchestra's French horn player.

Most cities in Europe have a symphony orchestra as well as a radio and television orchestra and choir supported by the government and directed by major conductors. I was discussing this with a Belgian government official at a reception in the American embassy following a recital Mary Alice and I had performed. When I expressed how wonderful it is that many cities in Belgium have their own symphony orchestra, he said, "In Belgium, we believe that classical music is essential. It is critical to our well-being and sensitivity."

We travelled throughout Western Europe attending concerts and operas whenever possible.

It was terrific to hear Mozart in Vienna and Salzburg, cities in which he composed much of his music. It was inspiring to visit homes in which Beethoven, Wagner, and Strauss lived and worked. We heard great masterpieces performed in magnificent venues by great artists.

Living in Europe, especially as Fulbright scholars, presented us with opportunities to see the works of the world's most important artists. We saw works by masters like Leonardo, Michelangelo, Van Gogh, Rubens, Rembrandt, and Caravaggio in museums like the Louvre, the British Museum, the Rijksmuseum, and in cathedrals, castles, small churches, and government buildings. I am proud that I am in the Conservatory's catalogue as a notable alumnus.

The experience of living and studying in Belgium for an extended period was a major factor in my artistic development. During my time in Europe I performed as a recitalist, occasionally with Mary Alice, had professional engagements, and taught pre-conservatory students at the Royal Conservatory. I received the Premier Prix and Diplome Superieur in performance and composition.

My saxophone teacher, François Daneels, was an extraordinary artist and teacher; his artistic sensitivity, work ethic, dedication, knowledge, polished technique, and insight into music influenced me greatly and was a model for my development. My composition professor, Marcel Poot, insisted that his students were well grounded in fundamental compositional techniques, and I was required to compose in the styles of major composers from Bach to the Impressionists.

The trip from Brussels to Paris was only three hours by train. Mary Alice and I took advantage of that and spent much time in Paris. Paris afforded me the opportunity to take lessons with Olivier Messiaen, one of the iconic composers of the twentieth century. I could take the early train to Paris, have my lesson, and return to Brussels the same day on a later train.

ABOVE
Belgian Saxophone Septet in a filming session for a documentary of Adolphe Sax.
Author Collection.

One of our Fulbright colleagues was Wayne Barlow, a widely published professor of composition at the Eastman School of Music. Dr. Barlow was an exchange professor of composition at the Conservatoire Royal de Mons. I composed an art song for one of my composition assignments to a poem I had written and asked Dr. Barlow to look at it and offer suggestions before I turned it in. He examined it for several minutes and said, "Well, the music is pretty good but the poem is terrible! Why did you waste your time setting music to a poem that bad?"

I never told him that it was my poem. It was the last time I attempted to write poetry. I decided to just stick to music from then on.

TWO

My Early Career

After the completion of my studies in Brussels, I applied to many universities, conservatories, and colleges for a teaching position. Mary Alice and I narrowed down the possibilities to two offers: one from the State University of New York in my hometown, Fredonia, and the other, a graduate assistantship stipend to pursue a doctorate at the University of North Texas. We decided on UNT because Mary Alice's parents lived in Sweetwater, which was only about a three-and-a-half-hour drive from Denton, and were having health issues. Also, a doctorate is important to have for a professorship on the university level. So in 1965, we returned to Texas. I enrolled in the PhD program at UNT in the fall of 1965.

Our first child, Anne, was born shortly after our return to Texas. We now have three married children: Anne and Steve Lasko, who have a daughter, Natalie; Ellen and Stewart Austin, who have two children, Sarah and Elizabeth; and John B. and Veronica Giordano, who have two children, John Charles and Mia.

University of North Texas

Upon completion of my PhD studies, I was offered a position at UNT to teach saxophone, and clarinet and theory as needed, to fill my teaching load. That was never necessary, as I soon had a full load teaching just saxophone.

While at UNT, I introduced film scoring and jingle writing classes in addition to teaching saxophone. I designed two courses that complemented UNT music students enrolled in its outstanding jazz program. The courses were Composition for Film Music and Composing Commercial Jingles. Both classes were popular among upper-level and graduate students interested in pursuing a career in commercial music. Several professional jingle composers, who had little knowledge of the technical aspect of feature film composition, registered for the film composition course. My approach was to make both classes practical.

In the jingle course, I required the students to compose the music, create the text, perform and record the instrumental part, sing and record the jingles, and function as the recording engineer. The university's radio station used the better jingles created by the class.

Computers for music and electronic keyboards did not exist. The class used my editing equipment that included a moviola machine in which the visuals, dialogue, sound effects, and music are synchronized. Film composers were superb musicians who also created music for more than motion pictures. Many considered them to be current-day opera composers. Several skilled traditional composers for film

ABOVE
Anne, John B., Mary Alice, John R., and Ellen at the Multicultural Award Ceremony. Author Collection.

ABOVE
Grandchildren John C. Giordano, Elizabeth Austin, Mia Giordano, Natalie Lasko, and Sarah Austin. Author Collection.

ABOVE
John B., Ellen, Anne, and Mary Alice in 1985. Author Collection.

ABOVE
Family, Thanksgiving 2010.
Author Collection.

RIGHT
Saxophone publication. The first royalty check was for 95 cents.
Author Collection.

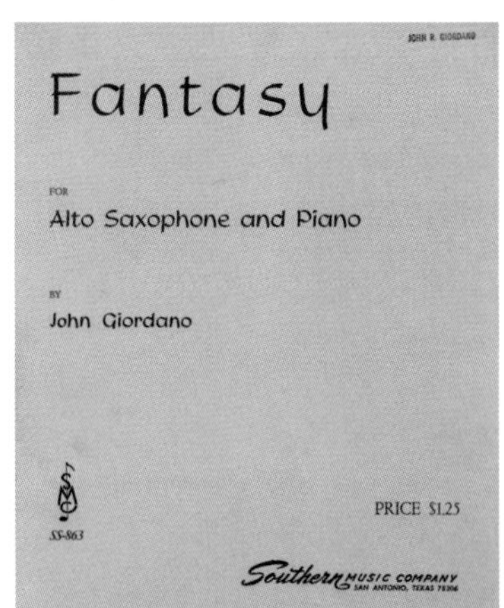

FILM SYNCH—Lew Gillis, right, of the North Texas State University music faculty, works with graduate student Ron Cook in new film scoring class at the Denton University.

NEW MACHINES—Phil Statser, another NTSU student, works at the controls of electronic machinery used for synchronizing music to the sound track of television and movie films.

TIMING—John Giordano, right, conductor of the Fort Worth Youth Orchestra and a member of the NTSU music faculty, works with Gillis on timing music to sound track.

NTSU Students Learning Technique of Scoring Films

DENTON (Spl) — The talents of North Texas State University music students are being utilized in the matching of film, action and musical compositions to produce radio-television commercials — heretofore thought to be only a professional art and rare to most college curriculums.

A film scoring course, taught by John Giordano of the School of Music faculty, who is also conductor of the Fort Worth Youth Orchestra, is the only such course in a university curriculum. Giordano says the only other place a student can formally learn the mechanics of film scoring is in Hollywood, in a small, expensive class for working composers. The other course, radio-TV music writing, may be offered at one or two other schools, according to Lew Gillis, NTSU's jingle writing instructor.

* * *

IF THE NTSU courses are the first, how did their teachers, music faculty members Gillis and Giordano, learn the techniques?

Both learned the difficult way, and their courses are designed so that working musicians, mostly NTSU jazz students who do not plan to teach music, can avoid some of their teachers' lean years.

Giordano said he learned film scoring techniques "the hard way. I did a couple of film scores some years ago, several play backgrounds and some commercials. I got with film editors and learned by talking, reading . . . trial and error."

Gillis, an active Fort Worth composer and arranger whose credits include music for Eddie Arnold, Six Flags, the Miss Texas Pageant and the Fort Worth Fat Stock Show, started his music writing career as band director at TCU in the early 1950s.

"I had to organize a dance band and write a 15-minute broadcast every week. This is how I got speed in writing," he said. When Gillis quit teaching to write full time, he supplemented his income by being a radio announcer, music store owner, musician and singer. "In 15 years, Lord I did an awful lot of different things to try to make ends meet until I got established as a writer," he recalled.

* * *

WITH WHAT they learn in his course, Gillis' students shouldn't have to repeat his experiences. "But regardless of whether they ever use it or not," he said, "the students should come out of school ready to meet any contingency in the music world. If they're performers and they don't get enough work, they can fall back on their resources.

"What John and I are trying to do is give these guys an inkling of what there is to be done professionally. If we can offer them one more way to make a living in this business, it's great. Then if they do get hit in the mouth and they can't play their horn, they can still make a living in music," Gillis said.

NTSU's courses are only two years old—so new that they can't be found in the school catalogue except under an assumed name. They are taught as special sections of senior theory and senior orchestration, but the courses are now being officially approved and named. Both will be offered during the spring 1972 semester.

* * *

NEW AS IT is, Gillis' course already has a success story. Arris Wheaton, Dallas graduate student, took some jingles he wrote in class to a Dallas jingle company and was hired on the spot. He now draws a full-time salary while still a student at NTSU, where he is taking film scoring from Giordano, directing NTSU's 5 O'Clock Lab Band and writing a thesis on a curriculum in jingle and film scoring.

Wheaton's station identification spots are played on radio station WLS in Chicago and on New York radio stations. He has written commercials for department stores, clothing stores, auto dealers and home builders. His work is also heard on 1090 Soul Express from Mexico.

Gillis said there are at least six others in his course who write jingles of professional quality, "who would be ready to move into a jingle company right now and do professional work if there were identification spot; and how to write for television action, or situation writing. The last, since it involves working within time limits, leads into Giordano's course in film music.

* * *

IN WRITING jingles, students first learn the various jingle forms, such as the "doughnut hole," where music begins the advertisement, an announcer follows, and music closes the spot. They practice writing in different styles, like Tijuana Brass, Dixieland or "hard rock," so that they can write for any advertiser.

Basic recording techniques are learned while the students record all their jingles in class, "using home type equipment," Gillis commented. "We're trying to come up with as professional a sound as we can, but what we come up with is a very amateurish thing, soundwise."

Budgeting a jingle to write, record and sell it at a profit is a major part of the course. For budgeting, the class has set up the "Jim Dandy Jingle Co., Denton, Texas," a mythical firm which produces commercials. Its budgets include everything from musician's time to the cost of "wining and dining" the jingle client.

Station identification spots are especially important to NTSU musicians — 90 per cent of the spots are produced just 40 miles away, in Dallas where "it's big business," Gillis said. The spots are sold to radio stations all over the United States, France and Belgium.

Gillis' television situation writing assignments force his students to develop versatility. They include hypothetical screen situations such as "the villain creeping up on the hero," "drug withdrawal pains," "a parade" and "a man trapped in a room."

* * *

WHEN THEY go on to Giordano's film music course, the students learn to mold all that versatility and creativity to an absolutely rigid timetable—the film.

Coordinating 40 film frames per minute, 60 seconds per minute and the musical measures per minute takes sophisticated mathematics. "It's really primarily a math course," Giordano said. "Ninety per cent of it is calculation of algebraic formulas."

The students do learn the types of films that need scoring. Drama, comedy, cartoons, musicals, documentaries, television commercial films — all need different kinds of music. Giordano's students score a cartoon, "which is the most difficult thing to do because it has so much action," he said.

Using special Hollywood score paper, with lines for music, dialogue, action and sound effects, the student composers score the film, using mathematics to make the music and sound effects precisely match what shows on screen.

The music is recorded in class and played while the cartoon is shown, so that everyone can see if each composer got his calculations right. If he did not, a mouse may be seen bashing a cat with a bat, while the music is still sounding like a tiptoeing rodent. When that happens, it is back to the practice room to try again, and again, until the music and action fit precisely.

Former Student Will Return With Chorale

DENTON (Spl) — When Milvern Ivey brings his Loyola University Chorale to sing at North Texas State University this week, he will really be coming home.

Ivey is a former music student at NTSU having graduated in 1967 with a master of music degree.

The choir from the New Orleans school will sing at 8:15 p.m. Friday. The concert, in the NTSU Music Recital Hall, is open to the public at no charge.

The 40-member group is on a tour of Southwestern Louisiana and North and East Texas. It will sing a varied program of works by Giovanni Gabrieli, J. S. Bach, W. A. Mozart, Johannes Brahms, Francis Poulenc and Innes Randolph.

During the last three years, the Loyola Chorale and Grand Chorus have combined with the New Orleans Philharmonic - Symphony Orchestra to present several large scale works and participated with the symphony in a recording of special arrangements of the "Star Spangled Banner" and "America The Beautiful." It was one of two

ABOVE
First film scoring class at the University of North Texas (UNT).
© Fort Worth Star-Telegram, 1972.

still exist, including John Williams, the extraordinary creator of music for several Academy Award-winning motion pictures.

It is much easier to compose for contemporary movies in today's digital age of computers and keyboards. Editing is much easier and flexible. Subsequently, music can be adjusted to fit the movies without the need for a contemporary film composer to have any knowledge of mathematical formulas. Some contemporary film composers are not formally trained musicians and cannot even read music. Many are talented and create excellent and appropriate music playing by ear on electronic keyboards.

A Missed Opportunity

When I was engaged to arrange or compose music, I never requested a specific fee and frequently received very small royalty remuneration. Lew Gillis admonished me to set appropriate fees and never accept any job for a royalty.

"Always get your money up front," he said.

I had composed background music for award-winning documentaries but never had written music for a feature film. I wanted to have that opportunity.

In 1972 I received a call from Joe Camp, the producer for Mulberry Square Productions, an independent film company. He explained that he was producing a feature film that was going to be filmed in the Denton, Texas, area. He said that they had a small budget and couldn't pay a large fee for the music but could offer me a generous royalty. I declined, explaining that I only worked for a set fee, then I quoted a high number that under most circumstances was quite reasonable.

He apologized and explained that they didn't have that amount in their budget. He asked me to recommend someone else.

I suggested they contact Euel Box, one of my talented students, and gave them Euel's phone number. Euel had his own recording studio in

FAR LEFT
Returned from Belgium to pursue a classical saxophone concert career. Author Collection.

LEFT
DownBeat *magazine ad featuring jazz.* Author Collection.

Dallas and has written many well-known jingles and commercials.

Euel accepted the offer to compose the film score for *Benji!*, the well-loved movie about a golden mutt who saves the day. Euel won a Golden Globe Award for Best Original Song and was nominated in the same category at the Academy Awards. And while I was overjoyed for Euel and his success with the film score, I was disappointed that I had passed up such a golden opportunity.

Classical Saxophonist Career

When I enrolled in the PhD program at the University of North Texas in the fall of 1965, my primary goal and mission was to develop a solo career as a classical saxophonist and champion the cause of the classical saxophone.

My saxophone students grew from twelve my first year in 1966 to 110 when I resigned in 1973, and I also had several graduate assistants. I continued to concertize extensively in the US and Europe and became a clinician for Carl Fischer Music Corporation. My symphony orchestra performances included those in Fort Worth, Dallas, Austin, San Antonio, El Paso, San Diego, Brussels, Paris, American Symphony in New York, and Buffalo. I also performed with the Belgian National Symphony, Belgian Radio and Television Orchestra, and the BBC orchestras.

BBC - Johnny Dankworth's Cigar Cutter

In 1969 I was invited to perform and record the Ibert Concertino da Camera and Glazunov Saxophone Concerto with the BBC Chamber Orchestra in London conducted by Francis Chagrin.

I had a day off between recording sessions and visited the Wurlitzer Music Store, known worldwide for brokering rare string instruments in addition to selling contemporary musical instruments and equipment.

John Dankworth, who was a pioneer of jazz in Britain, a composer, performer, and leader of the best "big band" in England that also featured his wife, Cleo Laine, entered the store. I had always admired his band, his playing, arranging, and film scoring, and introduced myself. We had a pleasant conversation.

He told me that he was there to trade in his old Selmer saxophone, "Cigar Cutter," on a new Selmer Mark VI. The Selmer "Cigar Cutter" was produced between 1930 and 1933 and was nicknamed that because it has a uniquely designed octave key mechanism that resembles a cigar cutter. It has a bold, rich, dynamic tone quality. However, its awkward mechanism makes it difficult to play virtuosic passages.

I wanted to play a "cigar cutter" in repertoire that calls for a dark mellow tone quality and doesn't require virtuosic technique. I asked him how much he wanted for the instrument, and he quoted a ridiculously low price of $100, which was what the store was going to give him for a trade-in. I immediately bought it, but sadly I have rarely used it. The instrument now is a collector's item, and the provenance of it having been played by Johnny Dankworth makes it even more valuable.

Julius Keilworth

My classical saxophone career continued to grow, especially while I was teaching at UNT. I performed concerti with several symphony orchestras throughout the US and Western Europe, gave clinics in several all-state band and orchestra festivals, was an artist sponsored by the instrument manufacturer Carl Fischer, and toured with the University of Northern Iowa band performing a work that Dr. William Latham composed for me. When I accepted the position with the FWSO in 1973, my solo career began to wane because the demands for my time with the symphony and the Cliburn became extremely time consuming.

Julius Keilworth, a German saxophone manufacturer, attended a concert I played in Belgium that was part of an international saxophone conference in Dinant, the birthplace of Adolphe Sax, inventor of the saxophone. I met Keilworth after the concert. He told me about a new metal alloy he was working on that he felt would improve the tone quality of saxophones and revolutionize their manufacturing. It was a gold alloy that did not require the usual coat of lacquer applied over highly polished brass. Also, since the density of the metal on brass instruments has a profound effect on their tone quality, he theorized that his dense new alloy would improve the instrument's sound.

He gave me a prototype to evaluate and shipped it to me through his US dealer, Herbert Couf. I like the tone quality very much, but the instrument is extremely heavy and awkward to play. I still have the saxophone but have never played it in public because of its weight and cumbersome key mechanism. The gold alloy model never was universally accepted. It's possible that my instrument is the only one in existence.

My Conducting Career Begins

Shortly after starting at UNT, I auditioned for Ezra Rachlin, conductor of the Fort Worth and Austin Symphony Orchestras, to play a concerto with both orchestras. Rachlin was a child prodigy pianist and a superb conductor. Rachmaninov coached him on his third piano concerto when Rachlin was twenty-two. He taught at the Curtis Institute and studied with Fritz Reiner.

After the audition, Rachlin asked me to visit with him in the FWSO office in Scott Theatre.

"Bravo," he said. "I would like to engage you as soloist with the Fort Worth and Austin Symphonies."

"Thank you, Maestro," I said. "It is an honor to meet you, and I am thrilled to accept the engagements."

Though I may have sounded calm and collected accepting his offer, I think I was in shock at the opportunity to begin a performing career on a professional level.

He continued, "Have you ever considered conducting?"

"Maestro, I am familiar with much of the orchestra repertory because my degrees are in composition and I have studied and analyzed the standard orchestral and piano repertoire, but conducting them is a different matter."

"You are an artist," he said, "which is something you can't teach, and after learning the repertoire and developing your conducting techniques, you could be a very good conductor.

"We are organizing a youth orchestra in Fort Worth and I am looking for an assistant—someone who eventually would become its conductor. If you are interested I will give you free conducting lessons. You should continue to develop your career as a soloist. The two disciplines will complement each other."

Although the saxophone has an extensive repertoire, a fact that few realize, the preponderance of classical saxophone music was French at that time. Its repertoire has expanded greatly since then. It does not include music by eighteenth and nineteenth century masters. It was invented in 1846 and did not emerge as a respected concert instrument until the early twentieth century. I realized that the opportunity to study conducting and symphonic music with someone of Rachlin's stature would be priceless, so I eagerly accepted his offer.

"We will begin with a conducting lesson. Can you meet with me in about a week?"

"Yes sir!" I still was stunned.

"I want you to memorize the first movement of the Beethoven First Symphony for your first lesson."

Thus began the turning point of my career from playing to conducting.

The assignment was not overwhelming to me because I had analyzed the entire work for a composition class I had in Brussels. When I showed up for my first lesson, Rachlin spent a considerable amount of time working on downbeats.

He told me, "You must spend much time on simple gesticulation fundamentals. Various beat patterns are relatively simple, but clarity of your baton technique is essential. Now let's turn to the Beethoven. Sing the second violin part beginning after the introduction!"

It seemed to be a simple request. Frequently the first and second violins played in either unison or octaves during that period in music history. I began to sing what I assumed was the second violin part, the same as the first violins. He stopped me immediately.

"That is completely wrong!" he exclaimed, admonishing me. "I asked you to memorize the piece. Memorizing means you learn every part in the score and its function. That is the first violin part. Concentrate and try once more."

I envisioned the printed page in my mind and remembered the second violin part. It was a trick question. The second violins had a very simple accompaniment for the first four measures

ABOVE
Youth Orchestra concert in 1973. Author Collection.

consisting of quarter notes. C–G–G, G, G. It was a lesson I carried with me my entire conducting career: learn the entire score in detail!

Maestro Rachlin was a taskmaster and perfectionist. He refused to allow the Youth Orchestra to play a concert until they were fully prepared to perform on a high level. He was also extremely selective when it came to the prowess of the young musicians accepted into the program. Consequently, there were only thirty-five members in the original Youth Orchestra. They performed the first concert well, but the string section was small. That posed serious balance problems, especially in the Romantic and twentieth-century repertoires. Also, a major thrill of performing in an orchestra is being enveloped by the rich, beautiful sound of a full string section. I wanted the YO members to have that experience.

Following Rachlin's resignation from the Youth Orchestra, I became the music director and immediately went on a quest to increase the size of the orchestra with the best available young musicians, with a focus on string players.

THREE

The Fort Worth Youth Orchestra

The Youth Orchestra has always had a dedicated board of directors and outstanding administrative leadership. Beverly Cardona, then executive director of the FWSO, was also the executive director of the Youth Orchestra when I was appointed its music director. Subsequently, Betty Utter, a talented musician, composer, and administrator, became the executive director of the Youth Orchestra. Betty and I joined forces, and in 1965 began the process to create one of the most outstanding YO programs in the US.

LEFT
Betty Utter, executive director of the Youth Orchestra, 1965. Author Collection.

Betty and I made a concerted effort to enlist the support of high school music teachers in Tarrant and Denton Counties and encouraged them to have their most advanced young artists audition for the YO. When the YO was established, there were twelve high school orchestra programs in the Fort Worth public school system. After a period during which the focus on developing the orchestra programs waned, the FWISD has now restored them to their previous outstanding status. In 2019, thirteen of those FWISD orchestra programs earned a UIL Sweepstakes Award for Division I in both concert and sight-reading.

In most high school orchestras, there is a dramatic discrepancy between the levels of a young musician's technical capabilities. A youth orchestra provides an outlet for the advanced musicians. For practical reasons, school conductors must select repertoire according to the level of the average student. That limits the quality and amount of important music that can be performed during a school year. That is frustrating to the more advanced musicians.

Betty possessed a unique acumen for public relations and promoting. She was an organized administrator as well. Her tireless efforts promoting the Youth Orchestra and securing funding for the organization afforded us the wherewithal to purchase better instruments and develop the program.

We initially had a serious problem in recruiting instrumentalists at the level we required because the average high school director would not cooperate with us, fearing that their best players would drop out of the school program when they experienced performing symphonic masterpieces with talented musicians. To alleviate their fears, we required members of the YO to remain members in good standing with their high school organization. To recruit the instrumentalists we needed, I visited school orchestras, listened to their rehearsals, conferred with the directors, and assured them that we would support their programs. It was difficult to convince them that the experience their most advanced musicians would receive by participating in our program would greatly contribute to their groups as well. I explained they would be performing unabridged original versions of masterpieces and not simplified arrangements. Most high school directors complied with our requests, and many were of great help; we even engaged some directors as sectional coaches.

All artists want to perform in special venues, such as professional concert halls, for a large audience. Artists also think it is important to have the experience of performing in cities outside of their own for a broader audience. Betty did all within her power to provide those opportunities.

The Youth Orchestra's philosophy was as follows:

1. To create an environment for outstanding instrumental music students in which they can develop their artistic skills and talents to the highest degree possible.

2. To provide members with the opportunity to perform music of the highest level with peers of a comparable level.

3. To give young artists the opportunity to work with professional conductors.

4. To provide a venue and artistic environment for young artists to rehearse, prepare, and perform classical musical masterpieces, not simplified arrangements.

5. To maintain a good relationship with school systems and music teachers.

6. To use professional section rehearsal coaches whenever possible.

The Youth Orchestra in Switzerland

Charlie Abdoo, a retired professional opera singer, attended a YO concert at my request. He was impressed with its quality and informed us that the inaugural International Youth Orchestra Festival was going to take place in San Moritz, Switzerland. It was going to be composed of youth orchestras selected from America, Canada, and Western and Eastern Europe. He suggested that we apply to be included. We submitted our application, which included a recording of our last concert, and were one of four YOs from the US selected.

We didn't want to secure underwriting with projects normally used to raise money for student organizations, like selling magazines or candy door to door. Instead we opted to solicit funds from parents, patrons, and corporations and to create projects that would generate funds and improve the musicians' skills.

Betty devised a unique fundraising idea. She put together a "Tour of Homes" that included several unique, beautiful homes and private gardens in Fort Worth. We charged a general fee for the tour. Betty acquired permission to use the homes of various patrons of the orchestra, and I organized chamber music groups from members of the orchestra. We placed them in various locations in the homes (i.e. a flute trio playing in a sumptuous bathroom, or a string quartet performing in a garden).

The event was extremely successful. Chamber music compels one to play sensitively and precisely with collaborators. The music is transparent, and the performers must blend together. Musicians always enjoy playing chamber music because most of it is remarkable and artistically fulfilling. The Tour of Homes improved the quality of the YO because the same elements of precision, blending, and sensitivity that the players experienced carried over to the full orchestra.

I selected repertoire for the San Moritz Festival program consisting primarily of American music. "American Youth Performs" was an overture composed for the occasion by Dr. William Latham, a professor at the University of North Texas School of Music and the parent of one of our flutists, Carol. The rest of the program included: Bartok's Rumanian Dances, featuring Robert Barney, the principal bassist of the Cincinnati Symphony and a charter member of the YO; and Giannini's Second Symphony. The Youth Orchestra was recognized as the model orchestra of the festival. Our members were the youngest in the festival, ranging from eleven to eighteen years old. All the other orchestras were composed of eighteen- to twenty-five-year-old musicians.

American Youth Performs

In 1968, Charles Abdoo created a program he called American Youth Performs (AYP) to give gifted high school singers and instrumentalists opportunities to perform with peers of similar ability. AYP differed from the regional and all-state choirs, orchestras, and bands that already existed throughout the US in that AYP's participants were not limited to public school students or any region. The ensembles formed by AYP were also later given the rare opportunity to perform in major concert halls like Orchestra Hall in Chicago, Dorothy Chandler Pavilion in LA, Powell Hall in St. Louis, etc. AYP also helped to launch careers of promising young instrumental soloists, singers, and conductors. Major conductors such as Walter Susskind, Carmen Dragon, and Leopold Stokowski participated in the program.

C. R. Smith, CEO of American Airlines, agreed to have AA underwrite the program and provide air service.

AYP consisted of two parts:

1. To assemble the finest high school musicians from bands, orchestras, and choirs in several regions of the US. They performed in the area's major professional venue. The first half of the concerts were all orchestral, consisting of major works conducted by an aspiring young conductor and featuring a talented young soloist. The second half was conducted by an established, internationally recognized professional conductor performing a major choral and orchestral work. The performances took place in the various cities in major venues such as Orchestra Hall in Chicago and the Dorothy Chandler Pavilion in Los Angeles.

2. At the end of the spring semester the most outstanding young instrumentalists and singers from all regions of the US were selected to form a National Orchestra and Chorus. They were flown via American Airlines to Washington, DC, where they spent a week rehearsing under the direction of a young conductor whose professional career was on the rise. These conducted the first half of the concert; for the second half a major choral/orchestral work like *Carmina Burana* was conducted by an internationally prominent conductor such as Susskind, Dragon, or Stokowski. The concert was performed twice, the first concert in the JFK Theater in Washington, DC. The airline then flew the entire entourage to NYC, where the concert was repeated in Carnegie Hall.

Charlie Abdoo attended a performance of mine when I was the saxophone soloist with the El Paso Symphony Orchestra playing the Ibert

Concertino da Camera and Glazunov's Saxophone Concerto. He subsequently asked me to join the AYP program as a soloist. I performed under the auspice of AYP throughout the US in their regional concerts and with the National AYP Orchestra in Washington, DC, and at Carnegie Hall.

After Charlie attended a concert of the YO I conducted, he asked me to also participate in the AYP program as a conductor. The highlight of my experience with AYP occurred when I conducted the first half of the National AYP orchestra's DC and Carnegie Hall concerts. I was also to prepare the orchestra for the second half of each concert, the choral/orchestral performances to be conducted by Milton Katims, Carmen Dragon, Walter Susskind, and Morton Gould. I later had the unique opportunity to prepare the International Youth Orchestra in San Moritz for Leopold Stokowski.

Columbus, Ohio, for AYP

In 1969, I went to a small town in Ohio to clinic an all-region high school orchestra under the auspices of AYP. The local airport was too small to accommodate large jets, so I had to change planes in Columbus and take a small regional airline that serviced smaller cities.

The regional airline used Gate 1A. I arrived in Columbus and tried to find Gate 1A. I found Gate 1 but not Gate 1A. I asked the agent at the Gate 1 desk the location of Gate 1A, and she pointed to a door across the lobby on which there was a "No Entry" sign. The "No Entry" was crossed out with a pencil mark and an 8 1/2" x 11" piece of lined yellow notebook paper was taped to the door with Gate 1A printed on it in pencil. I opened the door and walked down a staircase to the tarmac level.

A small, wooden podium in disrepair sat at the foot of the stairs with another 8 ½" x 11" piece of paper taped to it marked 1A. A coat rack upon which two hats, jackets, and a pair of coveralls hung stood behind the podium. A gentleman in a navy-blue blazer who stood behind the podium took my ticket and asked me to sit in the small folding chair. He then changed into the coveralls, put on a hard hat, picked up my luggage, and carried it to a small single-engine prop plane parked on the tarmac close to Gate 1A. He placed my luggage behind the pilot and co-pilot's seats, returned to the podium, removed the coveralls, and hung them and the hard hat on the rack. He then donned a brown leather pilot's jacket with captain's epaulets, put a pilot's hat on, and escorted me to the tiny plane. He instructed me to sit in the co-pilot's seat and fasten my seat belt. The ticket agent/luggage handler/pilot sat in the pilot's seat, removed his hat and jacket, fastened his seat belt, and handed me a headset.

He taxied to the runway and took a place in line between two 727s for takeoff. While in line he recited the standard commercial airline's safety instructions. After takeoff, he gave me a dramatic aerial tour of the city flying between skyscrapers. It was much too close for comfort for me.

We safely reached our destination. The return flight to Columbus was not as dramatic.

Carnegie Hall, Saxophone Soloist

AYP engaged me to be the soloist with the National Orchestra for the Washington, DC, and Carnegie Hall concerts. I performed the Ibert *Concertino da Camera* conducted by the talented young conductor, Louis Campiglia. The major conductor of the concert was Walter Susskind, music director of the St. Louis Symphony.

Susskind was a brilliant and flamboyant conductor. Just before the concert in Carnegie, I went to his dressing room, knocked on the door, and saw him applying stage makeup.

"Maestro," I said, a little shocked. "Are you putting on stage makeup?"

"I always do; after all, we will be on stage!" He said as if the answer were obvious.

"Yes, but you will be facing the orchestra, the audience only will see your back," I explained.

"Of course, but I'll have to bow and that will be towards the audience!"

While I was waiting to perform I nervously paced around backstage observing autographed pictures of legendary artists, such as Rachmaninov, who had performed in Carnegie Hall. I became extremely nervous and went to Susskind's dressing room again.

"Maestro," I said, "I can't do this. I'm not qualified to perform in this sacred place!"

"Come with me," he said.

He led me to the Green Room, in which there was a small one-way window from which one could observe the audience.

"Look," he said.

The house was filled with standing room only.

"Thanks a lot Maestro, now I'm positive I can't do this."

"You don't understand—playing music is nothing to be afraid of. See all those people?"

I looked out at the audience again. "Seeing them doesn't help any, Maestro. That's what frightens me!"

"You are looking at it the wrong way. They are here to be entertained and have a wonderful experience. They want you to play well. Something to be afraid of is if you were in Vietnam wondering if every move you make would be your last. Now, go out there and make wonderful music!"

The performance received standing ovations, and the *New York Times* gave a great review that compared the orchestra to a first-class European orchestra. Several years later, in 2008, when I was teaching at TCU, I was given a CD of the concert that I didn't know existed. Richard Gipson, director of the TCU School of Music, has a close friend in New York City, Jim Wayne, who is a professional recordist, and he recorded my concert. His company was the first to produce CDs. During a social event in New York in 2003, Wayne mentioned to Richard that his first recording in Carnegie Hall featured a saxophonist. Richard asked: "Was it John Giordano?" Wayne replied, "Yes! How do you know him?" Richard told him that I was a faculty member at TCU. "What a coincidence!" Jim Wayne exclaimed. When Richard played the recording for me, I was overwhelmed; it brought back wonderful memories.

Conducting American Youth Performs in Carnegie Hall

My second performance in Carnegie Hall was one where I conducted the first half of the AYP National Orchestra's concert. My program included: Shostakovich's *Festival Overture*, "Adagietto" from the Mahler Fifth Symphony, and Stravinsky's *Firebird* Suite.

The second half's work was Rachmaninov's *The Bells* for orchestra and choir, conducted by Milton Katims, the renowned violist and conductor who was music director of the Seattle Symphony.

I was assigned to prepare *The Bells* for him. It is an extremely complicated, thirty-five-minute work that is rarely performed because of its difficulty. I called Katims, score and notepad in hand, to take notes of his instructions for my preparation.

"Maestro Katims? I am John Giordano. I have been assigned to prepare *The Bells* for you for the AYP concerts."

He responded, "Yes, Mr. Giordano. I am aware of that. Mr. Abdoo informed me of your assignment. Do you have a score and are prepared to take notes? As you know, I have very limited rehearsal time so your preparation will be critical."

"Yes, Maestro," I answered. "I have the score and pad and pencil at the ready."

His instructions were unbelievably detailed.

"Turn to page thirty-seven. Mark the third eighth note in the fourth measure in the clarinet part mp. Then turn to page thirty-nine. Mark pp in the first violin part for four bars."

This continued for a half hour, and we weren't even one third of the way through the hundreds of pages. I was becoming more and more frustrated with his extremely detailed instructions. I interrupted: "Maestro, excuse me. If you are asking me to balance the piece, I can do that. I basically need to understand your interpretive instructions regarding tempi and phrasing so I can properly prepare the orchestra for you."

"Well then," he said, "simply follow Rachmaninov's indications. I always adhere to the composer's wishes. Please don't hesitate to call if you have any more questions."

"Thank you, Maestro, I will. I'm looking forward to meeting you in person and observing what you will do with this masterpiece."

Katims turned out to be a pleasant and charming individual. He was an accomplished conductor, and his interpretation of *The Bells* was breathtaking.

Harold Schonberg's *New York Times* review of the concert stated that if he had closed his eyes he could have been listening to a major orchestra's performance. He gave special recognition to the Mahler and Stravinsky as the high points of the concert. Several years later, when he was on the Cliburn jury, he brought up this performance to me and was highly complimentary.

Leopold Stokowski

Several of our outstanding members were selected to participate in an all-star orchestra conducted by Leopold Stokowski. Playing for one of the finest and most famous conductors in the world was a rare opportunity for them. The featured work was Beethoven's Seventh Symphony.

I was asked to prepare the orchestra for the Maestro. Several months before the festival I telephoned Stokowski for instructions. I was anxious and surmised that he would give me even more detailed instructions than did Katims. I felt an enormous amount of pressure. Nevertheless, I gathered up my courage and called him.

"Maestro, I am John Giordano and have been assigned to prepare the Beethoven for the International Youth Orchestra in the San Moritz Festival. Do you have any specific instructions for me?"

"As a matter of fact, I do."

He paused for several seconds, while I waited anxiously for his instructions. I anticipated that I would have to make a plethora of detailed notes throughout the lengthy score.

Then, in his stentorian voice, the great Maestro said, "Make it musical!"

I breathed a sigh of relief, but the relief only lasted a short while. His simple instructions made the task even more challenging, because making a work "musical" is the most difficult aspect of performing!

Maestro Stokowski learned that I spoke French, so he asked me to translate his instructions to the orchestra during rehearsal. I stood on one side of the orchestra translating into French, and Maestro Walter Susskind stood on the other translating into German and Russian.

The overwhelming success and publicity of our Youth Orchestra that we garnered after the festival launched the orchestra into the limelight. Its status as an outstanding ensemble became well known throughout the metroplex. Extensive recruiting was no longer necessary; the large number of applicants allowed us to be very selective, and we improved exponentially.

Acquisition of Orchestra Hall

The Youth Orchestra was rehearsing in church recreation rooms that were inadequate in size for our eighty to eighty-five members and had poor acoustical properties.

Harriet Woldt, principal cellist of the FWSO, a TCU faculty member, and a YO board member, informed me that she noticed a Church of Christ for sale in a convenient location.

Betty and I assessed the church and determined that it had the potential to fulfill our needs. The FWSO also desperately needed a venue in which to rehearse, along with office space and a room for its fast-growing library. The asking price for the property was quite rea-

sonable. Betty and I met with Val Wilkie, director of the Sid Richardson Foundation, who was an enthusiastic supporter of both the YO and the FWSO, and he agreed to help. The funding came from grants by the Richardson and Amon Carter Foundations. The facility was to be used by both the YO and the FWSO. However, both parties agreed that it be deeded to the YO.

The architectural and acoustical firm of Jaffe-Holden renovated the sanctuary of the church. They successfully transformed it into a functional five-hundred-seat concert hall with good acoustics.

We christened it Orchestra Hall. It provided both organizations with administrative offices, teaching spaces, rehearsal spaces, and a library capable of holding an extensive collection.

The Youth Orchestra's European Tour of 1973

In 1973, the Youth Orchestra embarked on its second international tour. This time we had acquired enough funds to make the trip a reality without having to undertake a major fundraising effort. The parents paid a substantial amount of the cost for their own children. Betty again secured underwriting from corporate sources including Aggie Pate, the owner of Texas Refinery Corporation, a company that had strong ties with the Grand Duchy of Luxembourg.

Through Aggie we became acquainted with Adrien Meisch, who was director of Political and Cultural Affairs of the Grand Duchy of Luxembourg. Adrien was also a concert pianist. He later served as ambassador to the United States from 1974 until 1983. Our friendship had a major

ABOVE
Building the stage for the Youth Orchestra's home, Orchestra Hall. Author Collection.

impact on the development of the FWSO and the Cliburn when he served as ambassador.

This tour was very different from the first sojourn to Europe in that it was a concert tour in which the YO performed in several venues through Western and Eastern Europe. We scheduled performances in major venues in Luxembourg, Brussels, Prague (the Mozarteum), Salzburg, Vienna, and Amsterdam.

The United States' relationship with the Soviet Bloc countries was strained at the time, but I was able to arrange for a performance in Prague through my friend, Karel Husa, one of the premier Czech composers. I met Karel when I performed his Concerto for Saxophone and Concert Band.

The YO had grown in quality and had attracted outstanding young musicians, many of whom now have major careers in a variety of disciplines. The orchestra was composed of the finest young musicians in the Dallas-Fort Worth Metroplex. We performed works by Tchaikovsky, Beethoven, and Dvorak, and premiered several works by American composers. The major work on the tour was the Ninth Symphony in E Minor by Antonin Dvorak, *The New World*.

Prague

After a successful performance in Luxembourg, we were on our way to Prague. We encountered an unexpected delay at the Czech border, however. After we passed to the Czech side, the border guards had no idea what to do when three busloads of American musicians, their entourage, and their instruments and other equipment unexpectedly appeared. The captain of the Czech military border guard was also taken aback. The guards searched every piece of luggage, insisted on unloading the truck containing our equipment and instruments, and forced every male member of the party to shave any facial hair not matching the photo on their passports. As you might surmise, this took an interminable amount of time. They even insisted we disassemble the large drums and timpani. That difficult task would have taken several more hours to accomplish.

I fell sound asleep in the lead bus while all of this was going on. When I awoke about an hour later I saw that nothing with our situation had changed.

I was angry and said to Mary Alice, "How dare these fools keep the kids on buses for several hours? Can't they see how tired, confused, and scared they must be?"

I pushed past the guard who was standing at the door of our bus.

Mary Alice pleaded with me to stop. "What are you doing? Do you want to get yourself killed?"

I ignored her and addressed the guard: "Take me to the officer in charge this instant!"

Although surprised by my outburst, the guard realized I was someone of authority.

The guard's superior officer, hearing my outburst, walked over to our bus.

"Do you speak English?" I demanded.

"Yes!" he answered defensively. I could tell he was also surprised by my anger.

I handed him our invitation from the Czech Republic's Ministry of Culture.

"I am in charge of this group. We are official guests of your government, and I demand you either let us continue to Prague or return to Austria. If you keep us here any longer there will be an international incident, and you will be in serious trouble.

"And where is the guide from the Department of Culture that we were promised? Has the Department of Culture even been informed that we are at your border?

"What have you done to our instruments? If any of them are damaged in any way I am holding you responsible. We are official guests of your government. I demand you report our circumstance to your superiors immediately!"

Mary Alice was standing at the door to our bus during my monologue, still pleading for me to return.

"You are going to be shot, John. Come back

here," she pleaded.

"Not until this is settled," I said.

"Come with me," the officer ordered and led me to his commander.

I was angry, and I knew from my own military experience that most military personnel of his rank can be intimidated by one of higher authority. I surmised that he was concerned that he had placed himself in an awkward situation, and his rank might be in jeopardy.

As we walked, I continued to rant. "We are official guests of your government. Your behavior will be reported to the proper authority. I demand that you call your superiors and have us released immediately, or this will become an international incident that will embarrass your country and probably result in severe punishment for you."

The officer ushered me into the border commander's office and handed the Ministry of Culture's letter of invitation to him.

I waited in his office while he phoned someone who sounded very angry. After what obviously was a stern admonishment he turned to me and said, "I have checked with the authorities in Prague, and they have granted permission for your group to continue on your journey to Prague."

"Thank you, captain. Where is the guide that was supposed to meet us here and be with us during our visit to your country?"

"Your Czechish guide will meet you on the way to Prague."

And just like that, we finally left the border behind and were on our way to Prague. Sometimes a little anger and an authoritative demeanor can get a lot done.

After travelling a few miles, we encountered a woman who was standing in the middle of the road. She signaled our buses to stop. Our driver opened the door, the woman entered our bus, exchanged a few words with the driver, turned to us, and said, "I am your Czechish guide. Welcome to Czechoslovakia! I am eager to hear you perform."

She was delightful, obviously well educated, and knowledgeable on every aspect of her country's history.

"I apologize for the terrible inconvenience you experienced at the border," she said. "Your arrival was very unusual to the border patrol, and they didn't know how to deal with you. I realize that it is not a good excuse for their behavior.

"The officer in charge should have informed us immediately of your arrival. Someone in the cultural department did not tell them to expect you. But it is over and I hope you will have a good experience here."

We arrived in Prague with no further incidents. The busses pulled up to our hotel and the guide entered the lobby while we waited. A few minutes later she returned.

"I am so sorry but there is a further embarrassment," she said. "It seems that this hotel is over booked. There are no rooms for you here, so we will place you in another hotel. It is not as nice as this one but it should do. Mostly Czechs use it. They are very friendly there."

They were very friendly, but the hotel was a hovel by US standards. However, we had no choice; we were exhausted and did not complain.

The next morning our Czechish guide gave us a tour of the beautiful city. It was a wonderful experience and one that made us appreciate our freedom in the United States. Russian tanks were stationed at every major intersection with their gun tubes parallel to the street, ready to quell any potential uprising. Soviets were not loved in Czechoslovakia, especially after the invasion in 1968, during which the Soviet Union invaded Czechoslovakia to crack down on reformist trends in Prague. They devastated the country.

Upon our return to the hotel our guide was waiting in the lobby.

"Maestro, I have more bad news for you. There has been a terrible mistake and the concert hall in which you were to perform has been rented to another entity. But don't worry, we have found another place for you to perform."

"Well we will just have to make the best of it. Where is it?"

"It actually is not in the city but in a town not too far away."

I think the Soviet-controlled government was concerned that we might be too successful and cause a problem. We accepted our fate and traveled to the village where we were assigned to perform.

That performance proved to be another Czech experience that we never shall forget, but this one luckily did not include being detained or interrogated.

We performed the overture we had been performing for the first week of our tour. There only were a handful of people in the audience when we began. As we played, more and more people congregated until the facility was overflowing with an adoring and enthusiastic public. The final piece of the concert was Dvorak's New World Symphony. It received an astonishingly warm reception. The entire audience stomped their feet in unison and demanded we perform several encores. After the concert the audience was overcome with emotion. They picked flowers from their gardens and handed them to members of the orchestra asking for their autographs. It was one of the most moving experiences one could imagine. The attempt by the Soviet-controlled government to isolate us from the Czech people had failed miserably.

Vienna, Salzburg, and Amsterdam

The rest of the tour was relatively calm compared to our experience in Czechoslovakia. Our next stop was in Vienna, where the orchestra gave another splendid performance. The reviews were enthusiastic. One critic stated that the orchestra was of such a high caliber he was in a quandary as to whether he should review the concert as he would a professional orchestra's performance.

One of the most thrilling performing experiences for the group was the opportunity to perform in Salzburg's Mozarteum. It was a magical and inspired concert performed in a city where Mozart had created so many masterpieces.

On an originally unscheduled stop in Mainz, Germany, a very anxious circumstance took place. Professor ("Prof") James Jacobsen, director of bands at TCU, was the chairman of logistics, responsible for seeing that the chaperones were executing their duties properly, equipment was handled efficiently, and that we remained on schedule. We assigned him that responsibility because of his exacting disciplinary reputation and attention to detail.

The French hornists in the group asked if we could stop in Mainz because it is home to one of the most important French horn manufacturers in the world: Alexander. We made arrangements for our French horn section to have a brief tour of their factory. We gave the rest of the orchestra free time to briefly explore the charming city. Prof Jacobsen set a deadline for departure from Mainz and threatened that anyone late would be left behind. At the appointed time a hasty roster check was made, and we left.

After a few miles of driving, Elisabeth Adkins shouted: "Stop the bus! We left Chris behind!" Her brother, Chris Adkins, currently the principal cellist of the Dallas Symphony, was the youngest member of our orchestra. He was late for the bus's departure. Elisabeth, our concertmaster, was beside herself. We stopped at the next place that had a telephone and called the Alexander factory. Fortunately, he was still there, and we arranged for him to join us at our next destination. Surprisingly, he was not frightened; instead, he expected us to realize his absence, so he patiently awaited his rescue.

The final concert was in Amsterdam's famous Vondel Park amphitheater. It was a fine performance, and we had the largest audience on the tour.

The flight back to the US was uneventful, especially in comparison to the events of the tour. As the plane landed in the US our entire group spontaneously sang the national anthem; there wasn't a dry eye on the airplane.

Washington, DC

After the European tour, the orchestra continued to grow artistically, garnering national recognition. We were invited to perform in Carter Barron Amphitheater in Washington, DC. Lorin Hollander was the piano soloist for the concert. The amphitheater is an excellent venue for orchestral performances and frequently features the National Symphony.

The program contained two major works: Dvorak's Eighth Symphony and Khachaturian's Piano Concerto. We had one rehearsal scheduled in the venue. It turned out to be an unusually hot and humid day, so we decided to rehearse the concerto first and finish as soon as possible.

The sun was shining directly on the string instruments, causing the varnish on many of them to soften.

We stopped the rehearsal after the concerto and returned to the hotel. However, I was very concerned with the readiness of the Dvorak, since we hadn't played it for some time, and felt that it needed more rehearsing. We were faced with a dilemma: there was no place to rehearse and, even if there were, our equipment and larger instruments were stored and only available for the performance.

I assembled the orchestra in the lobby of our hotel. It was the only available space large enough to accommodate a group of our size. I explained that since there was no venue available in which they could play, they were going to sing the entire symphony. I had them sit on the floor in the orchestra's usual seating configuration and conducted them as they sang the entire Dvorak Symphony complete with all its nuances. It took a while for them to get into the spirit of things, but once they did, they sang with enthusiasm. (The voice is the ultimate instrument, and as my father taught me when I was a preteen, instrumentalists should play is if they were singing.)

The performance that evening was a dramatic example of how singing for instrumentalists greatly improves their artistry. The performance was exceptionally sensitive and the intonation, balance, and ensemble playing exemplary.

The Youth Orchestra's Development

During my tenure as music director the participants in the Youth Orchestra program expanded from thirty-five student musicians to three hundred.

Some of the former Youth Orchestra members are now playing in major symphony orchestras; one was an Air Force officer; and others are surgeons, teachers, and lawyers.

The Fort Worth Youth Orchestra's program continues to thrive and improve. It currently consists of a Suzuki School, a Beginning String Orchestra, a Junior Youth Orchestra, the Youth Orchestra, a Chamber Music Program, a facility for the library, and office space for the administrative staff, the music director, and artistic staff. The artistic staff's high quality begins with the current music director, Germán Gutiérrez, one of the finest conductors of young musicians. The orchestra has developed artistically to an extremely high level, capable of performing the entire symphonic music repertoire.

As Maestro Rachlin predicted, the YO was the foundation of my career as a conductor. It influenced the direction of my life, propelled my artistic development, and inspired me to learn and delve into the substance of a great deal of the world's greatest music.

FOUR

The Fort Worth Symphony Orchestra and the Van Cliburn International Piano Competition

After the success of the Youth Orchestra in the San Moritz and the subsequent visibility it garnered through several prominent concerts and publicity that Betty Utter, executive director, attained for it, I became somewhat well known in the Fort Worth music community. Several members of the YO Board of Directors as well as other community leaders, including the executive director of the FWSO, Beverly Cardona, encouraged me to apply for the music director position vacated by Ezra Rachlin.

My audition took place in the 1971-72 season. I programmed a variety of musical styles for my concert: Shostakovich's Festive Overture, Dvorak's Eighth Symphony in G Major, and Ginastera's "Estancia Dances." The pianist Barry Snyder played Liszt's Piano Concerto in E-Flat. After my audition, I was offered a one-year contract for the 1972-73 season. As a result of that season, I was given a three-year contract as music director/conductor beginning the 1973-74 season.

During the 1972 season, in addition to the eight concerts I conducted with the FWSO, Anshel Brusilow, the music director of the Dallas Symphony, engaged me for the season to perform saxophone solos in a number of park and community concerts and to function as his assistant conductor. In that capacity, he assigned me to conduct several student and community concerts that season. Maestro Brusilow gave me conducting lessons as part of my compensation. When he learned of my appointment as music director of the Fort Worth Symphony Orchestra, he sent a very encouraging note.

"Rely on your talent and you will do extremely well," he wrote.

The day my appointment was announced, a telegram arrived from an English professor, John Pratt, who was a colleague at Tarleton State University where I taught in 1963-64. It read:

"Congratulations! Remember—Speak loudly and carry a little stick!"

No matter how thrilled I was to be named music director, my position with the FWSO was basically a part-time job, and Mary Alice and I couldn't rely on its income alone to make ends meet. Mary Alice was also the alto soloist at Saint Andrew's Episcopal Church, a paid position, and she taught piano lessons. At the same time, she was able to care for our children. Even with Mary Alice working, however, it still would have been difficult to survive on my FWSO salary and Mary Alice's part-time positions. Thus, it was serendipitous that the conductor of the TCU orchestra, Fritz Berens, retired in the spring of 1973. TCU and the FWSO always worked closely, so TCU offered me his position at the beginning of the 1973 fall semester, and between the FWSO and TCU job, I could earn a reasonably decent living to help support my family. My teaching load consisted of conducting the university orchestra and teaching a conducting course and a music appreciation course for non-music majors. As if I weren't already busy enough with my positions at the FWSO and TCU, when another opportunity presented itself in 1973, I just couldn't say no. Thus began my relationship with the Van Cliburn International Piano Competition.

The Van Cliburn International Piano Competition

Serving as music director of the Fort Worth Symphony changed the course of the lives of our family. We purchased a home in Fort Worth and moved there in the summer of 1973. My forty-year relationship with the Van Cliburn International Piano Competition began as a serendipitous surprise.

When I received the phone call from my friend Catherine Russell, who was asking me to step in for Howard Hanson for the 1973 Cliburn Competition, I told her I would help her in any way I could. She instructed me to arrive at TCU a half hour before the jury orientation meeting and that she would provide me with all the necessary instructions and materials. "It won't be difficult for you at all," Catherine told me. "All you have to do is to just make certain that everything runs smoothly regarding the jury."

Make everything run smoothly during one of the most prestigious international music competitions? Easy enough, I thought.

"I don't feel qualified to vote without a great deal of preparation and much more knowledge of the competition." I told her.

"You do not have to vote; you simply have to administer the proceedings."

I told her I could handle it, and I hoped I was right.

I arrived the next day a half hour before the scheduled orientation for the jury and asked Catherine for the jury handbook that should contain all the information the jury needed, including the rules and regulations along with an explanation of the scoring system.

She said: "There is no handbook. You're the jury chairman—you decide!"

I was puzzled and replied: "There is nothing distributed to the jury with that information?"

"John, you're the jury chairman. It's your job to make those decisions."

I was dumbfounded. "What? There are no written regulations and voting methods?"

"Of course not," she replied. "The jury chairman decides all those things. Come and meet the jury. We're running behind schedule."

And so my forty-year affiliation with the Van Cliburn International Piano Competition began.

* * * * * *

I entered the jury meeting room, and, before leaving the room, Catherine introduced me to the jury; they were luminaries, such as major performers Lili Kraus, Leonard Pennario, Nicole Henriot-Schweitzer, and James Dick, and major teachers such as Abram Chasins and his wife Constance Keene.

After the initial pleasantries, Leonard Pennario asked: "What scoring system are we using?"

I improvised. "We will use a system like that used at many Olympic events. We will score the competitors, assigning a numerical evaluation from 1 to 25 to each competitor. After each stage, we will drop the top and bottom scores and average the others."

"Will the scores be cumulative?" Leonard Pennario asked.

"No," I answered. "We will deliberate after every stage."

"What about the system for the finals? Will it be the same?" another juror asked.

"No, we will list them from one through eight—one being the best. We then will total the scores, and the finalist with the lowest cumulative number will be the winner."

Catherine entered the room and interrupted. "John, we're running late. We must go to the hall now."

As we exited the room behind Catherine, Abram Chasins, a brilliant American composer, pianist, piano teacher, lecturer, and musicologist asked me:

"John, where do we sit?"

That's a strange question, I thought.

"In the auditorium, Mr. Chasins," I said, while trying not to sound sarcastic.

"Yes, of course. But where?"

I was amazed that someone so sophisticated and brilliant would ask such a question

"I'm certain there will be a section cordoned off for us," I answered.

He replied, impatiently, "Yes, yes, I assumed that! But what are our seat assignments?"

"Just take your place anywhere in the jury section."

"No, no, even though we are married, Connie and I must sit on opposite sides of the jury. There is a reason that she lives in New York and I in Los Angeles!"

Catherine took me aside. "Excuse me, John, but we really have to get started right now. We have set up a microphone in the center of the front row and that's where you will sit."

Again, I was puzzled. "Why do I need a microphone, Catherine?"

"You'll need that to talk with the contestants and tell them what piece and which section of the work you want them to play. We think a bell is too shocking."

At that time, major competitions normally required competitors to design a program consisting of works from categories that the competition requires and will stipulate a time limit for each stage of the competition. For example, a competition might require a forty-five-minute program of works to be selected in Stage One from composers like Mozart, Beethoven, and Chopin. Stage Two might be a sixty-minute program of works of Liszt, Brahms, Scriabin, etc. I never imagined that a jury chairman in any competition would request certain works and/or parts of works on the spot.

"What? You mean they don't play entire works, and I select what they play?"

"Of course, John. It's always been like that!"

I couldn't believe it. "They don't know what they're going to play before they're on stage?"

"Of course not. They are required to prepare all of the repertoire on the list they prepared for the competition, and you choose what you want them to play."

That really set me back, but I had no choice at this point. I took my seat in front of the microphone.

I opened the program to the repertoire page and couldn't believe my eyes. The program contained all of the competitors lists, which included an overwhelmingly vast amount of works from the Baroque, Classical, Romantic, Impressionist, Twentieth Century, and Modern periods. It looked like the entirety of the modern piano repertoire.

I couldn't understand how anyone could learn that much music. It was like a conservatory final exam, the kind of exam I had experienced throughout my musical education as a student and professor. As a theory and composition major, I had studied a great deal of piano music but was not familiar with much of this unbelievably extensive list.

Just before I called for the first competitor, Abram Chasins, sitting immediately behind me, leaned over and whispered: "John, it isn't necessary for us to hear more than a few measures of each piece."

"You mean that you want me to stop them after they only have played a few bars? Surely we need to hear more than that."

"If any member of this jury can't make a decision after eight measures they don't belong on an international jury!"

I ignored him, followed my instincts, and requested a variety of works that would give the jury what I perceived to be the most insight into each competitor's artistry. I also decided that I would poll the jury throughout each competitor's performance to ascertain when everyone had heard enough.

I summoned Catherine and asked her to provide me with scores.

"We never have provided any scores, John," she informed me. "Surely you all know the music well enough to do without it. No one ever has asked for that before. If the jury doesn't know all of the repertoire by memory we have the wrong group!"

Nothing surprised me after that.

There was no way I could implement any changes at that point. I requested sections of major works according to what I felt was necessary for the jury to evaluate each pianist. It was obvious that it had to differ for each competitor.

I interrupted the performances at points that were the least disturbing and chose logical sections. For example, if they were playing Liszt's Piano Sonata in B Minor, I might interrupt, "Thank you, now please skip to the fugue." I requested whatever I believed to be necessary for the jury to make a proper decision until either the competitor's time was up or the entire jury was satisfied.

But Abram Chasins was relentless. After a few measures of every piece, he leaned over my shoulder and whispered: "We don't need any more of that. Stop her now for God's sake. I'm sure everyone has heard enough!"

Despite Mr. Chasins's chidings, I stayed the course, designed the programmatic contents of the competitors' programs to give the jury as much information as they needed to make a proper evaluation, and directed the competition sessions as I saw fit.

* * * * * *

Since Catherine Russell's phone call on September 16, 1973, I immersed myself in the Van Cliburn International Piano Competition. The 1973 Cliburn Competition was important to me in a myriad of ways. I acquired many close friends and learned an enormous amount of piano repertoire. I also helped to develop my artistic growth by listening to some of the world's best young artists' interpretations of magnificent masterpieces.

My First Cliburn Competition, 1973

There were many interesting moments during the 1973 competition, and some humorous. Lili Kraus sat next to me during the competition sessions; we became close friends, and I soon considered her to be a member of our immediate family. She was often mischievous during the competition sessions. After every performance she would, in a dramatic, Hungarian accented loud stage whisper, either exclaim: "Superb!" or shake her head and say: "Poor boy/girl." Lili was a very popular, flamboyant, and highly visible international figure; the audience watched her every gesture because she was an icon in Fort Worth. After several of her demonstrative reactions, and many complaints from her jury colleagues ("John, please do something about Lili"), I spoke with her and asked that she be more discreet and not make any physical reaction to the performances.

As discreetly as possible I grabbed her arm during the performances when I felt she might

ABOVE
Van meeting with competitors discussing his artistic philosophy. Courtesy of The Cliburn.

dramatically over-respond to a particular performance. Sometimes it worked!

The Van Cliburn International Piano Competition was unique in many ways, but one thing that set it apart from other international competitions was Van Cliburn's insistence on including chamber music in the competition at its inception. All collaborative performances are based on chamber music playing. Chamber music is transparent and difficult and reveals essential aspects of a performer's musicality. Whether one is performing a sonata with a solo wind or string instrument, a trio, quartet, quintet, or orchestra, the fundamental musical content is identical. Collaborating artists must listen carefully to each other and exchange musical ideas as they are playing and working together to create a common musical goal. If they don't the result is neither artistic nor satisfying. Individuals in ensemble playing should not insist on the interpretation of the work; the performance should reflect a combined and cooperative effort. The same elements are critical in concerto performances: if the soloist in a concerto hears one of the instruments playing a phrase in a way the soloist hadn't conceived of and likes it, a fine artist will incorporate that idea. An outstanding, thrilling performance of any ensemble is enhanced to a large degree by that collaborative effort. Van epitomized that concept in his concerto performances, and subsequently conductors and orchestras loved to perform with him. That contributed to his performances' great successes.

The optimum vehicles in which to evaluate a pianist's chamber music ability probably are trios and quartets. They reveal the performers' skills to the highest level. The problem with those is that they take much rehearsal time and it is almost impossible to find an extant violin, cello duo or a violin, viola, and cello string trio. That would necessitate hiring separate musicians and arranging for their rehearsal time prior to the competition, logistically a daunting task.

Subsequently we settled on using piano quintets. That also gave us the opportunity to engage some of the finest quartets: The Tokyo String Quartet, the Brentano String Quartet, the American String Quartet, the Takács Quartet.

Walter Susskind, music director of the Saint Louis Symphony, conducted the final phase of the competition with the Fort Worth Symphony. Since Maestro Susskind was my former conducting teacher, I insisted that I transport him and his newest bride from the airport to their hotel and to his first rehearsal with the Fort Worth Symphony. The Tarrant County Convention Center was the venue for the finals and all the rehearsals, and performances took place in its JFK Theater. The theater was a multipurpose hall and had a large door designed for vehicles to drive into the backstage area to unload scenery and large equipment used for stage productions of shows, ballets, and operas. When I entered the theater's parking lot with Walter, I noticed that the huge loading-dock door was open, so I drove into the building and parked at his dressing room.

"My God John, is this the way they do things in Fort Worth? Is your parking space in front of your dressing room?"

"Of course," I answered. "Isn't this the way it's done in St. Louis?"

Walter had a wonderful sense of humor. All the finalists were required to perform Beethoven's Fourth Piano Concerto in addition to a virtuosic one of their choice. That meant that the orchestra and conductor had to play the Beethoven sixteen times including rehearsals and performances.

We were driving Walter and Jennifer to their hotel after one of the concerts. There was a popular TV ad that went something like: "I dreamed I was playing in an all-girl orchestra in my Maidenform Bra."

Mary Alice asked Walter, "Walter, how is everything going? Is there anything you need?"

"Well, Last night I fell asleep and was dreaming. I dreamed I was conducting Beethoven's Fourth. I woke up, and I was!"

I was fortunate in that every problem I encountered during the 1973 competition was resolved, and the competition was a great success.

Van Cliburn

I met Van Cliburn in 1973 when my tenure as jury chairman of the Cliburn Competition began, and it was an experience that I will never forget.

Van will always be remembered as one of the greatest pianists of our time. His triumph in Moscow in 1958 changed the complexion of the relations between the United States and the Soviet Union at a time when there was considerable tension between the two superpowers. This extraordinary event—one that never can be repeated—emphasized the significance of classical music in our society and confirmed that it transcends politics, geography, and ethnic boundaries. Van became the hero of the free world overnight and, through his music, made us believe in the sanctity of the human spirit.

Before we were introduced, I was very nervous and anxious. I was meeting a living legend, the great artist who charmed and captured the hearts of Russia and changed the course of the Cold War! When we met, I knew that I was in the presence of someone special, but there was no need to be nervous. Van was warm, self-effacing, humble, and dignified—qualities that were reflected in his performances. They were always electrifying.

Van had a particular philosophy when it came to performance. He would often say something along the lines of:

"We have the sacred responsibility to reproduce the works of the great masters to the highest level of our ability. It must be as if we had plucked the most beautiful flower in full bloom from our garden and are handing it across the footlights to our precious audience. It is a serious and considerably important responsibility."

Van was a champion of classical music; he always strove to perform on the loftiest level and never considered his performances to be adequate. He often stated: "The more I study and practice, the more I learn something new and the more I realize how little I know."

I collaborated many times with Van, and it always was a special occasion for everyone on stage as well as for the audience. The concerts were inspiring, exciting, and fulfilling. The musicians were on the edge of their seats trying to emulate Van's every musical inflection. He rarely said a word in rehearsals—he didn't have to. His music making spoke for itself. When his part was subservient, he gave the orchestra full rein, and when he had the principal part, we all knew what he wanted.

Van sympathized with young artists, always supporting their developing careers. Van appreciated and admired artists in every musical discipline. All classical music, especially opera, touched him deeply, and he was effusive in his compliments to the performers.

Van was a great storyteller; his prodigious

RIGHT
Van performing in the recital stage of the Tchaikovsky International Piano Competition in 1958. Courtesy of The Cliburn.

RIGHT
Van's ticker tape parade following his victory in the Tchaikovsky International Piano Competition in 1958. Courtesy of The Cliburn.

LEFT
Rehearsing with Van and the Fort Worth Symphony Orchestra (FWSO). Courtesy of The Cliburn.

ABOVE
Celebrating with Van Cliburn after a FWSO performance. Author Collection.

LEFT
Leaving the stage with Van after a FWSO concert. Author Collection.

memory enabled him to recount fascinating events in detail. Van loved to laugh, and it was so infectious that when I recall those many humorous moments it is difficult to restrain from laughing out loud. He was the best storyteller imaginable and could thoroughly recount fascinating events. Through his extraordinary music making, his definitive recordings, his charm, his charisma, and his caring spirit, he has enriched the world with a legacy that will last forever.

Van's Father's Funeral

Van's father died January 14, 1974, not long after my first Van Cliburn International Piano Competition, and soon after the formidable Martha Hyder was named the new chairman of the competition, a seat previously occupied by Adelaide Fuller. Martha would prove to be a transforming force for the Cliburn Competition, and for myself. Adelaide was Van's close friend, and she continued to be involved with the competition. She invited me to accompany her and Martha in her private plane to attend Van's father's funeral in Shreveport.

The flight was uneventful until we began our approach to Shreveport. Adelaide asked the copilot what arrangements he had made for a limousine to pick us up.

The pilot answered, "I'm so sorry, Mrs. Fuller, but I forgot."

Adelaide demanded that he immediately see to it that there be a limo waiting for us on the tarmac.

After a few moments, the copilot returned and informed Adelaide that every limo in Shreveport was already reserved. Adelaide was livid; she then demanded that he engage a taxi to meet us instead and arrange for it to stay on hand for us the entire day.

When our plane landed, we saw a filthy, dented, and dilapidated Yellow Cab with torn seats parked at the bottom of the plane's exit ladder. The driver, a large, muscular woman dressed in dirty coveralls, was smoking a cigar. The taxi had a large sign on its roof advertising "OLD CROW." Unfortunately, we had no choice but to accept this transportation. So there we were: two beautifully dressed, elegant women and me in a black suit, seated in a hot, stuffy Yellow Cab on our way to the home of one of the world's most famous and respected artists to attend his father's funeral.

"Please turn on the air-conditioning," Adelaide requested.

"Air-conditioning?" The driver responded. "What the hell do y'all think this is—a damn limo? Y'all are damn lucky; this is the last car we got in town! And don't worry, ladies, I'm a damn good driver."

Adelaide and Martha were horrified.

When we finally arrived at Van's home, sweating and likely smelling like cigar smoke, Van was standing on his front porch awaiting our arrival. When he saw our vehicle, Van—the personification of decorum—handled the situation with aplomb.

"I'm so, so embarrassed, Adelaide and Martha, please let me arrange for proper transportation."

Adelaide replied, "I am the one who is embarrassed, Van. Please forgive us."

The driver, cigar still in hand with her left elbow resting on the taxi, chimed in: "What are y'all talkin' about? There ain't a damn thing wrong with this car! If y'all are too damn good to ride in this cab, just tell me and I'll get the hell out of here."

I calmed the driver and begged her to remain until we knew what we were going to do.

We paid our respects to Van and his mother, Rildia Bee. Van invited us to join him and his mother to attend the graveside services in the family limousine. Adelaide declined and said we probably should be returning to the plane. Van insisted that we join the procession immediately following his limousine. In deference to him and his mother, we agreed.

Adelaide said, "As you wish, Van. However,

we will follow the procession at a distance that will not embarrass you."

Van insisted. "No, no, Adelaide. You are too important to Mother and me. After all, you are family. I insist that you be the next car following Mother's and mine."

The taxi driver interrupted. "Dammit!" she yelled. "There ain't nothin' embarrasin' about this car!"

Adelaide pleaded with the driver to at least remove the Old Crow sign.

The driver said, "This sign stays right where it is. I don't give a damn how fancy y'all think y'all are; Old Crow is paying me a hell of a lot of money to have this on my roof."

Thus, we followed Van's black limousine to his father's graveside in our non-air-conditioned Yellow Cab with the Old Crow sign on the roof, and our driver, elbow on the window, smoking a cigar.

Van and I laughed about this almost every time we got together.

The Cliburn's Martha Hyder Years, 1973 - 1977

The Van Cliburn Competition had an enormous influence on my artistic development and personal life. I attribute much of it to Martha Hyder. An extraordinary woman in every regard, Martha was intelligent, regal, energetic, and industrious.

Martha chaired the 1977 Van Cliburn Competition after Adelaide Fuller passed her the torch. (Adelaide was the chairman of the 1973 competition. She was an elegant, generous, and gracious woman. Her husband William, a successful businessman, supported her philanthropy.)

From the first moment I met Martha during the 1973 Cliburn Competition, I knew she was a special individual. After the competition that year, she invited me to her fabulous home on Crestline Drive to begin planning for the 1977 competition. The home is remarkable, only challenged for its uniqueness by her other home, Casa Hyder, in San Miguel, Mexico. The Crestline home is filled with priceless art and collections of objects d'art from everywhere. Both Martha and her husband Elton Hyder Jr., a prominent attorney who garnered his fame from his role as a prosecutor in the Tojo war trials after WWII, collected items from Degas paintings to Russian icons to ancient dueling pistols to crowns of Russian tzars to African spears. Martha never did anything less than 100 percent, including decorating her home. One time Martha was decorating her lake house for a Cliburn party. She had a new next-door neighbor whom she had yet to meet. When she knocked on his door, he answered and she immediately said: "Hello, I'm your neighbor, Martha Hyder. I'm having a party and would like to paint the side of your house red to complement my color scheme. I know you won't mind since there aren't any windows on that side so you won't be able to see it from inside your home." He let her do it!

Everything with Martha was an adventure, no matter if we were abroad or even in our own home state. One time, Martha, Mary Alice, and I travelled to San Antonio to hear the Russian pianist Vladimir Viardo's premier performance with the San Antonio Symphony. Viardo was the Cliburn competition's 1973 gold medalist. Martha invited Lady Bird Johnson, one of her close friends, to attend the concert since Johnson City is less than an hour's drive to San Antonio. Lady Bird graciously declined and invited us to the LBJ Ranch for lunch.

It was fascinating to hear about many of Lady Bird's experiences in the White House. She began with the circumstances surrounding the assassination of President John F. Kennedy from her viewpoint, including the swearing in of her husband, President Johnson. She talked in some detail about her current project of planting Texas wildflowers along the highways

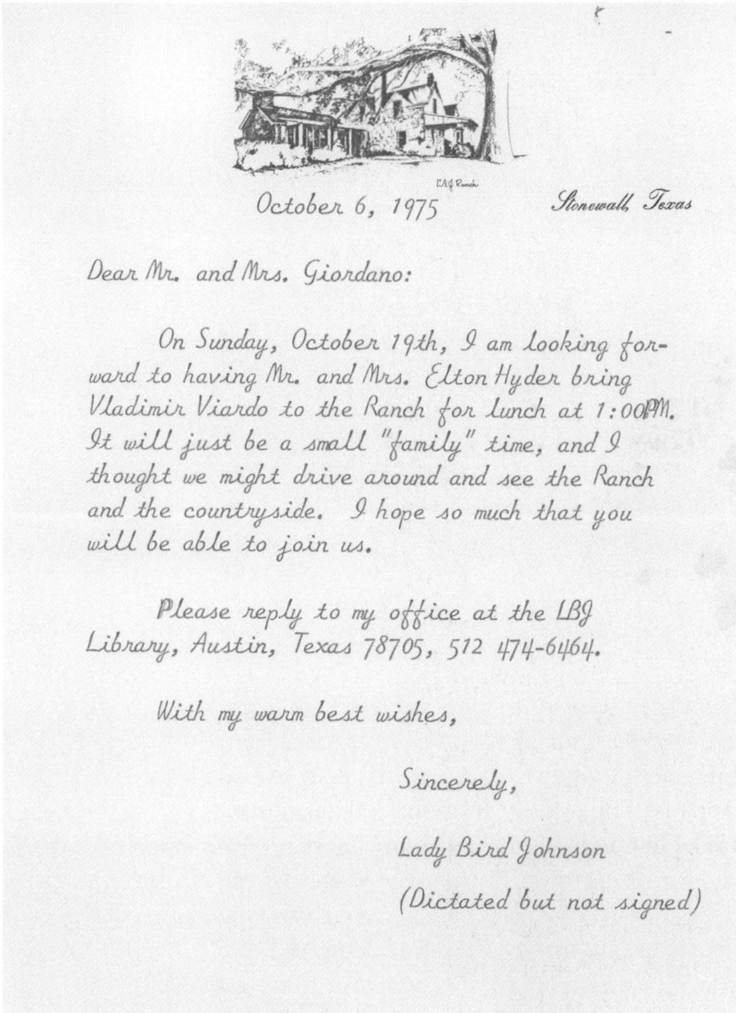

October 6, 1975 Stonewall, Texas

Dear Mr. and Mrs. Giordano:

On Sunday, October 19th, I am looking forward to having Mr. and Mrs. Elton Hyder bring Vladimir Viardo to the Ranch for lunch at 1:00PM. It will just be a small "family" time, and I thought we might drive around and see the Ranch and the countryside. I hope so much that you will be able to join us.

Please reply to my office at the LBJ Library, Austin, Texas 78705, 512 474-6464.

With my warm best wishes,

Sincerely,

Lady Bird Johnson

(Dictated but not signed)

ABOVE
Lady Bird Johnson's invitation to lunch at LBJ ranch.
Author Collection.

throughout Texas.

Martha's circle of friends included some of the most influential people in the world. Once, when I was in LA, I called Jimmy Stewart at Martha's request to ask him to be a member of an international board that she was putting together. His first words when he answered the phone after I introduced myself were: "How is Martha? I haven't heard from her in some time." Martha's circle was composed of heads of state, CEOs of major international corporations, and political leaders in several countries including the Soviet Union and royalty in the Far East, Middle East, and Eastern and Western Europe. These connections contributed greatly to our success. In fact, I never have met someone of international and national standing who did not either already know or at least know about Martha. Pretty much no one was immune from the amazing effects of Martha's influence, myself included. For example, on a 1980 trip to Beijing, where I was on a mission to recruit pianists and jurors from the People's Republic of China for the 1981 Cliburn Competition, I met the minister of culture. He first greeted me with, "Welcome to the People's Republic of China, Mr. Giordano." But his second sentence was, "Tell me, how is Martha Hyder?"

Diplomatic relations were strained between the US and the PRC at that time. I was the first US citizen admitted as an individual to the PRC immediately after the Cultural Revolution and am certain Martha Hyder's sphere of influence contributed to my admittance.

Martha was determined to make the 1977 Cliburn Competition the most important one in the world. Her first statement after giving my wife, Mary Alice, and me a tour of her incredible home was "How can we make the Cliburn the best? What do we have to do to make major improvements?" Martha also planned to produce a documentary film of the 1977 Cliburn Competition to bring more attention to it.

I gave her my suggestions of things we should improve to achieve her goal. "Young aspiring performers want to have many engagements in significant venues with orchestra as well as in recital; they want to be judged by a jury composed of the most important artists and teachers; and the repertoire and voting system must be improved—currently it is much too comprehensive, and the process is conducted like a conservatory final exam. If we are seeking young artists ready to be launched into a major career, they will probably be focused on specific repertoire such as Lili (Kraus) is on Mozart, Schubert, and other classical composers, or Van, who concentrates on Romantic works."

I continued my list of suggestions. "They want to have major management like Columbia Artists or Hurok; we must have a fully professional staff with a qualified executive director; we must recruit the finest young pianists—the ones who already have budding careers are skeptical of taking a chance of doing poorly in a competition; and we have to raise the quality of the Fort Worth Symphony, because even though it performed well in the competition, there will be much more international attention on the Cliburn in the future and the orchestra must be on the very highest possible level."

Martha agreed with most of my suggestions. But she added, "Why spend a lot of money to hire a fully staffed administration when we have the best, most knowledgeable, and dedicated volunteers in the world?"

"That's true Martha, but as dedicated, expert, and wonderful as our volunteers are, they can't possibly devote the time necessary to accomplish your goals. We must have experienced professionals leading the foundation. An experienced executive director will know exactly what to do and will have the necessary contacts and knowledge."

After further contemplating my suggestions she said: "This makes sense; we will do it all!" And she did.

Martha proceeded to read every book on classical music she could find. She researched and studied every major competition in the world. She even studied the careers of other competition winners to determine the effect the prize had on their careers.

One of Martha's first accomplishments was to hire an executive director. I suggested Bob Alexander, who was formerly the executive director with the FWSO. We were fortunate when he accepted the position.

Martha threw herself indefatigably into anything that interested her. She was the most determined individual I ever have met, often working and studying all night, frequently until daybreak. (This was a perfect formula for dealing with Van, too, since he studied and practiced all night.) But this meant that Martha would sometimes call at all hours of the morning. She would call at 3:00 a.m. and ask, for example: "I'm reading several books on classical music and listening to as much music as possible because I want to be an expert. What are the best recordings of Brahms's symphonies?"

One night, or rather morning, at about 2:00 a.m. Martha's phone call woke me, and I answered.

"I am ready," she said. "We are going to see every major conductor, major administrator, and important artist management in the world, and we are going to put together the best jury that ever has been assembled. John, you will meet with the conductors and I with the executive directors. Together we will make a great team."

It was impossible to be angry after being woken up by a phone call like this. Martha's enthusiasm and dedication inspired me to work harder so we could accomplish those goals. She was right—we were a great team. Martha and I had great ideas, and we executed them well together. Not *all* of her ideas were great, or even safe, though. Once Martha asked me to help smuggle Russian religious icons out of Moscow in my luggage. I told her that if I were caught, I would spend the rest of my life in a Soviet prison. She was nonplussed and said it was improbable that they would search my luggage at the airport (this was decades before today's security). Martha is a hard person to say no to, but I was adamant and told her that I really did not think I should smuggle anything out of the Soviet Union. That was the power of Martha's confidence, though. She was willing to risk life in a Soviet prison for some relics.

We began with New York. Martha and I visited with Leonard Bernstein to ask if he would help us. We also met with Carlos Moseley, the New York Philharmonic's president. Martha persuaded him to engage our winner. He agreed conditionally, based on the music director's blessing. With that success under our belts, we visited every major orchestra in the United States, sometimes without an appointment. Martha never accepted no for an answer. She convinced almost everyone that engaging our gold medalist would be in their best interest. In almost every instance we were successful. This venture was, and still is, unprecedented in the annals of international piano competitions.

Soon after that success, Martha called again. "Now that we have done so well getting engagements for the first prize winner, I want Mary Alice to do the same thing for the second and third prizes."

Mary Alice, who is also an articulate, fine musician, was energetic and successful, booking an amazing number of orchestral engagements for our second and third place winners.

Our executive director, Bob Alexander, put together an outstanding staff and followed Martha's directions to the best of his ability. However, Bob didn't indulge in idle conversation; his discussions were brief and to the point. Martha wanted to have daily and detailed conversations with him. One day she called me and complained, "I am so angry with Bob, he never calls me unless he has something to say! That is how I learn; I must have someone who talks to me several times every day."

Bob and Martha's relationship was strictly business. Bob was often frustrated with Martha because he couldn't accomplish all of her requests as fast as she requested they be done, though he always completed them. Bob resigned after the 1977 competition.

Martha always will be important to Mary Alice and me. She was a sensitive, caring, and faithful friend. It is not well known that she played an important part in the development of the Fort Worth Symphony. She introduced me to leaders of Fort Worth, which created opportunities for me to promote the development of the symphony.

The Cliburn Retreat and its Influence on the FWSO

In the spring of 1974 Martha asked Adelaide and William Fuller to host a retreat for community leaders at their Weatherford ranch. They invited several of their close friends, including Mr. and Mrs Charles Tandy, Mr. and Mrs. Perry Bass, and Mr. and Mrs. Bayard Friedman. Few people knew about the retreat.

Martha explained the importance of developing the Cliburn Competition as the leading international piano competition in the world, or as she phrased it, "I want to make it the best." She emphasized the impact it could have on Fort Worth as well as on classical music worldwide.

To achieve these goals, Martha stressed that more underwriting was a necessity. She asked me to explain the process that I envisioned to improve the FWSO. I presented an abridged version of the outline that I later presented to the Fort Worth Symphony Orchestra Board. Many of those at the retreat were the same as those who supported the FWSO and also served on its board of directors. They enthusiastically supported my plan based on acquiring the necessary funding. Their support helped me obtain official approval from the FWSO Board of Directors.

Lili Kraus

Lili Kraus was the Artist in Residence at TCU when I met her in 1973, during my first stint as the jury chairman for the Van Cliburn International Piano Competition. We subsequently became close friends and performed together on many occasions with various orchestras in the US and abroad.

In addition to being one of the most insightful performers of the twentieth century, Madam Lili Kraus was also one of the truly unique individuals I have ever met (in the best way). A survivor of a WWII Japanese prison camp, she charmed her captors and laid the groundwork that was to become an extraordinary and positive relationship. The Japanese developed a deep affection for Lili, who became an icon in their country.

Lili was one of the leading performers of Mozart and Schubert. Her recordings of the Mozart concerti are quintessential, and she was respected and admired by her colleagues as well as by lovers of Mozart's piano music.

Lili possessed a special insight into music. She emphasized the importance of delving into the composer's lifestyle, the period of history in which the composer lived, and made a detailed technical analysis of their works. Since Lili was the Artist in Residence at TCU, where I had just accepted an appointment to the faculty as conductor of the TCU Symphony Orchestra, we formed a collegial and close relationship. This relationship gave me a rare opportunity to acquire her insight into the Mozart piano concertos.

She gave me private lessons, emphasizing her methods of determining her interpretations of Mozart. She explained why she approached her performances from a structural as well as philosophical standpoint.

In the first session, Lili related stories she fashioned for each concerto. For example, she perceived Mozart's D Minor Piano Concerto, K466, as an instrumental version of his opera *Don Giovanni*.

"This concerto is *Don Giovanni*. You must remember that Mozart was first and foremost an opera composer, and all of his concerti are operas."

She demonstrated how various musical themes in the concerto reflected phrases in the opera. She demonstrated how his piano concertos, as well as many of his other compositions, should be analyzed as if they were operas and be interpreted accordingly. She pointed out that all Mozart's music depicts life's experiences including passion, tenderness, anger, peacefulness, tranquility, and turmoil.

We also discussed analysis of Mozart's works from their structural perspective. During the sessions, I played the orchestra/piano reduction on one piano and Lili the solo part on another. She demonstrated how the performer should reach beyond the basic and obvious signs of loud, soft, long, short, speed, and accents. Less obvious aspects such as harmonic structure as well as rhythmic and thematic development must be studied and should influence one's interpretation. (Major artists who have insightful interpretations recreate works based on in-depth technical analysis.)

We needed a better piano at home, and Lili also was in the market for a piano. Together we chose and purchased two "twin" Yamaha six-foot grands.

The First Cliburn Trip to Europe

In January 1974 Martha planned our first trip to Europe to begin our quest to accomplish the goals we had set for recruiting competitors, acquiring important engagements, and procuring European management for the winner. We landed in London and checked into Claridge's Hotel. That evening we attended a concert at Royal Festival Hall in which Radu Lupu, one of our gold medalists, was performing with the London Symphony. After the performance we dined with Radu, then returned to the hotel around midnight. We were tired and suffering from jet lag.

When I returned to my room I realized it was Father's Day and decided to call my father. Before I had a chance to place the call the phone rang. It was Mary Alice.

"John, I'm so very sorry to tell you," my wife said, sounding composed but clearly upset. "Your father died suddenly of a heart attack last night."

I was in complete shock and could only respond by saying that I would take the first available flight home.

I called Martha's room to inform her of my father's unexpected death. Martha was amazing. "I'll be right there," she said. Within a few minutes she was in my room. As I sat in shock, frozen, sitting on the edge of my bed, Martha began packing my luggage and arranging for me to take the next available flight to Love Field. She even hired a limousine to take me to the airport.

Martha continued on our planned trip by herself and spent most of her time in Moscow. She visited Vladimir Viardo, and together they met with Madame Furtseva, the Soviet Union's minister of culture, who had a reputation of being a severe and unyielding administrator. Martha, unwavering as usual, insisted on the participation of Soviet artists in the next competition and requested that they provide a juror as well. Mme. Furtseva agreed to Martha's every request. (Martha also managed to smuggle several Russian religious icons in her luggage to add to her collection!)

Imelda Marcos's Leftovers

After Martha's Cliburn recruiting trip to Moscow, Mary Alice, Martha, and I traveled to New York City together to attend Vladimir's Carnegie Hall debut. Imelda Marcos, the controversial First Lady of the Philippines, was in New York at the time and invited Martha, Mary Alice, Van, Vladimir, and me to a post-concert reception at her penthouse in the Waldorf Astoria.

Martha asked us to meet her and escort her to the concert. We arrived at her room about thirty minutes before the concert. Martha, who always was appropriately and beautifully attired, greeted us at the door to her suite, and Mary Alice immediately exclaimed, "Martha, what a beautiful gown! You look fabulous!"

Martha responded, "What are you talking about Mary Alice? This is my dressing gown."

After the concert our group reconvened at Imelda Marcos's penthouse in the Waldorf Astoria. It even was more opulent than we expected, with enormous bouquets of exotic flowers on every surface. The glamorous Mrs. Marcos dramatically greeted us in the elegant and warm demeanor for which she was famous. She was a gracious and attentive hostess, and after a few minutes we all felt comfortable. At one point, one of her staff entered and whispered to her. The "First Lady" excused herself. She soon reappeared and announced: "Everyone, Ferdinand just called. He just received news that Franco died. We must go to Madrid for the funeral. Ferdinand is on the way to pick me up."

Mary Alice happened to be standing next to her. She turned to Mary Alice and said: "Mary Alice, of course you and John will accompany us to the funeral."

"I'm very sorry, Mrs. Marcos, we won't be able to join you."

"Why not?"

"I'm afraid we have to get back to our babysitter."

Mrs. Marcos, obviously incredulous that any of her acquaintances could not go to Madrid on a moment's notice, continued, "I truly apologize for having to leave you so suddenly. There are several 'leftovers' in the fridge. Please take them with you."

We all looked at each other and Van said, "Oh no Imelda, we can't accept your kind offer."

"Van, I insist. We won't be back here for some time and they must be consumed." She turned to a staff member. "Please take my friends to the kitchen and give them all of the leftovers they can carry!"

We obediently followed her staff member to the kitchen. She opened the refrigerator and began distributing the "leftovers." They were bottles of vintage Dom Perignon champagne. We took as many bottles as we could carry.

The Great Cliburn European Adventure of 1975

Martha decided it was crucial that we make an extensive tour of as much of Western Europe and Eastern Europe as possible. She assembled an entourage consisting of her twins Brent and Whitney, Adelaide Fuller, and me, and planned an itinerary to secure engagements for the gold medalist, recruit competitors, interview prospective jurors, and learn as much as possible about other major international competitions. As is usual with Martha, several unusual events took place.

Brussels to Paris

Martha and Adelaide had engaged a car and driver for our appointments in Brussels. Because of the frenetic schedule we set for our appointments and our continuous laughter over unusual happenstances, like losing our way in the Netherlands and going to the wrong city for a meeting with one of the potential management companies, our driver, Andre, referred to us as "my crazy Texans."

After a successful sojourn in Belgium and the Netherlands, we were scheduled to take the high-speed train to Paris, a three-hour trip. We were to gather in the hotel lobby, load Andre's car, and go to the Gare du Midi. Brent and Whitney were on time, and we all loaded our luggage into Andre's Chrysler. Martha and Adelaide were not present, albeit Adelaide's luggage was, which we placed in the car. We were concerned since it was becoming uncomfortably close to the train's departure time.

Brent suggested that we go to Martha and Adelaide's suite to check on them. Upon our arrival in their room we discovered Adelaide impatiently pacing the floor.

"Is there a problem Adelaide?" I asked.

"Martha still is not ready. I've told her a million times that we will miss the train if she doesn't hurry."

She called to her, "Martha, you must come right now! We will miss the train if you don't come this instant!"

Nonplussed, Martha responded, "Don't worry, I am all dressed and ready to go except for my bath!"

Somehow we managed to gather everyone and make it to the station a half hour before the train was scheduled to leave. Andre summoned a red cap and assisted him in taking the luggage to our compartment. He left the car running and parked in a loading zone while they carried our luggage to the compartment. Adelaide had arranged for a private car with hors d'oeuvres and champagne to toast our success in Belgium and the Netherlands. Andre, still enamored with his "crazy Texans," remained with us and joined the party. I noticed the time, and understanding that the efficient European trains always functioned on a strict schedule, warned Andre that the departure time was imminent. "Don't worry Mr. Giordano, I have plenty of time." As he uttered those words, the second hand struck the departure time, the doors automatically closed, and the train started to move.

Since it was a nonstop high-speed express train he had no choice but to travel all the way to Paris.

Andre's car was still parked in the short-term loading zone in front of the Gare du Midi in Brussels with the engine running. Andre's wallet, containing his driver's license, carte d'identité, credit cards, and cash were in the front seat of the car.

When we arrived in Paris we said goodbye to Andre and took a taxi to our hotel. He wasn't upset whatsoever about his plight and wished us well. He assured us that he would be able to return to Brussels with very little trouble.

Two years later I was guest conducting the National Symphony of Belgium and staying in the same hotel. The competition requested that I schedule meetings on their behalf while I was in Brussels. I decided to rent a car and driver for the day.

When my car and driver were scheduled to arrive, there was a knock on my hotel room door. I opened it—and there stood Andre! We both began to laugh uncontrollably. After we both regained our composure, I asked about his train fiasco to Paris.

"Well Mr. Giordano," he began, "after explaining my dilemma to the train's conductor in Paris, he agreed to let me return to Brussels on the next train."

"What happened to your car with all of your documents and cash? How did you explain your experience to your wife?"

"It was no problem. The car was still parked in front of the station and nothing was disturbed. As for my wife; I never told her!"

I forgot to ask him if the car was still running.

Vienna and Herr Gruen

We traveled to Vienna to acquire Austrian and German management. Our appointment was with the influential artist manager, Herr Gruen (Mr. "Green"). His office had a green carpet, the walls were green, the furniture was upholstered in dark green leather, the rest of the decor was in shades of green, and he wore a dark green suit with a green tie.

During our conversation, his door opened and an unkempt figure dressed in wrinkled clothing entered the room; we thought he was part of the cleaning crew. Herr Gruen excused himself, left the room with the man, and returned a few minutes later. We assumed he was chastising the man for his rude interruption.

The appointment was successful, and we completed an agreement with Herr Gruen for his agency to represent the next Cliburn winner. Herr Gruen invited Martha and me to be his guests that evening to a concert by the Vienna Philharmonic with the legendary pianist Arturo Benedetti Michelangeli performing Schumann's piano concerto.

The orchestra performed the opening work splendidly, as expected. The atmosphere in the hall was filled with excitement as we all eagerly anticipated Michelangeli's entrance.

There was an uncomfortably lengthy pause and the audience became restless. Several minutes later the stage door finally opened. Michelangeli and the conductor made their entrance to enthusiastic applause.

We immediately recognized him; he was the unkempt figure in Herr Gruen's office who we assumed was one of the cleaning crew!

The conductor took his place on the podium and Michelangeli approached the piano bench. He immediately turned around and left the stage. A stagehand then went to the piano and moved it at an imperceptibly different angle. Michelangeli made a second entrance to a slightly less enthusiastic ovation, approached the piano, shook his head and left again. The same stagehand reappeared and moved the piano to the previous angle. Michelangeli entered shook his head again; the stagehand reentered again and adjusted the height of the piano bench.

This routine was repeated several times, each time to less applause. Finally Michelangeli sat down and played the opening phrase of the Schumann. It was an extraordinarily beautiful performance and well worth experiencing the unusual and entertaining opening routine.

Martha and Karajan Meet in Paris

Martha Hyder was not intimidated by anyone. She and I attended two concerts in Paris by the Berlin Philharmonic conducted by Herbert von Karajan. The programs consisted of all four of Brahms's symphonies. After the second evening's concert, she asked me:

"Do you know Karajan?"

"No, I've never met him."

"It doesn't matter, I want to go backstage and ask him to engage the winner of the '77 competition."

"Martha, I'm certain they won't allow us to go backstage."

"Why not? Of course they will."

I led Martha to the backstage door. She opened it and a guard was standing just inside.

"This is Maestro Giordano, I am Martha Hyder," she said. "We are here to see Maestro Karajan. Where is his dressing room?"

He spoke no English, but she was so authoritative he assumed we were official and pointed to Karajan's dressing room.

A man the size and stature of a Dallas Cowboys linebacker stood in front of Karajan's dressing room at attention with his arms folded across his chest. Again, Martha stated, "This is Maestro Giordano, I am Martha Hyder. We are here to see Maestro Karajan."

"Nein" he said sternly. He was staring past us and didn't even glance at us.

Martha said, "Nonsense, we represent the Van Cliburn Piano Competition in Texas; he will see us!"

With that, she took him by surprise, pushed past him, opened the door, and we entered.

"Maestro von Karajan, this is Maestro John Giordano, I am Martha Hyder. We want to speak with you regarding your engaging the winner of the Van Cliburn Piano Competition."

The guard at the door entered and stepped menacingly toward us. Karajan nodded at him and gestured for him to leave.

We spoke with Karajan for a few minutes and explained our proposal. He was very gracious and said he would consider our proposal but would have to audition the winner before he would offer an engagement. We thanked him profusely for giving us the courtesy of speaking with him and left.

Galina and Varley Panov with Vladimir Viardo

Shortly after our return from Europe, I was engaged to conduct the Fort Worth Ballet in a Dallas performance featuring Valery and Galina Panov. They were two prominent Russian/Israeli dancers who, in 1974, had recently defected to Israel from the Soviet Union to a great deal of publicity and controversy and were making a rare appearance in Dallas. Valery was one of the greatest virtuoso dancers in the Soviet Union. Their defection increased the international tension between the Soviet Union and the Western world.

The Panovs were engaged to perform in Dallas soon after their defection, and I was invited to conduct the performance. Their appearance in Dallas generated worldwide attention.

The Panovs' flight was late, and they missed their only rehearsal with the orchestra for the performance. They had their own music for their act, which they planned to distribute to the orchestra at the rehearsal. They feared they were under constant surveillance by the KGB and had to be secretive regarding their accommodations and private activity during their public appearances. They were afraid they would be captured and forced to return to Russia. They arrived at the theater an hour before curtain time. Valery and I met briefly, for about five minutes, to discuss the tempos of their music before they were to perform. Fortunately, I knew the music well. Valery asked, "You know our music, no?"

I responded that I had performed it several times and that I wanted to discuss the tempos. Valery said, "Is not problem; all is standard tempo. If too slow, I raise thumb up; if too fast, down." It worked, and the performance was extraordinary.

Vladimir Viardo, the Russian pianist and gold medalist of the 1973 Cliburn, happened to be in Fort Worth visiting his former host during the competition, Martha Hyder. He was touring the US as a soloist with the Moscow State Symphony. The orchestra had a few days off during their tour, and Vladimir surreptitiously flew to Fort Worth to visit with Martha.

Vladimir learned that I was conducting the Panovs' performance with the Fort Worth Ballet in Dallas. He asked me to arrange for a secret meeting with them after their performance to discuss the details of their defection, because he too was considering defecting.

After the performance I spoke with Valery alone in his dressing room and told him of Vladimir's desire to meet with him to discuss Vladimir's plans to defect. Valery consented, but only if it could be done with utmost secrecy. Around 11:00 that evening after the performance, Mary Alice and I parked in front of their hotel. The Panovs were nowhere to be seen. Suddenly, Galina and Valery appeared out of the shadows and quickly entered the back seat of the car through a door Mary Alice had opened. They were trying to hide. They did not sit up in the car, remaining in a crouched position, until we were on the interstate highway between Dallas and Fort Worth.

We arrived at Martha Hyder's home around midnight. There, the Panovs and Vladimir discussed with Vladimir how they escaped from the Soviet Union and the details of their defection until daybreak. Valery interrupted their conversation and turned to me. He said, "John, please we go back to hotel now. Is late and dangerous for us."

They ended the conversation with Vladimir, and we drove them back to their Dallas hotel. As they got out of the car, Valery turned to me and said, "John, thank you for good performance. Have good life!" They quickly rushed into the hotel.

It was a surreal experience.

During a rehearsal with the FWSO the next day, my assistant, Sylvia Stoddard, handed me a note with a phone number and a message that stated: "Please call the Soviet embassy as soon as possible."

I called at the next break. A man gruffly answered:

"Is Mr. Giordano?"

I affirmed that it was.

"Is Maestro who conduct Soviet dancers, Panovs in Dallas, Texas?"

Again, I affirmed that I was.

"Is true you drive them to Crestline Road in Fort Worth, Texas, where they meet with Soviet pianist Viardo and discuss defection from Russia?"

At this, I was taken a bit off guard by the known details of our supposed clandestine interaction. "Yes, why?"

"We are very angry that you help Soviet citizen defect to West."

Now, I was angry. "Sir, this is the United States, not Russia, and I can take anyone anywhere I please. Do not call me again!" I slammed the receiver down. Later, when I reflected on the phone call and previous evening, I realized that a Russian agent must have followed us the whole evening because they knew exactly where we went and the content of the conversation that took place. I guess I'm not cut out for life as a secret agent.

Amsterdam Engagement, Pickpocket, Claridge's, and a Lost Passport

Martha learned of my engagement during June of 1976 with the Amsterdam Philharmonic at the Concertgebouw and asked me to stop in London a couple of days before my rehearsals. We were trying to secure London management for the winner with Harrison and Parrott Artist Management, and Martha charged me with the duty of finalizing a contract with them. I scheduled the meetings with Jason Parrott, who was then married to 1969 Cliburn Gold Medalist Cristina Ortiz. Martha arranged for me to stay in Claridge's, the five-star luxury London hotel in Mayfair that caters to heads of state, international figures, and celebrities.

Following my Cliburn duties I had a morning flight to Amsterdam from Heathrow that was scheduled to arrive in time for a two o'clock rehearsal. The logistics of my travel plans had become complicated. My program consisted of American works as part of the Holland American Festival. One of the works was not published in Europe, therefore the publishing company sent the orchestra parts to me. They did not arrive in time before my flight to London, and it was too late to forward them to Amsterdam. When I explained the problem to Martha during a casual conversation, she arranged with one of her friends who was travelling to London and arriving on the morning of my flight to Amsterdam to take the music in her carry-on luggage.

Heathrow has intercontinental and international terminals. My plan of action was to meet Martha's friend at the intercontinental terminal, pick up my music, and go directly to the international terminal for my flight on KLM to Amsterdam. It was a tight schedule but doable. To expedite everything, I asked my taxi driver to wait for me at the intercontinental terminal and drive me to the international terminal.

Everything was going splendidly—the plane with my music was on time. I met the lady at the exit from customs, retrieved my package from her, and hurried to the waiting taxi. When we arrived at the international terminal, I reached into my jacket to get cash to pay the taxi driver and . . . Nothing! My wallet was missing. I had been pickpocketed. My wallet contained all my cash, traveler's checks, credit cards, ticket to Amsterdam, and most important, my passport. I didn't know what to do except return to Claridge's and ask them to pay the taxi fee. I then had to obtain more cash, call the Concertgebouw to tell them of my plight, and somehow quickly get a new passport.

When I arrived at Claridge's, the concierge met me at the door. "What happened Mr. Giordano?" he asked. "You are visibly very upset."

When I explained my plight, he said, "Please don't be concerned Mr. Giordano. you are a guest of Claridge's, and we take care of our guests." He paid the taxi, returned to the lobby, and said, "Mr. Giordano, how can we be of service? How much cash do you need? We will advance you what you need and you can reimburse us when you return to the United States."

I thanked him and asked if I could make a couple of phone calls that I also would repay.

I first called Amsterdam and explained my dilemma. They offered to have their assistant conductor conduct the first rehearsal that was scheduled for that afternoon. My second call was to Martha to get her advice on how I could have my passport replaced on short notice. In typical Martha style, she said, "That's no problem. I will call Anne Armstrong (the US ambassador to England). I'm certain that she will help you. In the meantime, why don't you have lunch with my friend who delivered your music? She is having lunch at Claridge's with Lauren Bacall and it will be a fun experience for you. I'll call her right now. Just wait in the lobby, and I'll call you right back."

As promised, she called in a few minutes. "I spoke with Anne. She said for you to take passport photos to the back door of the embassy. She will see that you have a new passport right away. They are expecting you and will have a form for you to fill out. Claridge's will help you acquire a photograph. Then go back to Claridge's and meet the girls at the restaurant. They'll be waiting for you."

Claridge's concierge arranged to have my picture taken at a shop around the corner. I took the photos to the embassy's back door, immediately filled out the form they handed to me, and returned to Claridge's for my luncheon date with Lauren Bacall. In about an hour, the concierge informed me that my passport was ready to be picked up. I bid the "girls" goodbye, picked up my passport at the embassy back door, and took a taxi to Heathrow.

When I checked in at the KLM counter to purchase a ticket to Amsterdam, the agent looked at my new passport and said, "Please wait for a few minutes, I'll be right back." She returned with my wallet.

"My goodness!" I exclaimed. "Where did you find that?"

She explained that it was found in a trash receptacle when they cleaned the terminal. I examined the wallet. Almost everything was intact—passport, credit card, travelers checks, photos, all my flight tickets—everything but the cash. The agent explained to me that it was commonplace for a thief to rob someone, take the cash only, and discard the wallet.

What a surreal day! I was robbed, a hotel paid for my taxi and advanced me cash, had lunch with Lauren Bacall, got a new passport in an hour, and was on an afternoon flight to Amsterdam. Martha did it again!

Cliburn, 1977

My involvement as a last-minute jury chairman for the 1973 competition, thanks to my friend Catherine, was just the beginning of my relationship with the Van Cliburn International Piano Competition. The 1977 Cliburn Competition was a result of the Martha Hyder years. We worked very hard in the years between the 1973 and the 1977 competitions to accomplish all of Martha's goals. We attempted to recruit the best young pianists in the world, assemble a jury composed of some of the greatest musicians in the world, acquire concerts for the winners (including first, second, and third place finalists), produce a documentary film, and include pianists and jurors from the People's Republic of China as well as the Soviet Union. We accomplished every goal.

The repertoire for the competitions prior to the 1977 Competition was overwhelming. It included a myriad of works from every period of music, from Baroque through Contemporary. It was so massive that many of the most talented potential competitors were dissuaded from entering. It resembled a final exam from a major conservatory.

We wanted to attract young pianists who were in the beginning stages of a career. If one already is on the performing circuit it's impossible to take the time away from preparation for recital, chamber music, and concerto performances to prepare the amount of repertoire we required.

It is a rare artist who enjoys a career by performing music from the entire piano repertoire. Most artists limit their scope to works from a few periods of music history. Some even base their career on a very limited repertoire, in the works of one or two composers such as Mozart and Schubert. For example, Lili Kraus limited her repertoire and became famous for her definitive performances of Mozart. On the other hand, Van made his mark in his quintessential recordings and performances of the Romantic repertoire by composers such as Tchaikovsky and Rachmaninov.

One of my major contributions to the competition was to allow the artist to select the repertoire, with the approval of our artistic committee. The only limitation we imposed was the time we allotted for the concerts. This gave the jury an opportunity to evaluate the pianist's programming as well as the quality of the performance. The jury now could focus on aspects such as: Was the program balanced and interesting? Were the works interpreted properly? Did the pianist understand the works and bring out the essence, shape, and proper emotional content? My idea was to create a setting in which to evaluate the competitors as artists who had the potential to develop a career with our support and direction, not as students playing primarily to please a jury.

It worked beautifully. We began to receive applications from budding young artists who were encouraged to participate by the repertoire change and were supported as well by their teachers and concert management. We continuously refined the format for every subsequent competition.

The 1977 Van Cliburn International Piano Competition will go down in the annals of its history as the turning point in its becoming the premier piano competition in the world—and that's largely due to Martha Hyder.

Martha outdid herself in the 1977 competition. She transformed Ed Landreth Auditorium from an institutional educational facility into a beautiful, international center for the arts. She ran into one stumbling block when she insisted on having the doors leading into the concert hall painted with a high-gloss black enamel.

The painters were preparing to apply the primer coat when Chancellor James Moudy learned of the painting. He refused to allow the project to continue. To my knowledge that was the only resistance Martha experienced. I think it was the first time in her life that someone said no to her, and she wasn't pleased, but she accepted the chancellor's decision.

We had the largest and most illustrious jury in the competition's history, which included legendary performers, teachers, critics, and conductors: Guido Agosti, James Dick, Rudolf Firkusny, Leon Fleisher, Alberto Ginastera, Lucrecia Kasilag, Lili Kraus, Nikita Magaloff, John Ogdon, Leonard Pennario, Nicolai Petrov, Pierre Sancan, Nicole Henriot-Schweitzer, and José Serebrier. The competition always commissioned a work for solo piano by a prominent American composer, and this time it was Samuel Barber.

The magnificent pianist, John Ogdon, was a juror for the 1977 competition. Unbeknownst to us he was having severe mental problems and always on the verge of a breakdown. One of the competitors, Boris Bloch, had been eliminated in the first round. In the deliberations for the semifinal round that took place one week later, I offered each juror the opportunity to voice their opinion before the vote was taken. Up to this point in the competition Ogdon had not uttered one word. When his turn arose, I asked if he would like to say something. He stood up and said "Yes." A hush fell over the entire room and everyone's rapt attention was on him. He took a deep breath and said, "Whatever happened to Boris Bloch?"

Our prize winners were: Gold Medal, Steven De Groote; Silver, Alexander Toradze; and Bronze, Jeffrey Swann.

Martha was responsible for the first documentary film produced by the Van Cliburn Foundation and directed by Peter Rosen. It chronicles the 1977 competition from the opening dinner through the final awards ceremony, and then accompanies Steven to his Carnegie Hall debut.

ABOVE
Steven De Groote's victory in 1977. Courtesy of The Cliburn.

OPPOSITE (TOP)
"Sheriff" Elton Hyder "arresting" jury members. Author Collection.

OPPOSITE
Martha Hyder and Nancy Lee Bass in the foreground of the staging for the 1977 awards ceremony. Courtesy of The Cliburn.

That year's opening dinner happened to be the scene of one of my most embarrassing moments. I was the evening's speaker. My opening line was supposed to have been: "It is a great honor to welcome this august gathering to the Fifth Van Cliburn International Piano Competition." Instead, I said, "It is a great honor to address this *austere* gathering."

One of the most difficult circumstances in which I ever placed myself was conducting the final stage of the competition. It was difficult because I had just added yet another responsibility to my primary job, which was shepherding and leading the jury. The preparation, execution, and pressure of conducting for six brilliant young pianists—each playing two complicated different concertos, on an international platform, with an audience of three thousand—would have been difficult enough, but pairing that with my jury chairman duties made the task daunting. I pulled it off, but not without a lot of stress.

Steven De Groote

Steven, the gold medalist of the 1977 competition, was an elegant, refined performer with enormous depth. At one of the jury delibera-

tions Ginastera stated, "We have a very difficult choice to make between a Hercules and an Apollo!" Steven was the Apollo, and Alexander Toradze was Hercules. Steven's stage demeanor was neither demonstrative nor choreographed. Alexander Toradze's (Lexo) stage demeanor is completely natural but very demonstrative and emotional.

Steven was an absolute joy with whom to perform. He was a wonderful artist, played chamber music with the conductor and the orchestra, knew the orchestral score intimately, had impeccable rhythm, and above all was a gentleman. He was never arrogant, and he treated his collaborators with the utmost respect. Every conductor appreciates that. His technique was amazing. However, that was not his focus—his focus was to strictly recreate the master works and honor the intent of the composer without distorting the musical intent of the work. He was interested in bringing out the inner meaning of the work to the best of his ability.

Steven was a well-read intellectual who did not indulge in small talk. He was more outgoing and relaxed when he was working on his Mercedes (he loved to detail it and even would come to our house and clean my car!), riding his motorcycle, or piloting a stunt airplane. He was much more socially comfortable when he was in a nonperforming milieu. Steven was a proud ambassador for his country, South Africa, and his license plate read jo–burg!

In 1985, Steven crashed his airplane while he was stunt flying over the desert outside of Phoenix. He suffered severe injuries and had to undergo surgeries and rehab, but he miraculously survived the crash, and his playing was even more insightful after the accident. Steven succeeded Lili Kraus as Artist in Residence at TCU in 1987.

Once I was returning from an engagement in Europe and changing planes in London. Before take-off I was reading my book and wasn't paying any attention to the other passengers when I heard a familiar voice say, "Hello Maestro." I looked up, and it was Steven! He had been assigned the seat next to mine. We talked almost the entire trip to Texas. As we were nearing our destination, Steven said, "There is something I want to give you."

He took off the gold watch that he was awarded in the Cliburn for the best performance of chamber music and handed it to me.

"I can't accept that, Steven!" I said.

"I want you to take it, please. I'm not going to live very much longer, and I know it will have a great deal of meaning for you."

"Don't be absurd Steven."

"No, I mean it. After my near-fatal plane crash I must take medication for every one of my organs to function. It's only a matter of time. My doctor suggested I get my affairs in order. I do not want any member of my family to have the watch, I insist that you accept it, please. It is very important to me that you do."

I accepted the watch; it was difficult to hold back my tears.

Steven died in 1989, shortly after that flight. I treasure the watch. Mary Alice and I consider Steven to have been a member of our immediate family.

The National Symphony Orchestra of Iran

Shortly after the 1977 Cliburn Competition, Mary Alice and I were invited to a reception at the Hyders' home. Martha's circle of friends included heads of state, CEOs of major industries, artists of international stature, and well-known celebrities. One of her guests was the personal bodyguard of Farah Pahlavi, the Shahbanu, Empress of Iran. I had read that she was interested in the visual and performing arts and very involved and influential in the modernization of Teheran.

The bodyguard was a devotee of Western classical music and was conversant with the finest recordings, important artists, major operas, and symphonic works. During our conversation, while he was describing plans for the modernization of Teheran, I formulated an idea to create an international symphony orchestra there and envisioned the construction of a Lincoln Center type of facility. I thought an orchestra and important facility would give Iran the image of sophistication and sensitivity in a manner impossible to accomplish by any other means.

I broached the subject with this gentleman and pointed out that the project could be a vehicle through which the rest of the world would regard Iran as a sophisticated center of the arts in the Middle East.

He was fascinated with the idea and said he thought the Shahbanu might be enthusiastic.

"How could this be accomplished?" he asked.

Improvising, I said, "With your country's resources, it would be relatively simple. First we should create an advisory board of directors comprising important figures in the classical music world."

"I wonder if that is possible considering the division that exists between us and the other countries in the area?"

"It could help to create better relationships. There is nothing political about a Brahms symphony; music communicates to everyone, regardless of religious or political views. For example, look at how Van Cliburn's victory at in the Tchaikovsky Competition changed the relationship between the Soviet Union and the United States."

"But if we established such a board who would serve on it?"

"I would ask important figures in music such as Isaac Stern; Stewart Warkow, executive director of Carnegie Hall; Rudolf Serkin; Leonard Bernstein; Samuel Barber; Alberto Ginastera; and Alicia Delarrocha."

"But many of those are Jews!"

"I think most of them would accept because of the potentially positive humanitarian impact it could have."

"Okay, for argument's sake, let's say these people accept. Where do we go from there?"

"We hire a consulting firm to explore the possibilities of the location of the facility, its scope, and estimate the costs."

The bodyguard was still skeptical. He said, "Then what? How do we develop an audience? How do we let the world know what we have? Where do we get the musicians? Who would the conductor be?"

"It is difficult to develop an audience for classical music everywhere; I think it might be easier in Iran because no precedent has been established. We could develop extensive music educational programs, have classical music playing on the school's sound systems as the students enter, develop classical music appreciation courses as early as elementary school, and form youth orchestras. The Iran Symphony Orchestra could perform in schools and give concerts in communities throughout Iran. We could do it properly from the beginning. And Iran has the financial resources to make it happen!"

"I think it would be very difficult to find musicians for the orchestra."

"I don't think so. We could recruit from everywhere. It would be a truly international orchestra. We would have to pay very well with many benefits and give them frequent vacations. There are many fine musicians seeking jobs. We might create a pool of maybe 150 musicians who would commit to signing a contract for at least a year at a time.

"Regarding a conductor, there probably should be a staff: a resident music director, several visiting guest conductors, an educational conductor, a pops conductor, and a major international figure as Honorary Music Director."

He was slowly getting on board and becoming more enthusiastic about my idea. He said, "We even could have an airplane customized for touring and have elegant housing for the musicians. It might work! Why not? I will bring it up to the Shahbanu as soon as I return to Iran. That is the first step. If she is interested eventually you should come to Iran to discuss everything and develop a specific plan.

"She is planning to join the Shah in his upcoming visit to Washington. I will try to set up a meeting for the three of us so that you can establish a relationship with her. I will be in New York in a few weeks. Could you meet with me at that time? Perhaps you could make a few inquiries about the interest in the project from a consultant and potential members of the advisory board."

I responded, "I would love to meet with you in New York. I will put together a preliminary plan for discussion and will speak with a few potential advisory board members to see if they would be interested."

Over the next days and weeks, I outlined a preliminary proposal for discussion and began to call some of the people on my list. Chris Jaffe, of Jaffe, Holden and Associates, was interested in being the facility consultant. Since I knew them best I contacted Alberto Ginastera, Stewart Warkow, and Isaac Stern to get their input regarding the entire project before I spoke with anyone else. They all were enthusiastic and felt that, as Isaac Stern said, "It is a very exciting idea. If the Shah wants to reach out to the rest of the world, this could be a major opportunity to bring people together that have been at each other's throats for centuries."

The Shahbanu bodyguard spoke with her. He said she became excited about the possibilities of the project and agreed to meet with me during her visit to Washington.

At this gentleman's suggestion, when he was in New York, we met at the Plaza Hotel for an initial planning session. I included Bill Perrotta, my personal manager. We refined my proposal to present to the Shahbanu. The bodyguard asked me to make plans for a visit to Iran and suggested a few dates.

The visit never happened. In 1978, the revolution in Iran began, and the Shah and the

Shahbanu sought refuge in the USA. Ayatollah Khomeini's regime began in January 1979, and all of our planning for the Iran Symphony Orchestra was for nothing. I often wonder if it could have become a reality and made a major impact on the world for the perception of Iran.

My Solo Trip to China

Martha Hyder learned that I had an engagement to conduct the Hong Kong Philharmonic in 1980, so she asked me to arrange for a visit to Beijing after my concert and recruit a competitor and juror for the '81 Cliburn Competition. The US had no cultural relationship with the People's Republic of China at that time, and subsequently the Cliburn Competition's attempts to communicate with them had not produced any results.

During the Fort Worth Youth Orchestra's trip to Europe in 1969 to participate in the International Festival of Youth Orchestras, we performed in Luxemburg. Adrien Meisch was Luxembourg's Minister of Culture and hosted the FWYO concert. He was a pianist as well, and we became friends.

Mr. Meisch served as Luxemburg's Ambassador to the US from 1974 to 1983. The US did not have cultural relations with the PRC at that time. In my quest to arrange for competitors from China and a tour of China by our chamber orchestra, it struck me that Luxembourg did have a good relationship with China, so I decided to ask Ambassador Meisch for help. When I called him I explained that I frequently conducted the Hong Kong Philharmonic and asked him if he thought that might be helpful. He said it might and offered to host a dinner at the Luxemburg embassy, where he invited one of his friends, Zhang Shu, who was Second Secretary of the Chinese Consulate to the US. Zhang Shu accepted the invitation. Ann Koonsman also attended the dinner, which was crucial because she and I desired to arrange for an extensive cultural exchange tour of China with the Chamber Orchestra.

During dinner I asked Secretary Zhang to arrange for me to meet with the PRC's Minister of Culture in conjunction with one of my engagements in Hong Kong. He said that my suggestion was an excellent idea and explained that, because of the current stressful political climate between the US and China, it would be much easier to arrange for a visit if it originated from a neutral site, and Hong Kong was perfect. He then voiced his opinion that our proposal also could help to improve the US – China relationship because music was politically noncontroversial. He also was enthusiastic about my including the Chamber Orchestra's tour in my request and thought that it might be the deciding factor for a positive response from the minister of culture.

Secretary Zhang opened the door for me to make a request of the minister, Wang Zicheng, to accept my communiques. He agreed, and all my subsequent communication for my trip to Beijing were made by telegrams between me and Minister Wang. My telegrams to China were simply addressed: Mr. Wang Zicheng, Minister of Culture, Beijing, PRC. I explained to Minister Wang that the purpose of my proposed visit to China was to establish a relationship with China through music and enlist the participation of a Chinese pianist and juror in the 1981 Cliburn Competition. I also explained that I wanted to arrange for a tour of the PRC by the Fort Worth Chamber Orchestra (called the Texas Little Symphony at the time).

Even though the Cultural Revolution ended immediately after Mao's death in September 1976, the relationship between the United States and China continued to be strained. Following much of my correspondence after the end to the Cultural Revolution, most of it through the Luxembourg embassy, my visit to Beijing was scheduled. We attempted to schedule it following my engagement with the Hong

NNNN L 5257

ZCZC HRC742 PHS912 TZ252

HXHK CO CNBJ 029

BEIJING 29/28 19 1812

MR JOHN GIORDANO

FURAM ROOM2825

HONGKONG

WELCOME YOU TO BEIJING ON24TH EVERYTHING SCHEDULED

YOUR TRIP IN CANTON WILLBE ARRANGED BY CULTURE

BUREAU WHO WILL MEET YOU ATAIRPORT.

WANGZICHENG

COL ROOM2825 ON24TH

ABOVE
Invitation telegram from Wang Zicheng, minister of culture, PRC to go to Beijing. Author Collection.

Kong Philharmonic in the spring of 1980.

During my stay in Hong Kong, while I was rehearsing the Hong Kong Philharmonic in preparation for my concert, I received two telegrams in succession from the PRC's Minister of Culture, the second contained instructions for my visit to the PRC.

In retrospect, I can't believe I bought a one-way ticket to Communist China during such stressful times between the US and the PRC. When I took my seat in the plane for my flight to Canton I realized it was a very old 727. It was very shoddy; the seats wouldn't recline and were broken. Instead of closed compartments for carry-on bags, the plane had a shelf designed for articles of clothing with a cord barely keeping the items in place. In this instance the shelf held heavy electric equipment like jam boxes and large items that had been purchased in Hong Kong. It was obvious that most passengers were businessmen bringing articles that were not available in China.

The pilots were ex-military. Take-off and landing were very dramatic—immediately straight up on take-off and nose diving to the runway in Canton. The runway in Canton was in ill repair and extremely short; our plane used every available foot to stop.

I was anxious after I deplaned and walked into the concourse. No one was holding a sign greeting me in English. In fact, there were no other Westerners, and almost everyone was wearing the blue or gray Mao outfits except those deplaning from my flight.

I thought, *My God! I just bought a one-way ticket to Communist China and the US has no relationship with China! What am I going to do?*

Just then, two gentlemen approached, and in perfect English one said, "Excuse me, are you from the West?"

Obviously, I thought.

I replied, "Yes."

"Are you John Giordano?"

"Yes," I sighed with relief.

They introduced themselves as representatives of the Ministry of Culture.

"Welcome to China. Your flight to Beijing doesn't depart until midnight. If you are agreeable we would like to give you a tour of Canton. We also would like to invite you to dine with us. We have very good food in Canton."

I felt that I was in capable official hands and said, "Thank you, that sounds wonderful."

As are most Chinese, my hosts in Canton were polite and pleasant, eager to make me feel comfortable. After only a few moments we established a friendly relationship. During the tour they described the heinous activity that took place during the Cultural Revolution and how the Chinese people were relieved and thankful it had ended. The tour was fascinating and the Cantonese meal was superb, even better than I imagined it would have been.

At 11:00 p.m. they escorted me to the airport and ushered me to the gate of the flight to Beijing. The area was packed with what seemed to be hundreds of people. I asked my guides, "Are all these people going to Beijing?"

"Yes, there is only one flight daily from here."

We waited until everyone had boarded. My guides then escorted me to a seat in what we refer to as "first class." Naturally it was not labeled as such since China has no class distinction. They politely asked a lady holding a young baby to give me her seat. She smiled and immediately stood, child in her arms. I said, "I can't sit here and take this lady's seat."

"This is your assigned seat, don't worry, she will be well cared for."

She was well cared for alright. She stood most of the flight, and during take-off and landing, a flight attendant held the baby and the lady sat in the restroom!

The flight was uneventful and landed safely in Beijing at around 3:00 a.m. The minister of culture, assistant minister of culture, chairman of the central conservatory, and the head of the piano department met me at the luggage area. The first words the minister of culture uttered were:

"Welcome to China Mr. Giordano. Tell me, how is Mrs. Hyder?"

How on earth he even knew who Martha Hyder was, and why she was the first person to whom he referred remains a mystery.

When I identified my luggage, the minister insisted on picking it up. He led me to a black limousine, placed my luggage in the trunk, opened a back door for me, and sat next to me. His assistant sat in the front seat and served as interpreter. Heavy black curtains covered all the windows. When I tried to move the curtain to attempt a glance at the surroundings, Minister Wang reached across me, smiled and pulled it back in place.

They took me to the Beijing Hotel, a huge monolithic edifice used for official foreign dignitaries. The expansive lobby had an extremely high ceiling and marble floors. It was dimly lit by what appeared to be a small damaged chandelier hanging a few feet from the ceiling using one thirty-watt bulb. There was no one at the desk.

The minister led me to a very shaky elevator. The entire entourage crowded in, and it slowly took us to a high floor, shaking as it ascended. I didn't know which floor it was because everything was written in Mandarin. He led the party to a very large three-room suite. We gathered in the parlor where a coffee table was elegantly set with hors d'oeuvres and tea. After a few minutes of polite conversation his assistant said, "It is late (about 4:30 a.m.), and we must leave you so you may rest. You will be met at 7:30 for breakfast and taken to the Central Conservatory. Minister Wang wants to know if there is anything you need."

"As a matter of fact, there is. Since I did not check in to the hotel, how do I get a key to my room?"

When he translated my request to Minister Wang, a silence permeated the room and everyone in the entourage froze in their steps. The minister's translator turned to me:

"Mr. Giordano, in China we do not need keys."

I smiled and said: "It is wonderful that the Chinese people are so trustworthy. Thank you for everything, I am looking forward to tomorrow."

But what I was really thinking was *That's fine, so I don't have to worry about the Chinese, but what about some foreign hotel guest who hates Americans? There are plenty of those!*

The whole time I was in Beijing, I was not permitted to leave the hotel without my official escort. He was Lu Zhengwu, director of the Arts Education Bureau in the Ministry of Culture. Mr. Lu is a well-educated, intelligent, kind, and considerate individual who was very accommodating.

Mr. Lu met me at 7:30 a.m. as promised, and we enjoyed an American breakfast and were driven to the Conservatory. I was welcomed by the chairman of the Conservatory and the head of the piano division. There was a brief

ABOVE
With Lu Zhengwu, director of the Arts Education Bureau in the Ministry of Culture of the People's Republic of China, during my trip in 1980 to arrange for participation of China in The Cliburn and the tour of China for the Fort Worth Chamber Orchestra (FWCO). Author Collection.

reception with tea and cookies. Everyone spoke English, which was a great relief.

After a few moments I was led to the concert hall where several of the Conservatory's better pianists played for me on an out-of-tune old piano in need of much repair. I heard several promising pianists but only one stood out—Zhu Daming. I then gave a masterclass in piano and another in conducting. We had a delightful lunch and I then rehearsed the orchestra for an hour.

I later learned that I was the first person permitted to visit China as an individual after the Cultural Revolution. Prior to my visit only official US groups were granted entrance.

I read a book about Chinese customs prior to my visit to the PRC. The Chinese can be very sensitive, and "saving face" is critically important to them. I didn't want to make a faux pas. One of the customs that I gleaned from the book was the toasting tradition of "gam bei," which translates, "bottoms up." The toast usually is made while drinking a very strong liquor, Mao Tai. The normal custom is for the host to begin by toasting the guest of honor. The guest follows suit, and several subsequent toasts usually take place. A rarely adhered to custom is if one is late to the function, the guest of honor may ask the person to catch up on the toasts he/she missed.

During the formal dinner in my honor, the obligatory series of toasts were initiated by Minister Wang through his translator:

"To our visitor from the United States—gam bei."

I reciprocated, "To Minister Wang of the great Peoples Republic of China, gam bei."

"To the Great State of Texas, gam bei."

"To the beautiful city of Beijing—gam bei."

This continued for several toasts, after which none in the room was feeling any pain. The chairman of the piano department, Mr. Wong, was very late to the event. I turned to the minister:

"Mr. Minister, I request that Mr. Wong make up for all of the toasts he missed."

The entire room erupted in laughter because apparently, no guest of honor had ever made that request. Minister Wang, after his boisterous laughter, gained his composure, turned to me, and placed his arm around my shoulder:

"Now, Mr. Giordano, tell me, why are you in China?"

I answered, "Sir, I would like to have a competitor from China participate in the Van Cliburn Piano Competition, a Chinese juror, and a tour of China for my chamber orchestra."

"Done, with one exception—you must choose one pianist from Beijing and one from Shanghai. The juror can be a teacher either from Beijing of Shanghai. Mr. Lu will assist you to make the arrangements for your orchestra's visit."

In his one official statement, all the goals of my trip were fulfilled and I could have returned home the next day.

Because there is a great deal of competition between the Beijing and Shanghai conservatories, at the minister's insistence it was necessary to include a competitor from each. Fortunately, there were several fine pianists in both conservatories, so I was comfortable in inviting two competitors, Zhu Daming from Beijing and Yu Jin from Shanghai. The juror whom I invited was Zhu Guangren, a concert pianist, well-known teacher, and charming woman from the Central Conservatory in Beijing.

When I packed for the trip to Shanghai, I discovered that one of my undershorts was torn and discarded it in the room's trash receptacle. When I entered the room in my Shanghai hotel I noticed a beautifully wrapped "present" tied with a lovely pink bow and placed on the bed. My first thought was that my Shanghai hosts had given me a lovely gift. I opened the package only to discover the undershorts I discarded in Beijing. They were beautifully repaired, ironed, and carefully folded.

I returned to the US, satisfied that all my goals had been successful. On the flight home I pondered my success and wondered how on earth the minister of culture knew who Martha Hyder was.

Zhu Daming

Zhu Daming, a former student in the Beijing Conservatory, was one of the pianists whom I selected to participate in the 1981 Cliburn Competition during that trip. His story reflects the difficulties Chinese musicians encountered during the Cultural Revolution, a sociopolitical movement that took place in China from 1966 until 1976 that paralyzed China politically and culturally. Set into motion by Mao Zedong, then chairman of the Communist Party of China, the Revolution's stated goal was to preserve "true" Communist ideology by purging remnants of capitalist and traditional elements from Chinese society, and to reimpose Maoist thought as the dominant ideology within the party. The Revolution marked the return of Mao Zedong to a position of power after the Great Leap Forward. The movement negatively affected the country's economy and society to a significant degree.

Purging China of all things Western was one of the Cultural Revolution's major goals. Western musical instruments, printed music, and recordings were destroyed. All instruments, including rare precious string instruments and pianos, were smashed, and along with sheet music were the contents of a large bonfire they set in the Conservatory's courtyard. Many professors and students who resisted this destruction were incarcerated and frequently physically abused, often using extreme measures, to assure they couldn't continue to pursue a career, even to the extent of making an example of a prominent piano professor by severing one of her fingers.

Daming was conscripted into the PRC army and assigned the duty of fertilizing crops with human excrement, using hand held buckets. Refusing to completely succumb to the Revolutionist's demands, he painted a piano keyboard on a wooden plank and secretly practiced on it to retain his technique. Many of his peers did the same. They also drew music staffs on plain sheets of paper and wrote by memory the printed music the revolutionists had destroyed. That frequently inaccurate and difficult-to-read music was the foundation of most conservatory libraries for some time after the Revolution had ceased.

Daming could play several different traditional Chinese instruments that were permitted by the regime. He entertained the troops by performing traditional Chinese music for them. He subsequently became well known and was transferred from working in the fields to troop entertainment and remained in that capacity until the end of the Cultural Revolution. When the Revolution was overthrown in 1976 Daming, along with his colleagues and professors, rejoined the Conservatory and continued to pursue his studies.

Daming was awarded the sixth prize in the 1981 Van Cliburn International Piano Competition out of several hundred applicants. Thirty-nine were selected to participate in the competition in Fort Worth. The popularity he achieved in China because of his success and the Cliburn Competition's enthusiastic urging convinced the Chinese government to let him stay in the United States under a temporary visa. He was accepted into the doctoral program of the prestigious Juilliard School and received a generous scholarship.

I conducted the Hong Kong Philharmonic frequently during that period and suggested that they engage Daming to be the soloist for one of my engagements. The Hong Kong Philharmonic administration agreed, realizing it was a unique opportunity to capitalize on his popularity in China.

When I walked out of customs after my flight to Hong Kong for the engagement, a representative of the Hong Kong Philharmonic's staff greeted me as usual. Daming was with him. It is unusual for a soloist to greet the conductor at an airport, but I assumed he was there because of the relationship we had established through the Van Cliburn Competition.

Daming was visibly upset. He explained that the Chinese government had demanded that he return to Beijing immediately after his two performances in Hong Kong. He wanted to return to the US, knowing that once he returned to China he probably would not be allowed to leave. I explained that they couldn't make that demand, because Hong Kong was still a protectorate of Great Britain, and China would not have official authority until it reverted to China in 1998. He informed me that prior to the Hong Kong engagement his US visa had expired. He had applied for an extension and was assured by the US State Department it would be granted and would arrive before his departure to Hong Kong. When it didn't arrive, he again contacted them and was assured that it would be sent to Hong Kong and would be there when he arrived. That didn't happen either, but instead, when he checked into his hotel, he was handed a communiqué from Beijing demanding that he return to China immediately after the concerts.

In my capacity as Jury Chairman for the Cliburn, I had established a relationship with a State Department official who had helped the competition acquire visas for competitors from Eastern European Communist bloc countries. It was extremely difficult to communicate with our State Department because the time differential between Hong Kong and Washington, DC, is twelve hours. My contact there was on vacation and wouldn't be back for a few days. To make matters worse, it was the weekend.

Knowing that saving face is extremely important in the Chinese culture, I called Joseph Polisi, president of The Juilliard School. I asked him to draft a letter and send it to Daming stating that if he did not return to NY immediately following the final concert he would lose his scholarship and would not be permitted to complete his studies. As per my request, Joseph sent a telegram to Daming insisting that he return to school. Daming gave the telegram to the chairman of the Communist party in Hong Kong who was the publisher of the Communist newspaper in Hong Kong. It was to no avail: the government still insisted that he return to China.

I then contacted the American and British embassies and requested assistance. They both agreed that we should help Daming. The embassies assigned staff members in cultural affairs to address the situation. They requested that we meet in my hotel room to formulate a plan, since that location would not be considered official. It was also critical that the discussions remain confidential. In the meantime, I had a cordial lunch with the Communist newspaper publisher and one of his reporters who was assigned to write an article about the concert and Daming's success in the Cliburn. The publisher had a great deal of influence in Hong Kong because he was leading the preparation for the 1997 PRC takeover. I avoided the subject of Beijing's demand.

We met again in my room and formulated

a plan of action. There still was the possibility that Daming's visa would arrive before the concert. We learned that there was a late flight to Tokyo. We arranged to have a car and driver waiting outside of the concert hall's stage door after the second concert and immediately take him to the airport for the Tokyo flight if his visa didn't arrive in time. My contact in the State Department offered to monitor the procedure in Washington, and if the visa was not issued in time he offered to send it by courier to the Tokyo airport. It was arranged for Daming to remain there until it arrived.

Daming was with me constantly during the week prior to the concerts in the hope that my presence would ward off any attempt to kidnap him and take him to the PRC. Everywhere we went—shopping, dining, traveling on the Star ferry between Hong Kong and Kowloon, and sightseeing—we noticed that the same two sinister-looking agents, probably for the Communist party, were omnipresent. They made us very uneasy.

The concerts were well received by the public, and Daming's performances in particular received an amazingly enthusiastic response.

On the day of the second concert I received a telegram from the State Department informing me that the visa would not arrive in Hong Kong in time and would have to be sent to the Tokyo airport. We decided to execute our plan.

The embassy officials and I met again in my room and formulated an emergency plan of action. There still was the possibility that the visa would arrive before the concert. In case it didn't, we planned to have a car parked outside of the stage door to take Daming to the airport immediately following his last performance and purchased a ticket for the late-night flight to Tokyo.

Two days before the final concert I contacted the State Department again. They assured me that if they weren't able to send the visa to Hong Kong before Daming's concert they would have it at the Tokyo airport in time for his arrival there.

After Daming's concerto performance at the second concert, he received an enthusiastic standing ovation. In response, he played a popular Chinese song that thrilled the audience even more.

I went to my dressing room during the encore to deposit my music, then went to the stage door to ensure the car was in place. I discovered the Communist newspaper publisher waiting for me in my dressing room.

He said, "Daming may return to the United States. Because of his great success, it will be in the best interest of the PRC for him to continue his studies in the United States. We have decided that his performances and popularity will substantiate the high international level of Chinese culture."

I was relieved, and we immediately cancelled our elaborate plans. After the concert, the four of us, the officials from the British and US embassies, Daming, and I celebrated the PRC's decision. When I returned to my room after our celebration, I wondered how the Chinese officials had learned of our plans, since our clandestine meetings were held in my room. I searched the room and discovered microphones placed behind pictures and in the mouthpiece of the phone.

Daming currently serves on the piano faculty of Soochow University in Taiwan. The cultural relationship has improved between China and the rest of the world. It now allows him to perform and teach in his native China, making it possible to help build an artistic bridge between the two long-estranged nations.

Richard Rodzinski

Richard Rodzinski was CEO of the Cliburn for twenty-three years, announcing his retirement after the 2009 competition. He is a brilliant individual who speaks several languages fluently, which was an immeasurable skill in his position with the Cliburn. As the son of renowned conductor Artur Rodzinski, Richard was reared in a rare musical environment. He has lived in several countries throughout the western world, and his close friends include the most important performers, composers, and music administrators of our time. I had the pleasure of working with Richard for all twenty-three years. During Richard's tenure, the Cliburn Competition grew into one of the most important international competitions. In his more than two decades at the Cliburn, he refined and innovated. Together we instituted live worldwide auditions. We made a great team and contributed much to the appreciation of classical music in addition to improving the Cliburn. A competition attracts a different audience—one that is not always seeking classical music. Richard's dream was to make the competition an integral part of the expansion of a young artist's musical development and as much of a real-world experience as possible. Richard also broadened the foundation's range, establishing a contest for amateur pianists. He created the Cliburn at the Modern concert series. He produced award-winning television documentaries and launched unprecedented live web coverage, reaching 156 countries. We had large audiences who weren't classical music lovers wherever we auditioned competitors in places like the US, China, and Eastern and Western Europe. Richard's innovations have been adopted by many international competitions. It was a privilege to have worked closely with him for so many years.

BELOW
Reviewing the judges' scores with Richard to substantiate their accuracy. Courtesy of The Cliburn.

Cliburn Screening Jury

During Richard's first year with the Cliburn Competition, the jury was still taping preliminary screenings, or screening via videos, rather than attending auditions in person. Our first competition together, contestants video-recorded themselves, which we perceived as an unfair and unbalanced audition, as some recordings may have been better in quality than others while the live music could have had the same quality. The next couple of competitions, we nixed the personal recordings and sent audio and visual people to record the contestants in person—that way, all of the recordings were with the same equipment and, presumably, of the same quality. While that helped a little, these recordings still didn't quite capture the real feeling behind the performances—the real passion behind the music.

Because the board members for the Cliburn trusted Richard and me so much, they allowed us to finally change our audition screenings, and Richard and I established the first international music competition in the world that consisted of a five-person jury selected from the full jury. It is a highly successful procedure because a live jury can take into consideration the different elements and conditions of the various locations, including different pianos, individual personalities, competitors' stage presence, and acoustical environments. Those elements are difficult to discern on recordings. This screening procedure influenced other competitions which have followed the Cliburn in various formats.

Frankfurt Airport

Perhaps one of the most eventful Cliburn Screening Juries was the 2005 one, which consisted of Jürgen Meyer-Josten, Marcello Abbado, Veda Kaplinsky, Tom Frost, and me. We were accompanied by Alann Sampson, chairman of the board, Wayne Lee Gay, the music critic for the *Fort Worth Star-Telegram*, and Richard Rodzinski, president of the foundation.

The flight schedule for the screening jury in the 2005 competition was not properly planned in that the travel agent rarely allowed enough time to make flight connections between audition cities. However, the flight from China to Moscow was properly arranged to give us enough time at the Frankfurt airport for the connection. We waited for the Moscow flight in the business lounge on the third floor of the concourse. The elevator to the concourse is located in front of the lounge check-in desk.

When our flight was called, all of us entered the elevator and someone in the group pressed the button for the concourse level. The elevator began to descend but suddenly stopped between floors. Jürgen and Marcello spoke German, so we didn't panic. Jürgen pushed the emergency button.

He explained to whomever answered the emergency call what had transpired and within a minute or two the elevator continued to descend but didn't stop at the concourse level.

It continued descending to the basement. The door opened and Richard, Marcello, Jürgen, Tom, and I stepped out of the elevator. We immediately realized that it was the wrong floor, but before we had time to re-enter the elevator, the door closed and the elevator ascended to the concourse level. The four of us found ourselves in a very small space in complete darkness.

Richard and I began to feel around the walls to see if there were a door that would allow us to leave the tiny, pitch-black enclosure. Richard discovered a door and opened it. It led to a well-lit staircase. We all walked up one flight of stairs and found ourselves on a landing facing a closed door that had a panic exit bar and a sign with the words (in German) "Warning! It is forbidden to open this door. Opening this door will result in the immediate closing down of the airport!"

We descended back down to our tiny cell. I groped around the walls again and found another door. I opened it and we discovered that it led to an enormously large, long, dimly lit tunnel. As we left the tiny dark room, the door closed after us and locked, trapping us in the tunnel. I spotted a door several yards down the tunnel and asked the others to wait while I went to check it out.

I knocked on the door. When I didn't receive a response, I opened it and discovered a small room with a uniformed man sitting behind a desk engrossed in his work. I startled him. He looked up at me and shouted:

"Who are you? It is forbidden for a non-official to be here. Get out immediately."

I understood even with my limited German. "I understand, but we can't! We do not want to be here. Please help us. We were trying to go to our flight but the elevator accidently took us to this floor. Please call someone to help us."

He seemed to understand me, but he said, "Get out! Only authorized personnel can be here."

By that time the others had joined me and Jürgen explained our situation to him. He was extremely excited and continued to insist that we leave immediately or he would call the authorities and have us arrested. Jürgen explained repeatedly that we did not want to be there.

We later learned that we were in a large maintenance tunnel located under one of the main runways. It had a myriad of cables and pipes affixed to the ceiling and designed to accommodate large equipment. Jürgen asked the man to call someone of authority to rescue us. He eventually calmed down and complied. After an obviously excited and nervous telephone conversation with the other party, he demanded that we not move. He jumped on a bicycle, disappeared down the long tunnel, and didn't return for at least a half hour. We had been trapped for well over an hour, missed our flight, and didn't know where the rest of our group was.

The bicyclist eventually returned and demanded that we follow him down the tunnel. We couldn't walk very fast because Marcello was not in the best of health, so the long walk, which seemed to be a mile, took over a half hour. We finally arrived at a padlocked chain link fence in front of a guardhouse that had a space between it and another locked chain link fence. A uniformed armed guard shouted, "What are you doing here? This area is forbidden."

Jürgen answered: "We understand, we don't want to be here. Please inform your supervisor that we are here and ask him to let us out."

The guard left, entered the guardhouse, placed a phone call, and accompanying his conversation with animated gestures, spoke with someone, then returned.

"Someone is coming for you, but first we must search you to be certain that you have no weapons or explosive devices."

We were forced to enter the area between the two fences one at a time. One guard thoroughly searched each of us while another held us under gunpoint.

When the guard was satisfied that we weren't terrorists, he ordered the bicyclist to lead us back down the tunnel to the original site where we entered. There we were met by an airport official who accompanied us back to the business class lounge.

In the meantime, while we were trapped in the tunnel, Wayne Lee, Alann, and Veda were at the gate waiting for the flight to Moscow. Alann and Veda were explaining our plight to the agent and requested that the flight be delayed until we could be found. The agent told them that it was impossible for us to be in the bowels of the airport but did agree to delay for a few minutes.

The only one from our party who boarded the plane was Wayne Lee. The plane departed. We couldn't understand what Wayne Lee thought he would do alone in Moscow without the jury.

Alann and Veda couldn't convince airport officials that the elevator was faulty and that we were trapped in the bowels of the airport. They insisted that a search be conducted, but they repeatedly received the same response, "That is impossible. A search is not necessary. Only authorized personnel are allowed on that level. The elevator cannot stop at that level without a special key! They are somewhere else in the airport, probably at the wrong gate."

It wasn't until Alann and Veda became very angry and demanded that they speak with someone of the highest authority that something was done to rescue us.

After we were rescued from our nightmarish ordeal we all returned to the business class lounge to wait for the next flight to Moscow. I went to the desk located in front of the elevator and informed the agents of the problem we had with the elevator. One of the agents said, "That is impossible, the elevator did not break down. We have been sitting here the entire day and never left the desk. We are certain that it functioned perfectly all day. The elevator never was stuck between floors. Only authorized personnel who have a special key can go to the lowest level. Your story is false."

Alann filed an official complaint after we returned home. She was informed that the incident never was officially reported because it was impossible for the elevator to descend to the lowest level.

When we arrived at the Moscow hotel I asked Wayne Lee what he thought he could accomplish for the competition by being alone in Moscow. His response: "I didn't want to miss the flight."

A Traditional Russian Meal

While we were in Moscow, a few of us wanted to dine in a traditional Russian restaurant other than one near Red Square. We asked one of our hosts for a recommendation. Something must have been lost in translation because, while it was an interesting experience, the restaurant was anything but a traditional Russian one.

It was in January and bitter cold, the streets and sidewalks covered in ice and snow. We ordered a taxi and were driven to a remote location several miles from the city center. When we entered the restaurant we saw that it obviously was not traditional Russian. However, our taxi already had left and we were hungry and had reservations, so there was no alternative except to dine there.

The food was very bad American-style cuisine. When we were served drinks, an awful, out-of-tune thirteen-piece 1940's style dance band began to play WWII songs. Just when we thought it couldn't get worse a female singer stepped up to the microphone. The poor girl was so bad it was almost comedic. The band finally took a break, much to our relief, and the Master of Ceremonies made an announcement. We asked our server, who spoke some English what he said.

"The show will begin in fifteen minutes."

I jokingly said to our group, "If the show is the female singer stripping, that's the last straw."

Well, it ended up being the last straw.

After the "show" and the unappetizing meal we asked to have someone call for a taxi. We understood the man to say that the taxi would pick us up at the corner in a few minutes. By now, it was at least 10:00 p.m. and unbearably cold. As we were waiting at the corner for what seemed to be eternity, a snow storm began. We were afraid to return to the restaurant for shelter fearing we would miss the taxi. It arrived at least a half hour later.

My Twenty-Eight Year Tenure with the Fort Worth Symphony Begins

If symphony orchestras had existed in the fourth century, the famous quote from the Chinese philosopher Xunzi would have read: "(Symphonic) Music is a fantastic peacekeeper of the world; it is integral to harmony, and it is a required fundamental of human emotion."

My goal was to make the FWSO become an integral and fundamental part of Fort Worth. I wanted Fort Worthians to say, when they spoke of Fort Worth, whether or not they were FWSO patrons, "This is a great city. We excel in all the arts and have a wonderful symphony orchestra."

The Plan to Dissolve the Fort Worth and Dallas Symphonies

Soon after my family's move to Fort Worth, following my acceptance as music director of the FWSO and my first Cliburn Competition in 1973, our board president, Frank Sherwood, informed me of a plan to dissolve the FWSO.

He invited me to a lunch meeting at Shady Oaks Country Club with the president of the FWSO Board and another board member; their agenda was to announce the creation of "The Texas Philharmonic."

After the usual pleasantries, one of the representatives from Dallas said, "The reason we called this meeting was to inform you all that we are dissolving the Dallas and Fort Worth Symphonies!"

"Oh, that's just great," I said sarcastically. "We just bought a new home!"

"Don't worry," he responded. "This is a good market. You'll be able to sell it without any problem."

The arrogance he displayed with this comment both surprised and infuriated me, but I maintained my composure.

The discussion continued, and the Dallas group enumerated the reasons the two organizations should be dissolved.

I interrupted, "Have you spoken with the Dallas Symphony leadership concerning these plans?"

One of them responded: "Not yet, but it's a moot point. They will have to accept it."

"Why?" I asked.

"Our orchestra will be so significant and well-funded that you both will be forced to shut down," he said with confidence.

"Who will conduct this 'Super Symphony'?" I was becoming increasingly annoyed.

"Herbert von Karajan, of course." This response showed me how ignorant they were of the way the symphonic world works. He didn't realize how ridiculous his assumption sounded.

"Why should he?" I countered. "He already has one of the best orchestras in the world."

"He will have to; we will pay him so much he won't be able to refuse."

They were so arrogant and naïve that I had to repress my desire to laugh in their faces, but I couldn't help but lash back with sarcasm.

"I see," I said. "I suppose he needs a bigger jet, a larger yacht, and a more lavish lifestyle. So—who will play in this super orchestra?"

Another in the group responded: "The very best musicians in the world. We will pay them so much they won't refuse. But don't be concerned, you and the Dallas Symphony's conductor will be retained as assistants for Karajan."

At this point, I was not only angry, I was disgusted. They had reduced everything to money. That monetary reworking included Karajan and every musician. Artistic fulfillment is the prime reason a musician pursues a career in music. Musicians don't play for money, they play because they are passionate about the music.

"Right," I answered. "Have you asked Mr. Karajan if he wants us to be his assistants?"

"That's another moot point. It will be a condition in his contract."

Their presumptuousness angered me, and I couldn't restrain myself further. I stood up, ready to leave.

"This entire project is naïve and ignorant. You obviously are not aware at all how the symphony orchestra world works. It can't succeed."

That remark ended the meeting, and I never heard about "The Texas Philharmonic" again. I kept my house and I kept my job as music director of the still-existing Fort Worth Symphony.

During my tenure from 1972 to 2000, I helped establish a close relationship between the FWSO and the City of Fort Worth. That relationship became a critical element in the fabric of the community. I hope my efforts contributed to Fort Worth's current pride in the orchestra.

The Fort Worth Symphony is an organization that will continue to serve a great city. It is an important element of the city's economic development. It is also a critical component of the Fort Worth Opera, the Fort Worth Ballet, and the Van Cliburn Competition.

We emphasized the need to bring great music to thousands of children annually, from preschool through high school. We performed in every quarter of the community to audiences of every economic level, ethnicity, and culture. We presented concerts in parks throughout the city: downtown Fort Worth, East side, Northside, Trinity River, Mayfest, Oktoberfest, Heritage Park, Sycamore Park, and Marine Park. We played the National Anthem at the memorable 1994 opening of The Ballpark in Arlington, with Van Cliburn as soloist. The African American community recognized our efforts to unite cultures, and I was named an honorary member of the African Bandits motorcycle gang, Mandinkas, an organization dedicated to promoting goodwill and brotherhood.

Tarrant County Convention Center

The FWSO concerts were held in the Tarrant County Convention Center, a facility that contained a large arena, exhibition hall, and the three-thousand-seat John F. Kennedy Theater. The theater was not designed for live unamplified music, did not have an atmosphere conducive to creativity, and had poor, unflattering acoustical properties. The Fort Worth Symphony, Fort Worth Ballet, and the Fort Worth Opera used it because it was the only option.

Val Wilkie recently had been appointed director of the Sid Richardson Foundation. He was a sophisticated, brilliant man who loved classical music. Val attended the opening concert of the 1973-74 season. He went backstage to introduce himself to me and to express his enjoyment of the concert.

"I am pleased that Fort Worth has such a fine orchestra, but we must do something about this hall, it is dreadful," he said. "The acoustics are perhaps the worst I've ever experienced."

Several years later Val would prove to be extremely influential in the creation of the Nancy Lee and Perry R. Bass Performance Hall.

My First Day with the FWSO

The FWSO's office was initially in the Scott Theatre building. The first day on the job I asked Beverly Cardona, manager of the orchestra, if I could examine the library. It is fundamental for a symphony orchestra to have a substantial library containing works such as the most frequently performed symphonies of Haydn and Mozart, all nine Beethoven Symphonies, the four Brahms Symphonies, the fourth, fifth, and sixth Tchaikovsky symphonies, frequently performed concerti, and major works by Bach, Handel, Dvorak, Schubert, Wagner, and Strauss.

Beverly's response was: "Close the door." Behind the door there was a small box. Beverly said, "It's in that box!" I was stunned. Every high school orchestra had a more extensive library than this. The Fort Worth Youth Orches-

ABOVE
James Galway rehearsing with the FWSO in the Tarrant County Convention Center JFK Theater. Author Collection.

tra's library was many times larger and had to be stored in a large room. The FWSO's justification for their meager collection was that they didn't have a place to store music, so they rented or borrowed. A proper library has a major impact on the budget of a professional orchestra because it eliminates much rental cost. It is also an important factor in an orchestra's artistic development. It was imperative that I increase the size of the library.

I analyzed the orchestra's programming for the previous several seasons. Programming is one of the most important elements for an orchestra's success. If nobody wants to hear what it's playing there is no reason for it to exist. Programming is also the foundation of an orchestra's artistic growth, determines its budget, creates public visibility, and makes or breaks its educational program's success.

The programs did contain many magnificent compositions but were lacking in the number of standard works by composers such as Mozart, Beethoven, Brahms, and Tchaikovsky. Those works are appealing to both audiences and musicians. They require relatively smaller instrumentation, therefore assist in controlling the budget. They are also a superb way to train an orchestra because they are technically difficult and transparent, requiring precise ensemble execution.

Mayfest

During my first season as music director of the Fort Worth Symphony Orchestra, the Junior League president, Phyllis Tilley, informed me that the league was organizing a Mayfest in Trinity Park and wanted the orchestra to be involved. She asked if there were something special we could play that would draw more attention to the festival and attract large crowds to the event. I suggested we perform the Tchaikovsky 1812 Overture in its original form, which requires a brass band, a battery of cannon, and fireworks. The National Guard unit agreed to furnish and fire 105" howitzers, and the Mayfest Committee arranged for fireworks. The novel use of cannon was appealing to the press, and curiosity about their use resulted in a much-increased attendance.

We placed the howitzers on the bank of the Trinity River and had the fireworks display originate from the other side. The performance was a rousing success and became a tradition and the highlight of Mayfest for several years.

The third year I wanted to do something different, so I added the rarely used choral part notated in the score, the Russian hymn, "O Lord, Save Thy People." The hymn's text was not in the score, only the musical notation. I couldn't find the Russian text or even an English translation. It only was a few days before the chorus rehearsal, and there was no time to continue my research; I had to act quickly. I made a phonetic version of the hymn using random phrases from my Russian tourist phrase book. I was certain that nobody would be able to understand the Russian words anyway.

I selected phrases with syllabic rhythms that fit the melody, such as, "Can you direct me to the closest restroom?" or, "I would like a beer and a bottle of sparkling water please," or, "Where is the closest post office?" I never revealed to anyone, including the choirmaster, what I had done.

The audience had one of the most enthusiastic responses to our performance that I ever have experienced. After the performance, John Loud, the associate professor of Russian and Latin at TCU, approached me.

"Thank you for performing the choral version of the 1812," he said. "It makes the piece much more meaningful and exciting. But the next time you use a choir please contact me and I'll work with you on the proper pronunciation. That was the only aspect of the performance that was not at all good. In fact, the pronunciation was terrible. It was so bad that at one point I could have sworn they were singing, 'Can you direct me to the closest restroom?'"

LEFT
Bev Henson, director of choral activities at TCU, during the choir rehearsal for the FWSO 1812 Overture performance at Mayfest. Author Collection.

1975 Fiftieth Anniversary Concert

During a conversation with a retired member of the Fort Worth Symphony in the fall of 1975, I learned that the symphony's fiftieth anniversary would be in December. I broached the notion of presenting a special concert to our executive director, Beverly Cardona, to celebrate the occasion. The board of directors approved the project, and I began to plan the repertoire. I selected the same works that Brooks Morris, the founding conductor of the orchestra, programmed on the first concert. It included Ferde Grofe's "Grand Canyon Suite."

Since I also was teaching at TCU and serving as jury chairman for the Van Cliburn Foundation, I had very little time to participate in any administrative detail other than those pertaining to the music.

About two weeks prior to the anniversary concert I asked Beverly how many tickets had been sold for the event. The concert was to be held in the JFK Theater in the Tarrant County Convention Center, where an audience fewer than two thousand would appear small and could be embarrassing for such an auspicious occasion.

I asked Beverly, "How many tickets have we sold for the anniversary concert?"

"Oh, they are selling," she answered, nonchalantly.

"How many have we sold?" I persisted. "It's only a couple of weeks away." She didn't respond.

"Two thousand?" I asked.

She shook her head.

"Fifteen hundred?" "No." "One thousand?" "Not quite."

At this point, I became extremely concerned. "Bev, please tell me how many we've sold."

"About eight hundred."

"Eight hundred?" I exclaimed. "We can't present our Fiftieth Anniversary Concert to eight hundred people in that huge place! We must do something to promote it. Has anyone asked Frank Butler to help?" Frank Butler was publisher of the *Fort Worth Star-Telegram.*

"No," she said. "But it won't do any good. The newspaper's policy is that they only will give us free space if we buy ads, and we can't afford them."

"This makes no sense. No one has asked Frank to help? We just assume that he won't do anything?"

"He won't," she said.

"Bev, please make an appointment for us to see him as soon as possible, and I'll try to convince him to help us. How could it hurt?" She agreed and made an appointment for us to meet with him.

The next day, we sat in Frank Butler's office, and after we exchanged a few pleasantries I broached the subject.

"Mr. Butler," I said, "in a couple of weeks, the Fort Worth Symphony Orchestra will be performing a concert to celebrate our fiftieth anniversary. We only have sold a few hundred tickets, and I think it's partially because we have received very little publicity from the *Star-Telegram*."

He paused for a few seconds. "I was not aware that this will be taking place," he said. "What can I do to help?"

"We desperately need some pro bono coverage in the paper," I answered. "It is the only thing that can save us. It will be very embarrassing to play a concert in that huge hall for such a small audience in celebration of such a milestone in the symphony's history."

"I'm very sorry, but it is impossible for me to do anything. It would set a difficult precedent. If we give extensive coverage to the symphony, we would have to do that for the ballet and the opera as well."

"That's fine!" I said. "When the ballet or the opera celebrates their fiftieth anniversary in twenty-five or thirty years, you can do the same for them!"

Frank was silent for a few moments. "Okay," he said, "we will help, but you have to give us something to write about. What is newsworthy about this event other than the fact that it is your fiftieth anniversary? That is only enough material for one short article."

At this point, Bev joined the conversation. "Ginger Rogers's mother was the first manager."

"Good, that is something we can use. What else?"

We were prepared with a few newsworthy topics. After we had exhausted our list, Frank said, "Okay, is there anything else? Like the music—anything that is unusual? Something that might grab our subscriber's attention?"

"I've programmed the same music that Brooks Morris programmed for the first concert. The last piece on the program will be the 'Grand Canyon Suite.' I guess I could ride a mule on stage, then there would be two jackasses!"

He laughed and said: "If you ride a donkey or mule on stage, I'll give you front-page coverage every day the week before the concert. But if you don't have either on that stage, you aren't going to like the next day's headline!"

"You're on! I'll do it!"

The first thing I did when we returned to the office was to call my assistant conductor, Tom Jensen. I told him to find a donkey or mule for us to use and said it didn't matter which as long as it was tame enough to ride. I jokingly threatened to fire him if he didn't succeed.

Tom located a small white donkey used in a Passion play in West Texas and arranged for us to use it. The *Star-Telegram* gave us the publicity they promised, and the concert was a sellout. As promised, I rode the donkey from the backstage area to the podium. Brooks Morris, the first conductor of the orchestra, a wonderful man and a great sport, led the animal. A photo of Brooks leading the donkey with me riding it appeared on the front page of the following day's *Star-Telegram*. Fortunately, the caption was not: "Big Jackass rides small jackass on stage."

Frank Butler fulfilled his promise to me, and we never failed to bring up the jackass incident any time we saw one another.

BELOW
Brooks Morris leading a donkey to the podium at the FWSO fiftieth anniversary celebration concert. ©Fort Worth Star-Telegram, 1975.

LEFT
Meeting Big Bird during the FWSO Sesame Street concert. ©Fort Worth Star-Telegram, 1976.

Sesame Street

Another serendipitous opportunity occurred at the beginning of my tenure with the FWSO. The extremely popular children's television program *Sesame Street* had scheduled a concert tour of the US featuring some of their characters such as Big Bird and Ernie. They offered concerts with symphony orchestras. Beverley Cardona, the orchestra's executive director, secured underwriting for the event, and we presented the concert in the arena of the Tarrant County Convention Center.

It was an overwhelming success. About ten thousand youngsters and their parents filled the arena. The quality of the program was splendid, garnered many additional friends for the orchestra, and increased its visibility. The next day the *Star-Telegram* published a front-page photo of Big Bird surrounded by children at the concert.

NBC Film

Shortly after our family moved to Fort Worth, the FWSO was approached by the local NBC affiliate and the Southwest Baptist Radio/TV center to be the subject of a documentary TV film that would be focused on a "Regional" symphony orchestra and its music director.

The project took place prior to a FWSO concert that featured Berlioz's "Symphonie Fantastique." A film crew followed my activities during that time, including my attending my son John's soccer game and programs in which my daughters Anne and Ellen participated. They also filmed various functions in which Mary Alice and I were involved.

The film featured the orchestra performing educational concerts, in ice rinks, at shopping malls, parks, and the chamber music ensembles in classrooms.

The film *Symphony* was broadcast on NBC and captured the relationship of a symphony orchestra and its conductor with the community. It received numerous awards from several entities as one of the outstanding documentaries of the year, and I feel honored to have been a part of it.

Music In

In the early 1970s there was a popular television comedy show called *Laugh In*. We just had begun the process of developing the Fort Worth Chamber Orchestra and had engaged full-time musicians for a very short season. I came up with the idea of creating an instrumental summer music camp program, primarily for underprivileged young children, and called it "Music In."

"Music In" extended the musician's season and added to their income. I was hoping it would develop into similar permanent music programs in community centers throughout the city. "Music In" provided an enjoyable supervised musical learning activity for children, one that most of the participating families would not have been able to afford. It also served as an educational and free day care center.

Beverly applied for a government grant that included instrument rental, salary for the musicians, and lunch for the children. Her application was successful. Our musicians coached our children for several weeks. At the end of the camp the children presented a public program in Will Rogers Auditorium as part of a brief FWSO concert.

We commissioned Lew Gillis to write an arrangement of a popular song for the FWSO that had very simple parts for the children to play. The program included a couple of pieces played by the children's group, followed by a brief concert by the FWSO. The concert ended with Lew's arrangement of a current popular song, "Sing, Sing a Song" that concluded with the children singing. It was a thrilling experience for the children and their families.

The grant only lasted two summers, and we were forced to discontinue the camp. The program drew attention to the FWSO and garnered attention from a new constituency—family and friends of the over one hundred young participants. Many continued by joining their school music programs. Unfortunately, we were not able to attain funding to continue the program.

Star Wars

Another extraordinary opportunity presented itself. George Lucas's *Star Wars* had just been released in 1977. An enterprising production company in Dallas, Showco, developed and produced a show/concert featuring a symphony orchestra and incorporated the use of lasers and other pyrotechnics, sound, and lighting effects in extraordinary ways never before attempted. They asked me to function as a music consultant for the show.

The musical foundation of the show was John Williams's film score to *Star Wars*. Showco's concept of the concert was to program traditional symphonic music and space film scores by Williams. I offered my suggestions of the symphonic classics to program for the first half of the show, the Introduction of Strauss's "Thus Spake Zarathustra" leading into "The Blue Danube" that was used in *2001, a Space Odyssey* followed by several movements of Gustav Holst's "The Planets."

The music in the first half was visually enhanced by the ingenious use of computer graphics displayed on a large screen suspended above the orchestra. The second half used lasers to emulate an actual space battle, with laser beams flashing above the heads of the audience. They combined that with more traditional pyrotechnics, lighting, and explosive sound effects.

I was also consulted in the design of a conductor's podium that resembled the command center of a spacecraft and made suggestions for non-traditional staging for a symphony orchestra. Showco used experienced, superb sound engineers to design the necessary acoustical support for performances in large venues. They placed contact microphones on every string instrument and designed special microphone patterns and placement for the other instruments.

The costume designers for Casa Mañana, a Fort Worth theater, fashioned two costumes for me to wear, one for each half. For the first half's traditional symphonic music, they added glitter and rhinestones to a set of white tails. The second half costume was a sweater-like garment made of silver and gold lamé that had a cape with the FWSO logo embroidered on it.

The concert proved to be such a huge success that symphony orchestras throughout the country booked the show. Performances were given in large arenas seating several thousands.

The concert attracted the largest audience for an indoor concert in FWSO history—more than fifteen thousand. It was the orchestra's most visible and popular single event. It garnered front-page coverage and was the subject of discussion throughout the city.

Subsequently, I conducted the program in several cities throughout the US, each to a very large audience. The FWSO and the Dallas Symphony Orchestra were the first to present the program. It was unique for a performance of symphonic music to have popular appeal of that magnitude.

FWSO Sunday Concert Series

Another proposal I made to the board was to repeat the Fort Worth Symphony Orchestra subscription concerts on Sunday afternoons.

I was certain that Sunday afternoon concerts would appeal to a different constituency and thereby expand our audience. It would create an opportunity for senior citizens who can't drive at night to attend concerts and establish a concert-going experience for families.

There is a false perception that symphony orchestra concerts are elitist. The atmosphere on Sunday would also help to alleviate that perception. I suggested we test the concept by using a smaller venue such as Ed Landreth Auditorium at TCU and initially offer a season of three concerts.

Repeated concerts do not incur a major increase in budget because additional rehearsal time is not necessary. They provide more income to per-service orchestra members and are an important component of the orchestra's artistic development.

Education Program

It was critical for us to expand the educational program. Presenting concerts to elementary school students is an important component of an orchestra's program. While one or two concerts during a child's twelve-year education is better than nothing, that limited exposure couldn't possibly develop many aficionados of symphonic music.

I wanted to develop an education program that would consist of several parts, somewhat patterned after Project Muse, a government-funded project that took place during Ezra Rachlin's tenure. We hired Ann Koonsman, who had extensive training and teaching experience in music education and had worked for Project Muse. She is a skilled violinist and was well versed in symphony orchestra structure. She was the perfect individual to administer the program.

We organized the program into four phases:

1. In addition to the string and woodwind groups under full-time contracts we added, on a per-service basis, a brass quintet consisting of two trumpets, French horn, trombone, and tuba, and a percussionist. We scheduled the ensembles to perform in as many classrooms as possible. Ann assisted them in choosing the music and designed their presentations to appeal to students of various age groups. The ensembles performed in the middle of classrooms surrounded by students sitting on the floor. They were close to the musicians and their instruments. Each member of the ensembles made a brief presentation.

2. We then bussed those students to the FWSO's venue where the full orchestra presented a concert for them. As opposed to the previous program, where students only attended one concert in their twelve years of schooling, with this new program these students will have already been exposed to the various instruments and could personally relate to the musicians with whom they had become acquainted in their classrooms.

3. We next scheduled the full chamber orchestra to perform in middle school auditoriums. That gave students an additional intimate exposure to symphonic music.

4. Finally, the entire FWSO played in as many high school auditoriums as possible.

This concept exposed students to the FWSO and to a wide variety of classical music four times instead of just once during their twelve-year education. The program was extremely successful. It's problematic today because the Chamber Orchestra no longer exists.

Memories of America

I was fortunate to have been at the right place at the right time on many occasions.

After the 1973 Van Cliburn Competition, I

became acquainted with one of Fort Worth's community leaders, Alann Sampson. Alann was involved with the Cliburn from its inception. One day Alann called and said, "John, I am in charge of the Bicentennial Celebration in 1976. I'd like to meet and discuss possibilities for Fort Worth's celebration."

"Great," I said. "I've been thinking about the Bicentennial and would like for the FWSO to be included in a major way."

We met and discussed several options. Alann explained that Fort Worth was one of several cities throughout the country selected by NBC to be featured on a July 4, 1976, special marathon telecast. Alann wanted the celebration to take place in Heritage Park, a park she was promoting for major development that was located on the outskirts of downtown Fort Worth. It was being established at the confluence of the two branches of the Trinity River, the original location of General Worth's Fort. We discussed several possibilities for the symphony's participation.

"I have an idea, Alann," I said. "Why don't we commission a major piece of music that could be premiered during the celebration?"

"That's a great idea, but don't forget the event will take place in Heritage Park and must be designed to appeal to the entire community. We must have a piece that would be appreciated by everybody. Whom do you suggest we commission?"

"Carmen Dragon. He's a good friend. He started the Hollywood Bowl and is a master of Americana music. His version of 'America the Beautiful' has been accepted as the unofficial but definitive version. Let's ask him to write a multimedia piece similar to the format of the 1812 Overture. It would be staged and use fireworks, cannon, two orchestras (the FWSO and the YO), marching band, chorus, a drill team, and maybe even a reenactment group."

"That sounds crazy but exciting. Wouldn't his commitment cost a fortune? We don't have a large budget."

"I don't think so. I think I could convince Carmen to do it for a reasonable fee because I'm sure it will turn out to be a standard for Americana programs and Fourth of July celebrations, and he'll make a fortune in rental and royalties. I'm certain the various groups would be happy to participate pro bono."

Alann loved the idea. She secured a grant for the commission, convinced NBC to air it, and we began to recruit the various organizations we needed.

I contacted Carmen and after some discussion we came up with a formula for the work. NBC wanted it to be between twenty and twenty-five minutes long. Carmen suggested that it be based on extant patriotic melodies. I asked Carmen to include the FWSO, the Fort Worth Youth Orchestra, a marching band, choir, drill team, reenactment group, fireworks, and howitzers. He loved the concept; it was along the lines of programs he created for the Hollywood Bowl.

He cleverly composed the work so that in addition to the huge forces we planned to use, it could also be performed by orchestra alone or by orchestra and choir. We had a multitude of conversations throughout his compositional process; he had many questions regarding the make-up and abilities of the participating organizations.

Before she died in 2012, Carmen's daughter, Kathy Dragon Henn, who ran Carmen's rental catalogue after his death, told me that "Memories of America" was "the most often rented and performed work in [his] catalogue."

It was complicated to put together because every component had to be rehearsed separately, and scheduling was difficult. Choruses normally do not sing in the summer months; marching bands do not march; schools are closed for vacation, etc. However, everyone cooperated, and we made it work. Mary Alice organized a hundred-voice choir. The Youth Orchestra agreed to participate, and we put a volunteer marching band together. The individual instrumental and choral parts were extrapolated from the score by hand and distributed to the various organizations. Everything was in place for a spectacular event, and NBC was thrilled with the concept.

Alann had a stage constructed on the banks of the Trinity River, and bales of hay were placed throughout the area to be used for audience seating. NBC constructed several towers upon which they placed cameras; the network brought in a special trailer used for remote broadcasts. We were ready!

About two hundred thousand people attended the program. They brought picnics and sat on both banks of the river on the hay bales, blankets, and the grass, while the rest stood.

The program began with the invocation, then the commandant of the Marine Corps, the guest speaker, began. He talked, and he talked, and he talked, and he talked . . . for over thirty minutes. The orchestra was on stage ready to play, the choir, marching band, and YO were in place. All the other participants including the reenactment group that included "George Washington" who was to float down the Trinity River on a specially constructed barge. We were ready!

Alann and I were in the control booth trailer. The NBC host in New York said, "And now we take you to a special celebration in Fort Worth, Texas featuring the premiere of a piece of music by Carmen Dragon."

But the general still was speaking.

"They're not quite ready in Fort Worth so let's go to . . . "

This was repeated several times, and he just wouldn't stop talking.

As Alann and I were anxiously standing in the control booth trailer waiting for the general to stop when we saw a black cloud approaching from the Northwest containing a whirling descending funnel. It was quickly moving toward our location, gaining momentum. Alann and I looked at each other. I said:

"No, it's not possible. Do you think that's a tornado heading towards us?

Alann turned to the stage director of the event:

"Get him off that stage! If we start now, we can finish before the storm hits!"

The general ignored everyone and continued to talk, and talk, and talk. He finally stopped, I ran up on stage to give the downbeat. The NBC TV director cued me. It was too late! Before I could raise my arms, the show's master of ceremonies grabbed the microphone.

"Everybody remain calm and seek immediate shelter. A storm is quickly approaching!"

The crowd ran in every direction seeking shelter. The tornado struck! TV towers toppled, the trailer was overturned, and the musicians and singers grabbed their music and instruments and ran for cover. I frantically looked for my children who were with my mother because Mary Alice was on stage in the choir. I glanced at the stage. My mother had taken our three young children, and they were huddled together under the stage among the electrical wiring!

Amazingly, no one was hurt. The storm briefly touched down on our site, skipped to another location, and dissipated.

We all were distraught. The planning, work, rehearsals, and costs were all for naught. Mary Alice approached me:

"Even though the orchestra and band have left, we want to sing the piece."

She gathered the choir together and they sang their part under my direction. What an amazing, emotional moment. "Memories of America" never has been performed with full forces.

Fort Worth Symphony Pops Series

One of the more exciting programs we presented was our Pops Concert Series. There are several reasons to justify a Pops Series for a symphony. It appeals to a much broader audience than classical music, so it will sell more tickets and subsequently become a good source of income. Most pop music is not as difficult as classical and requires fewer rehearsals, although the conductor must understand the various pop music styles, from country western to rock and jazz. My background in jazz, Broadway musicals, recording studios, and stage shows proved invaluable. We were fortunate to have several key musicians with similar backgrounds in the orchestra.

The FWSO concert season always included a Pops concert. A Pops concert inserted in a season of serious classical music forces patrons to buy tickets to a concert whether or not they enjoy it. On the other hand, most patrons who prefer Pops concerts buy single tickets because they have no interest in classical music. They are two different audiences.

The typical FWSO programming was not attractive to most potential Pops patrons because it didn't contain popular music! The programs primarily consisted of only light classical music, like Strauss waltzes and well-known overtures.

It was very difficult to convince the board to accept the concept of presenting a separate series. It helped when I pointed out that the Boston Pops is at least as successful as the Boston Symphony, and there is little audience crossover. They finally agreed to offer a separate series of three Pops concerts in addition to the classical series.

Ella Fitzgerald

I suggested that we open the Pops series by featuring one of the all-time great singers: Ella Fitzgerald. A few board members insisted that she wouldn't sing with a symphony orchestra because we wouldn't be able to afford her, and the orchestra couldn't play her style of music.

I explained that I knew her personally and had played for her, along with several other artists, when I was a teenager. I informed them that I played in "Big Bands" in Las Vegas, New York, and New Orleans, and in many venues where I met and performed with the finest jazz musicians as well as a variety of popular performers of every style. I told them that I thought I still had her private phone number and, if so, would ask her. I said that the worst that could happen was that she would say no.

Hoping I could speak directly to her and not have to go through her management, I searched and found Ella's phone number in some memorabilia I had saved from my "big band" days when I played her act. Serendipitously it was still valid, and she answered the phone.

She expressed a few concerns when I asked her to perform with us.

"Naturally I remember you Johnny, you were just a kid," she told me. "I've never performed with a symphony before and I have a few reservations. Can the brass section swing?"

"Absolutely, Ella," I reassured her. "We have one of the best first trumpet players in the country, and the trombone section has a couple of great jazz players. I'm certain you've worked with many of our players. All of our musicians have played many shows."

"I don't have any charts for a symphony."

"You have recorded many albums that have string parts, harp, French horns, and woodwinds. They will be fantastic played by a full symphony orchestra. Our string section of fifty players will sound wonderful, and I'm sure you'll love it! Also, you don't have to sing every song with the full orchestra. It's important that you bring your rhythm section and sing several songs without the orchestra."

I explained how important her appearance would be to the future of the FWSO and how desperately we needed the income that would be generated by a Pops series.

After a while, her concerns turned into enthusiasm. "Johnny, you've convinced me," Ella said. She assured me that she would ask her management to quote a reasonable fee.

The concert was completely sold out, and the audience's reception was overwhelming.

It was one of the best Pops concerts we performed during my tenure, and all it took was one phone call and an old friendship.

Ella appeared as a guest on *The Tonight Show* with Johnny Carson a few days after the concert.

Johnny asked her, "What have you been doing lately Ella?"

"I just played my first symphony gig in Fort Worth, Texas."

"That must have been a disaster, trying to make classical musicians swing."

"Absolutely not, Johnny, they were great! In fact, they have one of the best young lead trumpet players I've ever worked with."

Johnny turned to Doc Severinsen, his band leader, "How about that Doc, a symphony orchestra that swings."

Doc echoed Ella and told Johnny that he also knew Don Thomas, our first trumpet player to whom Ella referred, and emphasized how good he was.

The concert's success made it much easier to convince the board to present a separate Pops series.

We were able to engage several guest artists for the Pops, and some adjusted their fees for us because of my friendship with them in the mid-1950s, when I played their acts. A few others who performed with us were Tony Bennett, Doc Severinsen, Sarah Vaughan, Phyllis Diller, Victor Borge, Dionne Warwick, and Mel Tormé. That set a precedent, and word got out in the industry that we were a very good Pops orchestra. We continued to engage many well-known and superb Pops artists. It was invaluable that Ann Koonsman was an accomplished Pops violinist and knew how to deal with that aspect of the music industry as well as how to negotiate fees.

Mel Tormé

When we engaged Mel Tormé for a holiday concert, I conducted the first half and he the second. He asked me to play saxophone on some of his arrangements. That surprised many of the orchestra musicians who had no idea of my background in jazz.

The concert ended with Mel leading the audience in a sing-along. The last piece in the sing-along was the "Hallelujah" chorus. I had forgotten that Mel was Jewish and had no idea of the text. All he knew was the intermittent phrase: "Hallelujah, Hallelujah. Hallelujah," so he mimed the other words, keeping the microphone away from his mouth until that phrase came up. Then, each time the phrase came up he sang loudly and directly into the mic.

Tony Bennett

I had also performed with Tony Bennett when I was a teenager. Tony, in addition to his being one of the great popular singers of our time, is a superb artist. After one of his concerts with the FWSO, Mary Alice and I took Tony to hear his favorite blues singer, Big Joe Turner, who happened to be playing at the Caravan of Dreams. We sat on the front row with Tony and watched him draw several beautiful and expressive

BELOW
Beverly Cardona, Ella Fitzgerald, and Walter Echols after the concert. Courtesy of the Fort Worth Symphony Orchestra (hereinafter FWSO).

RIGHT
Backstage with Ella Fitzgerald.
Courtesy of the FWSO.

pencil sketches of Turner.

The opportunities to collaborate with the finest guest artists in the world were many of the most rewarding experiences of my tenure with the FWSO.

Bernstein Mass

In 1971, the Bernstein *Mass*, commissioned by Jacqueline Kennedy, premiered as part of the opening of the John F. Kennedy Center for the Performing Arts. The next performance took place in 1973 in Vienna by the Yale Symphony Orchestra.

Mass is an extraordinary work that requires a myriad of performing disciplines: a pit symphony orchestra, stage orchestra, jazz ensemble, marching band, full choir, dancers, rock band, boy choir, staging, lighting effects, costumes, a small ensemble of singer/actor/dancers Bernstein referred to as "street people," and the celebrant. It rivals grand opera in its complexity.

In May 1976, the Fort Worth Symphony Orchestra attempted to bring *Mass* to fruition. I had to convince the entire Fort Worth performing arts community along with technicians, stage hands, a stage director, and costume designer to participate. It was a perfect platform on which to capture the interest of the public and receive international attention. It was the third performance of the work and the first by a professional symphony orchestra.

It proved to be a project that would require every organizational and leadership skill that I could muster. Detailed rehearsal schedules for every element had to be made and implemented. That alone was an enormous task.

The effort was worth it. By involving so many different segments of the performing arts community, this collaboration created good will for the FWSO and established its leadership role. The media supported it because of its uniqueness and the local and national attention the performance garnered.

There is something mystical about the work. Everyone involved with the production, including administrators, performers, and stage hands, became *Mass* "groupies." The work ends with all the performers and audience holding hands and singing "Simple Song." The *Mass* had such a strong emotional impact that most of the performers and audience were in tears by the last note of "Simple Song."

The audience included people from every walk of life from throughout the US and Europe. Internationally acclaimed conductors such as Lorin Maazel, international impresarios, artist managers, well-known performers, dignitaries, and Bernstein's personal manager, Maggie Carson, all attended.

In 1976, the NY Philharmonic, which Bernstein was conducting, toured throughout the US and Europe to celebrate America's bicentennial. They performed an all-Gershwin program including *Rhapsody in Blue*, played and conducted by Bernstein. The historic London performance took place in Royal Albert Hall. I had made a stopover in London on the way home after having conducted the Belgian Radio and TV orchestra in an all-American program. I ran into the cellist Lynn Harrell, who had been performing in London, and we attended the NY Phil concert together.

Afterward Lynn and I went backstage to congratulate Bernstein on the performance. I

LEFT
Arthur Fiedler, longtime conductor of the Boston Pops. Courtesy of the FWSO.

LEFT
Editing session of the recording of my film score for Milepost 407: A West Texas Story, *produced by Mitchell Johnson.* Author Collection.

LEFT
Playing polo during the annual FWSO Polo for the Pops fundraising event at the Upchurch polo field. Author Collection.

had met him a couple of years earlier in NYC when I asked him to engage the Cliburn winner. Lynn had never met him and asked if he could join me. When we arrived at Bernstein's dressing room we were met by a guard who refused to let us greet him. I gave the guard my FWSO business card, wrote "Thank you for the Mass" on the back, and requested he give it to Bernstein.

As Lynn and I were leaving, we heard, "John, please come back." It was Bernstein!

We eagerly returned to his room. He was shirtless, perspiring heavily, with a towel draped around his neck. He approached me, embraced me, and kissed me on the cheek. He was crying profusely.

"John, Maggie told me that your performance of *Mass* was wonderful and the best. It is my favorite work and has a very deep, emotional meaning to me. I would have been there, but unfortunately your performance took place on the same date as the opening of *1600 Pennsylvania Avenue.*"

That was one of the most meaningful compliments I ever have received.

TCU Faculty Position

During my time as music director for the Fort Worth Symphony Orchestra, I simultaneously held a position at my alma mater, TCU, both as a faculty member teaching classes and as the director of the TCU orchestra.

Conducting Class

Part of my teaching load with my position at TCU was a junior conducting course.

Conducting is a junior-level course required of all music majors. Before one studies conducting it is imperative that one has taken several basic courses such as music theory, music history, orchestration, and form and analysis. Those fundamental courses are critical for conducting. One must understand how music is constructed, its harmony; have the ability to sight sing; be conversant with all orchestral instruments; have studied orchestration; and read full band and orchestra scores.

During the first class I gave the students a basic test that included an analysis of a simple Haydn string quartet, easy harmonic dictation, playing a simple hymn on piano, and fundamental sight reading. I didn't even include basic form and analysis or orchestration. Few students were conversant with every section of the exam.

The test results were absurd for junior-level students! One must understand music fundamentals and be able to know if the ensemble is making errors by reading the score. Proper gesticulation to communicate that knowledge is imperative, but conductors can't lead the ensemble to recreate music properly unless they completely understand the piece they are conducting.

After a week of teaching, during which I concentrated on music fundamentals, the chairman of the music department, Dr. Michael Winesanker, summoned me to meet with him. Dr. Winesanker was a superb musician and musicologist, and I admired him from the first day I met him. As always, he was calm and congenial. He handed me a note signed by the members of my conducting class.

It read: "Dr. Winesanker, Mr. Giordano is spending too much time teaching us music and very little time teaching us conducting."

"Dr Winesanker, that is one of the best compliments I've ever received!" I said. "How can one be a conductor and not know anything about music fundamentals? I don't understand why junior-level students are not more capable of taking melodic and harmonic dictation, playing a simple hymn on the piano, sight singing, or analyzing eight measures of a slow movement of a simple Haydn string quartet. It is impossible to conduct anything without those fundamental skills. It's relatively easy to teach them how to give a downbeat and conduct basic beat patterns."

Throughout his teaching and administrative tenure, Dr. Winesanker always championed the students' needs. He was dedicated to assuring that they received the best training possible, so, needless to say, he was extremely concerned when I explained the reasons for my approach to the class.

"Mr. Giordano, I felt it was important for you to know this. I will speak to them regarding your concerns and will investigate the courses that should have prepared them for conducting. In the meantime, I suggest you spend a little more time on gesticulation." He was not admonishing me but attempting to solve the problem I was facing.

"Thank you for sharing the note with me. I will spend much more time on gesticulation as you requested."

I left the room. It wasn't as if Dr. Winesanker was actually upset with me. He just was serious about giving students the best music education possible. He was concerned that there was a problem in preparatory classes for conducting. The students were not receiving a thorough education in certain subjects. Ultimately, he was right: I needed to focus more on teaching students gestures.

At the next class I addressed the students and explained that I will spend more time on gesticulation and also will expect them to learn the fundamentals of the music they were assigned to conduct. I informed them that knowledge of the music they were conducting will always be included on tests, and I expected them to be prepared at every class to explain in detail every aspect of the pieces they are conducting. Subsequently there was a positive solution to the problem.

Music Appreciation Class

My approach to the Music Appreciation course for non-music majors I taught was much different. The purpose of the course was to develop an appreciation of classical music, hence its title. My predecessor made the class very difficult and was determined to instill how complicated classical music is and how superior it is to popular music. That approach only alienates non-classical music listeners and perpetuates their perception of classical music as pretentious and something created for intellectual, condescending, supercilious snobs, which is far from the truth. The class should be designed as an opportunity to develop future audiences for classical music, not cause them to detest it.

I began the course by playing and discussing contemporary pop music and made analogies to classical music. Then I bridged the gap between styles by playing examples and explained how they related. I played recordings of exciting, beautiful, and approachable classical music and tried to make the class enjoyable. My tests consisted primarily of multiple-choice questions and identification of well-known classical music recordings, like the slow movement of the Dvorak New World Symphony, the negro spiritual "Goin Home."

It became a very popular course. Years later, a young man who was a former starting linebacker on the TCU football team and his wife came backstage after a FWSO concert. He expressed how my course influenced him to love classical music and that he is a season ticket holder to the Fort Worth Symphony Orchestra and plays recordings constantly in his home. I hope that there are many former students who experienced the same thing.

Artistic Development

The Fort Worth Symphony Orchestra had always performed on a high level, especially for a regional orchestra. This region is unique in that there is a pool of highly skilled musicians in the DFW Metroplex. There are several colleges and universities that have faculty members and many outstanding students capable of playing in any major orchestra. There are also several recording studios that attract prominent musicians to the area.

Great music must be performed on the highest level possible and not be an inferior facsimile. Although a photocopy of a great painting might be attractive and resemble the original, it isn't nearly as beautiful. A symphony orchestra must play together on a regular basis, preferably daily, to acquire the precision, balance, and artistry necessary to properly recreate symphonic masterpieces. To build an ensemble of a high artistic quality it is necessary to engage as many full-time artists as fiscally possible. Great music performed to bring out its beauty, excitement, and passion will attract patrons.

A problem in developing an eighty-five piece "major" orchestra in Fort Worth is that we are in the shadow of the Dallas Symphony. It would be possible but costly to develop that size orchestra in Fort Worth. The Dallas Symphony employed full-time musicians and had a budget of several million dollars for decades, whereas the Fort Worth Symphony's budget was approximately $80,000.

The English Chamber Orchestra

Lili, the ECO, José-Luis, and the Caribbean

Through Lili Kraus's recommendation, I was offered an opportunity to participate in a music tour of the Caribbean on a cruise ship during which she was performing recitals and concertos. The orchestra on the cruise was the English Chamber Orchestra, one of the finest chamber orchestras in existence. Among the renowned artists on the cruise were Henryk Szeryng, György Sándor, James Galway, Maurice Andre, Alexander Schneider, and José-Luis Garcia (José-Luis was the leader of the English Orchestra). The cruise turned out to be an experience that influenced my musical development in a profound way, led to close personal and professional relationships, and contributed to the success of the FWSO and eventual creation and success of the Fort Worth Chamber Orchestra.

During the three-week cruise the wonderful artists and the fabulous ECO often presented three concerts per day. Listening to rehearsals and performances by these artists was a rare opportunity to experience music making on the highest level within a concentrated time frame.

The most exciting musical aspect of the cruise for me was observing the technical methods employed by the rich-sounding string section of the ECO—how and why the sound varied according to the different soloists and conductors for the performance. The orchestra's leader, José-Luis Garcia, was the main reason for the orchestra's magnificent sound and artistic excellence. The leader of an orchestra such as the ECO is the concertmaster, and the person primarily responsible for overseeing and upholding its standard of excellence. In addition, because of the nature of the ECO's repertoire, José-Luis often played solos while conducting and frequently led works not requiring a conductor from his seated position in the orchestra.

José-Luis Garcia

José-Luis was a charming and humorous man who used off-the-wall phrases and was one of the most influential and masterful musicians I knew. He'd say things like, "He is as thick as two planks!" or "Thank Gawd for thaht," and, often, "When I was with Di and Charlie . . . " (referring to Princess Diana and Prince Charles, who were the Patrons of the English Chamber Orchestra. José-Luis played for their wedding in Saint Paul's Cathedral in 1981).

José-Luis was the leader of the English Chamber Orchestra for twenty-five years, during the period considered to be the orchestra's "golden years."

José-Luis was a protégé of Serge Celibadache and had a profound influence on hundreds of musicians. His recording of A. Vivaldi's Four Seasons with the English Chamber Orchestra is one of the bestselling classical music discs. One of his best among his many outstanding recordings with the orchestra was J. S. Bach's Double Concerto with Pinchas Zuckerman (1990) and later with Dmitry Sitkovetsky. He recorded a CD, on which I conducted, with the Fort Worth Chamber Orchestra that received rave reviews. (It was fun for my son John and me to see it in a music store's window in Oxford when we were on a trip together in England.)

José-Luis was a superb violinist and a master of developing a beautiful sonority in string sections. His input was inestimable in attaining international recognition for the Fort Worth Chamber Orchestra.

Our children adored him, as he did them. He traveled from London and played Mozart's "Adagio for violin and strings" at our daughter Anne's wedding. He also planned to perform for our other daughter Ellen's wedding but broke his arm a couple of days before his flight and couldn't play. He came anyway to give Ellen his support.

Mary Alice and I were fortunate to have been with José-Luis in his London home shortly before his death. He had recently been knighted into the Order of Alfonso X, The Wise, by King Juan Carlos for his musical contribution to Spain. He was enormously proud of what he considered to be the most important recognition in his life.

José-Luis was at times vain and proud, but he was also energetic, loving, and kind.

José-Luis had a profound influence on my artistic development. He was a great friend, one whom I could take into my confidence. He served as principal guest conductor of the Fort Worth Chamber Orchestra for several years. We remained close friends until his death on August 12, 2011, at the age of sixty-seven.

The most important benefit of the ECO cruise, besides acquiring many close friends and having the opportunity to hear great music performed by world class artists, was meeting José-Luis Garcia.

Henryk Szeryng

On one of the cruise's concerts the iconic, sensational violinist Henryk Szeryng conducted and played Bach's *Concerto for Two Violins and Orchestra*, with José-Luis performing the second solo part.

I was observing the rehearsal for the Bach. At one point Szeryng stopped the rehearsal and asked:

"John, would you please check the balance?"

"Certainly," I responded.

The rehearsal resumed. Szeryng stopped suddenly and said, "No, no, no John, you can't possibly do it from there!"

I was sitting at the bar, about thirty feet from the stage. He placed a chair directly in front of him, a couple of feet away.

"Sit here, where you can have a better perspective."

I knew he wanted to make certain that he was prominently heard above the second soloist. They resumed playing and I could barely hear José-Luis. He stopped again.

"Well John, how is it now?"

"It's perfect, Maestro!"

That pleased him greatly.

There were three concerts per day on the cruise, some orchestral and some solo recitals. One day the third concert began at 10:00 p.m. and featured Szeryng and György Sándor in a program of works for violin and piano. Everyone programmed short concerts. However, Szeryng and Sándor played a concert that was two hours long and consisted of heavy, lengthy, serious sonatas. This was at the end of a day, following two recitals. Even though Szeryng and Sándor were extraordinary artists, programming a long concert at the end of a music-filled day was not a great idea.

Jimmy Galway, José-Luis, Lili, and I were sitting together in the back row observing the audience as well as the performers. Despite the wonderful artistry of the performers, after a few minutes several members of the audience

RIGHT
José-Luis Garcia, principal guest conductor of the FWCO during the 1980s. Author Collection.

began to doze off, some lapsing into a deep sleep with their heads thrown back.

After the last lengthy sonata, which ended around 12:30 a.m., we looked at each other and Lili said, "I wonder if they would play an encore?"

"Surely not!" Jimmy responded.

José-Luis said, "Let's get everyone to stand and applaud vigorously and see what they'll do."

They responded by playing a twenty-minute, three-movement sonata!

After the sonata's last note, José-Luis said, "Do you think they would play another one?"

"No way!" I responded.

Again, we led the audience in another rousing round of applause. Szeryng addressed the audience: "Thank you, my dear friends, we now will play Mozart Sonata—"

Lili interrupted, "For goodness sake Henryk, enough is enough!"

The audience responded to Lili with the most enthusiastic applause of the evening.

The cruise with the ECO was very rewarding. However, there were some drawbacks. We were required to dress formally for almost every evening meal. The organizers rotated musicians from table to table to give passengers an opportunity to visit with them. Those meals often were stressful because we were bombarded with questions like, "Which recording of the Brahms Symphony no. 3 do you prefer?" or: "Why is Karajan's interpretation of the Mahler First Symphony so different from Bernstein's?" or: "Where did you receive your formal training?"

One evening the bass player of the ECO sat at the same table as I. He had little patience with the nonstop questions. The lady sitting next to him wouldn't relent from asking personal questions about his training, his hobbies, how many children he had, etc. He tried to change the subject. "Okay mum," he said, "enough about me. Now how about you? What does your old man do?"

"He's in oil."

"What is he? A bloody sardine?"

Creation of the Fort Worth Chamber Orchestra

The establishment of a chamber orchestra of top international quality was my first priority in the development of the FWSO. I didn't think that the metroplex could support two full-time major orchestras, and the Dallas Symphony was well established. I deemed it would be several years, if ever, that Fort Worth would be able to financially support a fifty-two-week, eighty-five-piece orchestra with full benefits that performed on the very highest artistic level.

Many orchestras in the US employed a "core" group of about thirty musicians. Their instrumentation normally consisted of full wind and brass sections, a very small string section, and a couple of percussionists. That ensemble could not perform on the highest artistic level. It didn't have enough strings to perform standard symphonic repertory properly and had too many winds and percussionists to perform music from the Baroque, Classical, and all repertoire requiring small forces.

A chamber orchestra was a different matter, and I was confident that we could develop a chamber orchestra to the highest musical standards in Fort Worth. It could present a fresh and varied repertory and not compete with the Dallas Symphony. My original concept was to create a "core ensemble" of the FWSO approximately the same size as the Italian ensemble, I Musici, which consisted of twelve string instruments and a harpsichord. Ours would consist of nineteen full-time artists (thirteen strings, five woodwinds, and a keyboard). I planned to add other instruments as needed on a per-service basis. An orchestra of this size would exponentially improve the full FWSO and be financially viable. An existing role model was the Minnesota Symphony Orchestra and the St. Paul Chamber Orchestra in the Twin Cities.

The chamber orchestra would be broken down to full-time musicians consisting of two string quartets, a string quintet, and a woodwind quintet. These smaller groups could also be an important part of a unique and extensive educational program. The full ensemble could play a series of concerts in a venue appropriate for its size. The musicians would be engaged for a thirty-two-week season.

My proposal to the board was approved based on the acquisition of funding to support it.

I started the process of creating an I Musici-size orchestra. Initially only the strings and harpsichord (keyboard) were on salary and woodwinds, brass, and percussion were added as needed. We played several concerts with that size orchestra, including a series at the Kimbell Art Museum. Lili Kraus was soloist on one of the concerts performing a Mozart Concerto.

The Texas Little Symphony

Before this chamber orchestra was officially named the Fort Worth Chamber Orchestra, we called it "The Texas Little Symphony—Portable, Affordable, and Flexible" and marketed that catchphrase to communities throughout Texas. One of the board members, Norwood Dixon, came up with the name. That promotional strategy was successful and provided income-producing services, gave name recognition to the orchestra, and improved its quality. During the seasons in the Kimbell we gradually expanded to the size of the English Chamber Orchestra and moved the concerts to Ed Landreth Auditorium on the TCU campus.

We were selected to be the touring orchestra of the Texas State Arts Touring program. That entity provided matching funds to assist local presenters. The ensemble was small enough to travel on a single bus, plus an equipment truck and a car for me and staff members. We performed a wide variety of repertoire: Baroque, Classical, Romantic, Impressionist, Contemporary, and Pops. The tours were very effective and cemented close relationships with several cities throughout Texas.

Rudolf Serkin

The destiny of the Fort Worth Chamber Orchestra came from a source I never would have imagined—the legendary pianist Rudolf Serkin.

My New York artist management at the time was the William Judd Agency, and one of his staff artist managers, Bill Perrotta, was my personal representative. I brought the recording of Lili's concert with me on one of my trips to NYC and played it for Bill. During that trip, Bill Judd invited Bill Perrotta and me to his apartment for dinner, and Rudolf Serkin, who also was on Judd's roster, joined us.

After dinner, Bill Perrotta suggested I play the recording. Both Judd and Serkin were impressed.

Serkin said, "This is a very good ensemble,

ABOVE
The Chamber Orchestra performing in the Kimbell Art Museum. Courtesy of the FWSO.

but I have a suggestion: I think that you should expand to the size of the English Chamber Orchestra and Academy of St Martin in the Fields. Then your repertoire would be greatly expanded. I would play any Mozart or Beethoven concerto with that size orchestra."

Serkin's suggestion made sense, and I decided to expand the chamber orchestra incrementally to accomplish that goal. The next season I added a few players and presented a series of concerts at the Kimbell Art Museum, for which we engaged artists such as the violinist Franco Gulli and guitarist Pepe Romero. The holiday concert was performed in an elegantly decorated setting in the Kimbell and became popular. The museum was full to capacity—standing room only. The combination of a beautiful environment and elegant music was a draw for the public.

Audience Development

Increasing the audience's size is paramount to the development of a professional orchestra. Conductors, board members, and many patrons of symphony orchestras unknowingly often create the perception that orchestras are elitist organizations that only perform music that can't be appreciated by the public.

A symphony orchestra should be a cultural resource and engender pride from every segment of its community. It should function as an aural museum capable of providing a variety of music from all periods of history and musical styles.

The Fort Worth Symphony improved artistically, became more locally and nationally prominent, and is now considered to be an integral and invaluable asset to the community. Much of the orchestra's popularity is due to the variety of music and uniqueness of our concerts.

We performed concerts throughout the community to citizens of every economic level and ethnicity. I put together programs that were enjoyable but not condescending. For example, in the Hispanic community we performed Latin music as well as standard repertoire and included the Ballet Folklorico as often as possible. In the African American community, we performed music by important black classical composers and featured black artists. We commissioned arrangements of current popular music.

The Chamber Orchestra performed in venues other than concert halls, like the Kimbell Art Museum, where the annual Christmas concert became a popular event, and the Museum of Modern Art, where we performed more adventuresome and unusual works.

The Fort Worth Chamber Orchestra made several recordings that received high acclaim. We performed in Carnegie Hall and toured throughout Texas, establishing concert series in several cities including Temple, Tyler, and

Waxahachie. We performed and toured with internationally acclaimed artists such as Alicia de Larrocha. We inaugurated a successful music festival in Ruidoso, New Mexico, and were the first chamber orchestra to perform a cultural exchange tour of the People's Republic of China. We also toured in Mexico and Spain.

Ann Koonsman

The most important development that determined the success of the FWSO and chamber orchestra was Beverly Cardona's engagement of Ann Koonsman as director of our educational and touring programs. The hire was critical to audience development, and the touring income helped to defray the cost of the full-time salaried musicians. Together, Ann and I significantly developed the orchestra.

Ann first served as education coordinator in 1974 and played in the orchestra. We had a policy that all musicians were required to audition, even for a part-time position. I had known Ann since she was an undergraduate at TCU, so I was already familiar with her playing. She is an accomplished violinist and was well qualified. When Ann was in undergraduate school at TCU she won the concerto competition on piano one year and on violin the next. In addition, she was in the Miss Fort Worth beauty pageant and wrote her own studio band arrangement for the talent portion.

Since I was very familiar with Ann's level of performance, an audition wasn't necessary for me to evaluate her qualifications, so while she played, I wasn't completely concentrating on her performance. I had turned my thoughts to the qualifications for her administrative position.

I was required to have her play all the music that I and the principal members of the string sections had selected. After she played several difficult orchestral excerpts and a portion of a concerto, she asked me, "Is there anything else?"

LEFT
The poster in front of Carnegie Hall advertising the FWCO's concert. Courtesy of the FWSO.

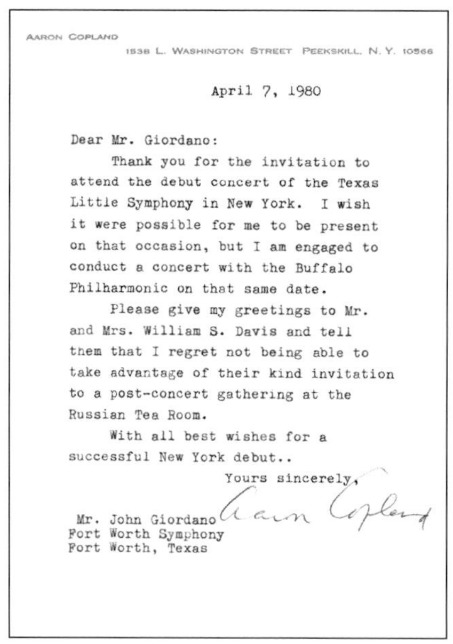

AARON COPLAND
1538 L. WASHINGTON STREET PEEKSKILL, N. Y. 10566

April 7, 1980

Dear Mr. Giordano:
Thank you for the invitation to attend the debut concert of the Texas Little Symphony in New York. I wish it were possible for me to be present on that occasion, but I am engaged to conduct a concert with the Buffalo Philharmonic on that same date.
Please give my greetings to Mr. and Mrs. William S. Davis and tell them that I regret not being able to take advantage of their kind invitation to a post-concert gathering at the Russian Tea Room.
With all best wishes for a successful New York debut..

Yours sincerely,
Aaron Copland

Mr. John Giordano
Fort Worth Symphony
Fort Worth, Texas

LEFT
Letter from Aaron Copeland. Author Collection.

ABOVE
The Chamber Orchestra's tenth anniversary celebration.
Courtesy of the FWSO.

ABOVE (TOP)
Texas Little Symphony performing in Carnegie Hall.
Courtesy of the FWSO.

"Yes," I answered. "As a matter of fact there is—can you type?"

In addition to Ann's musical talent, she has an extraordinary propensity for organization. She is persuasive, fiscally responsible, and willing to make difficult and decisive administrative decisions.

Ann lived with her husband Ron, an executive with Bell Telephone Co., in several cities throughout Texas, as his position demanded. In 1974 Beverly Cardona, who was the manager of the orchestra at that time, and I were seeking opportunities to augment the income of the musicians and improve the quality of our educational activities. Beverly applied to the Junior League of Fort Worth for funding to reestablish the concept of Project Muse. The grant was approved, and Ann was engaged to administer the program. This time when the grant expired we were able to continue the program, replacing the grant's funds with private funding, local foundation grants, and corporate gifts. Ann's responsibilities were expanded to include the acquisition of touring engagements for the Chamber Orchestra.

Ann was forced to move to Houston when Bell Telephone transferred Ron. She secured employment as director of educational activities with the Houston Symphony.

In 1980, our executive director was fired because the orchestra incurred much financial difficulty during her tenure. During the meeting in which the executive committee of the board of directors voted to terminate her, I recommended that we offer the position to Ann. The committee was aware of Ann's capabilities and unanimously voted to offer the position to her. After the vote, Leon Brachman, president of the board, left the room, and immediately called Ann in Houston to tender her the offer to be our executive director.

Fortunately, she accepted. Ron graciously agreed to support Ann's appointment and insisted she accept the board's offer. He subsequently resigned from Bell and created his own

LEFT
FWSO Concerts in the Garden performance. Author Collection.

LEFT
Lunchtime concert in Fort Worth's downtown Burnett Park. Courtesy of the FWSO.

RIGHT
Toasting the great tenor Luciano Pavorotti after his performance with the FWSO. Author Collection.

BELOW
Recording a commercial for the Fort Worth National Bank in its lobby. Courtesy of the FWSO.

ABOVE
Conducting lesson during an education concert with the FWCO. Author Collection.

company in the Dallas-Fort Worth Metroplex.

After the Koonsmans moved to Fort Worth, Mary Alice and I invited them to dinner to celebrate Ann's appointment. At dinner, we learned of Ron's new company, and Mary Alice asked, "Ron, what will your new company be?"

He responded, "I'm starting a telephone cellular service in the metroplex."

"What is that?"

"A new technology that will make it possible for everyone to have a portable phone to use in their car."

"Ron, that never will work," Mary Alice said. "What fool would want to have a telephone in their car?"

* * * * * *

Ann and I worked together until 2000. We established the only entity in the Fort Worth Musician's Union, Local 72, that gave classically trained musicians full-time employment. We always were fiscally solvent and considered the unique personality of Fort Worth while planning our concert season. We carefully and conservatively planned the orchestra's growth, with the goal to develop the quality of the FWSO and establish it as a critical component of the fabric of Fort Worth.

The Fort Worth Chamber Orchestra's Historic Tour of the People's Republic of China

Touring is an important factor in the development of a musical ensemble. It contributes immeasurably to the ensemble's maturing and the sophistication of its performances. The unique qualities of China, the world's oldest civilization, made our experience extraordinarily meaningful. Traditional Chinese music is completely different from Western music; it is based on different pitches, is primarily programmatic, and reflects many aspects of the

LEFT
Ann Koonsman.
Author Collection.

Chinese culture.

Prior to our China tour, the Texas Little Orchestra changed its name to the Fort Worth Chamber Orchestra. The name change was sparked one day when I was talking with some officials during an engagement with the Hong Kong Philharmonic.

"Maestro, I understand your children's orchestra will be touring in the PRC soon."

"Yes, except it is a professional orchestra."

"But don't you call it the Texas Little Symphony? In Chinese that name translates to the 'Texas Children's Symphony.'"

As soon as I returned to Fort Worth I called Ann and told her of the counseling I received regarding our name. Neither she nor I ever did like the label "The Texas Little Symphony." She said, "I agree; the name is incorrect anyway. Since we are a chamber orchestra in Fort Worth and funded in Fort Worth, why don't we simply change the name to 'The Fort Worth Chamber Orchestra'? After all that's what we are!"

She was right; how obvious. Ann presented it to the board for official approval, explaining my experience in Hong Kong, and they approved it unanimously without any discussion.

The FWCO's trip to China in 1983 was unique. China did not have official cultural relations with the US. The orchestra's tour of China was solidified during my solo trip there back in 1980 because of the relationship I had established with the PRC's Minister of Culture, Wang Zicheng.

Funding was a major stumbling block we had to overcome. Because of the strained cultural atmosphere with the PRC at the time, our State Department, while approving the trip, could not offer financial aid. Ann and I created a plan. She sought funding for the airfare and subsistence as per the union agreement, and my assignment was to appeal to the Chinese for help. Ann was fantastic. She acquired the airfare from AA and the extra funds needed for per diem etc. from Ed Bass. I was successful in getting China to agree to cover the expenses for everything in the interior of China.

All we had to do was to get to Beijing! That turned out to be a more daunting task than we could have imagined in our wildest dreams. What transpired made our trip quite meaningful, extraordinary, and historic. I believe it also helped to alleviate some tension between our two countries.

We planned for a true cultural exchange, which would not be as unwieldy as an attempted exchange with a large ensemble. As a chamber orchestra, we could perform in smaller venues in addition to the large concert halls. We could travel in fewer busses, have less equipment, dramatically lower expenses, and offer a diverse repertoire, flexible enough to include Chinese music. My major professor for my doctoral studies, the prominent composer Samuel Adler, wrote a superb work for the orchestra which we performed throughout the tour. It became an integral part of our repertoire and is one of his most frequently performed compositions.

As a major part of the exchange, our musicians gave masterclasses to the Chinese musicians, and in turn the Chinese musicians gave demonstrations, concerts, and master classes for us on their traditional instruments. That was a unique experience. Although ancient Chinese musicians used a notation called Gongche or gongchepu, which utilized Chinese characters, traditional Chinese music is now played by memory and passed from generation to generation. Many FWCO musicians purchased Chinese instruments and were coached by their Chinese counterparts.

During the Cultural Revolution, Western instruments were destroyed and music burned. Chinese musicians attempting to secretly perform, practice, and study Western music were severely punished. There were very few strings available for string instruments, reeds for the woodwinds, proper mouthpieces for the winds, and no proper editions of printed music. There were few instrumental technicians, especially those who could repair and adjust string instruments. Wayne Burak, our principal cellist, was an expert string instrument repair specialist. Wayne offered to adjust and make minor repairs on the Chinese musicians' Western instruments. Much of the Western music they were using was written by Chinese musicians relying on their memory and contained many errors. We gave them printed music, reeds for the woodwinds, mouthpieces for the brass, and strings for the violins, violas, cellos, and basses.

Everything was set for what we thought would be a truly exciting and historic adventure. Accompanying us was a physician (Dr. Ed Etier) and two photojournalists from Time LIFE who were assigned to document the tour and keep the AP and our local press informed.

We had a celebratory send-off at DFW Airport. Our first stop was a layover at Narita Airport in Tokyo, Japan, intended to help us overcome jet lag. The flight was uneventful and pleasant. We enjoyed a special dinner the evening of our arrival in Tokyo and retired with the hope that our jet lag would be alleviated and we would be better prepared for what looked like an exhausting schedule of concerts, workshops, rehearsals, sight-seeing, and travel.

I received a call at 2:00 am from the State Department asking if I was the person in charge of our tour. I explained that Ann was the administrator in charge and gave him her room number. I dressed immediately and went to her room. She was already speaking to the State Department. Sylvia Stoddard, our operations manager, and Robert Davidovici, our concertmaster, were also already there. The State Department informed us that the PRC had broken off all diplomatic relations with the US because the pro tennis player, Hu Na, had defected while we were in the air on our flight to Tokyo. They informed us that if we continued, we were on our own.

While deciding what to do we received a telegram from Ed Bass, who was at his hotel in Katmandu, Nepal, at the time. The telegram read: "Have courage, remember Marco Polo also had a difficult decision to make." After contacting the minister of culture's office in Beijing and learning that they still would receive us, we decided to proceed. We were not traveling under the auspices of the State Department and were sponsored by the PRC. We were permitted to continue.

Although it was never officially stated, I think that the decision to complete the tour and the positive results we achieved helped the US restore cultural relations with China.

That morning we continued with apprehension as to what difficulties we might incur because of Hu Na's defection. We were concerned about the reception we might have from the public as well as the Chinese government. We imagined that they might be angry with all Americans over the defection. As the tour progressed, we learned that the Chinese also were concerned for our safety. All these concerns turned out to be unfounded. Our reception wherever we traveled was marvelous.

Our schedule was filled with activity from early morning to late evening. The typical day would begin at 6:00 a.m. with breakfast, followed by master classes at the local conservatory, a several-course lunch, rehearsal at the concert venue, a tour of some important Chinese attractions such as the Great Wall, the Forbidden City, the Summer Palace, etc., and a heavy meal followed by a concert.

ABOVE
Debbie Brooks, cellist, and Richard Pliler, violinist, going over with me some of the music we were going to play in China. Courtesy of the FWSO.

In the US the schedule of rehearsals, performances, and touring is controlled by the agreement between orchestra management and the Musicians Union. Unions do not exist in China. One afternoon, after a long period during which the musicians had no time to address personal things such as doing their laundry, individual practicing, and shopping, most wanted to have some time off from official duties.

Mr. Lu, the associate minister of culture in charge of the tour, announced after a morning of master classes that we would have a tour of the zoo in Beijing immediately following lunch. The orchestra committee approached Ann and requested they be given an afternoon free of any organized activity. Ann agreed and explained that she was not in charge of the schedule, and suggested the committee communicate directly with Mr. Lu.

The chair of the orchestra musician's committee addressed Mr. Lu: "The orchestra has had a meeting and decided that they prefer to remain in the hotel this afternoon."

Mr. Lu said, "Thank you very much, now please get on the bus!"

And they did!

The orchestra was wonderfully received in every city. We performed to sold-out houses and enthusiastic audiences everywhere. They always demanded we play several encores. At the end of one concert we had played everything that we had prepared for encores. As I left the stage after the last one, I said to Alice McDaniel, one of our violinists, as I walked past her, "What can we play now?"

"How about the third movement of Dvorak's G Major Symphony?" she said.

It worked beautifully and remained in our encore repertoire.

After one particularly well-received performance, the stage manager had to turn out the lights in the concert hall to stop the applause.

The tour enriched our lives tremendously and considerably helped the orchestra to develop into a performing ensemble on an increasingly high level.

The FWCO's First International Tour in Mexico

On a few occasions, I have been mistaken for the internationally famous tenor Plácido Domingo and have even been asked for my—his—autograph.

One of the most memorable concerts on the Mexican tour was in Guadalajara. The city has an extraordinarily beautiful opera theater in which orchestra concerts are also presented. Our performance followed an opera that had closed the night before

We were fortunate to perform in that historic venue. The sold-out audience warmly received the performance and many, mostly attractive señoritas, demonstrated their appreciation by throwing flowers onto the stage after the final encore.

Our hotel, where most artists stayed, was conveniently located across the street from the theater. It gave us the opportunity to quickly change out of our concert attire before we attended the post-concert reception. The concert sponsors had arranged for Ann, our concertmaster Robert Davidovici, and me to be taken to the reception in the same car. After changing I was first to arrive in the lobby.

While I was waiting for the others, three beautiful young ladies holding autograph books approached me. One of the señoritas said, "Maestro, may I please have your autograph?"

I had forgotten that there was an opera the night before and assumed they had just attended our concert. I was flattered and replied, "Certainly, with great pleasure," and signed her book.

She sighed, backed away, and clutched the open book to her chest, never looking at the signature. The second followed suit. However, the third was staring at me and approached hesitatingly.

After I signed her book, unlike the other two, she looked at my signature and angrily exclaimed, "You are not Plácido Domingo!"

She stormed out of the lobby.

Concierto para una Fiesta

The creation of *Concierto para una Fiesta*, a composition that has become a major work in the classical guitar repertoire, was a milestone in the development of the Fort Worth Chamber Orchestra.

An orchestra has a critical responsibility to

ABOVE
Chamber Orchestra at the Great Wall. Author Collection.

ABOVE
Ann Koonsman making friends with a Chinese child at the Great Wall. Author Collection.

ABOVE
Jack Rumbly giving a masterclass to Chinese percussionists during the FWCO's cultural exchange tour of the People's Republic of China. Author Collection.

ABOVE
Teaching a conducting class to young Chinese conducting students during the FWCO tour of China. Author Collection.

encourage the creation of new works. However, without generous underwriting it is extremely difficult to accomplish, partially because, even with sufficient funding, new compositions infrequently become standard in the classical music repertoire.

Carol and Bill McKay, patrons of the arts, lovers of classical music, and supporters of the Fort Worth Chamber Orchestra, were determined to do something of significance for the social debut of their daughters, Alden and Lauri. They were inspired to underwrite the creation of a guitar concerto. The McKays and I had established a close relationship with guitarist Pepe Romero after his first performance with the FWCO, and we asked him to be included in the project.

Joaquin Rodrigo, one of the most significant Spanish composers in the twentieth century who had written several important works for guitar and orchestra, was a logical composer to approach. Pepe, a close friend of the Rodrigo family, was instrumental in convincing the maestro to compose another work for guitar and orchestra.

In 1982, *Concierto para una Fiesta* was born. The FWCO premiered the performance with Pepe as soloist on March 9, 1983. It is one of the rare cases in which a new composition has become a standard part of the classical music repertoire. *Fiesta* is a popular concerto in the guitar's repertory and is frequently performed by the greatest guitar virtuosi.

The Fort Worth Symphony League

The Fort Worth Symphony League is a major supporter of the FWSO and raises funds that are critical to its existence. A couple of seasons before I took the helm of the orchestra, the league organized an Oktoberfest that evolved into a yearly event in the fall that attracted thousands of revelers. The orchestra played a concert every year during the event that was the highlight of the festival. During my first season the Symphony League presented me with authentic lederhosen, which I wore for several Oktoberfests. We performed a variety of music that fit into the theme of the festival. The Oktoberfest concert afforded us another opportunity to reach out to another different, large segment of the community. It was also a great source of important income that helped keep the orchestra afloat.

Parking Lot

Parking Lot was an event (not a traditional concert) I produced intended to reach out to yet another segment of the population and bring attention to the orchestra. Symphony orchestras have a responsibility to encourage living composers and program contemporary music. Contemporary music has a stigma among many as being extremely dissonant, cacophonous, and unpleasant. However, many contemporary composers are creating fresh, exciting, and beautiful music in a wide range of styles that are appealing to a broad populace.

Much modern music includes multimedia, dancers, actors, lighting effects, etc. Many of these works have become part of the standard orchestra repertoire. Leonard Bernstein and John Corigliano, for example, are composers who have produced multimedia works that fall into that category. We publicized this aspect of the concert's program and didn't highlight that it was composed of "new" music.

The Parking Lot event was presented at Casa Mañana, a geodesic domed theatre in the round. I choose Casa because it gave me an opportunity to design and uniquely stage a variety of multimedia pieces that included dance and audience participation. I made the programming to take advantage of Casa's unique configuration. There were works with dancers and instrumentalists on stage, in the pit, and positioned throughout the theatre.

The program included my composition "Compilation" for jazz quartet, string orchestra, and dancers. The dancers performed throughout the entire theater, the jazz quartet performed on stage, and the string orchestra played in the orchestra pit.

Another work was Merrill Ellis's "Kaleidoscope," which required electronic sounds and audience participation in addition to the traditional orchestra. From center stage I directed the audience and asked them to make various spontaneous vocal effects on my command. After the Ellis, I remained on stage and led the last piece on the program.

It was an event that I titled "Parking Lot." Before the audience, performers, and musicians left the theatre I instructed everyone to whistle "Stars and Stripes Forever" while clapping their hands in rhythm. I asked them to follow me to the parking lot and react to my hand and arm signals when they reached their cars. They followed my instructions to a tee, marched into the parking lot, and entered their cars.

I had borrowed the TCU football coach's practice tower and strategically positioned it where I could be seen by the entire parking lot. From there I "conducted" the "piece." Following my various hand signals, everyone honked their horns, turned their windshield wipers on and off, and blinked their lights, all the while continuing to whistle "Stars and Stripes Forever." As part of the grand finale I had the cheerleaders from TCU run in between the cars in the lot waving sparklers.

For the climax of the spectacular grand finale I arranged for the Fort Worth Police Department to fly a helicopter over the parking lot on my command, covering the entire area with its roving search light.

The police department initially refused to participate. When I spoke to the officer in charge about it before the performance, he said, "I'm sorry but we can't even consider doing something like that. It could not be considered official police business by any means."

ABOVE
With Pepe Romero, guitarist, and Carol McKay. Carol and her husband, Bill McKay, commissioned Joaquin Rodrigo to compose Concierto para una Fiesta *for Pepe and the Fort Worth Chamber Orchestra. They dedicated it to their daughters, Alden and Lauri.* Author Collection.

"Don't you fly over the Casa Mañana parking lot every evening to check for miscreants?"

"Yes, we fly over that location several times every evening. It's a prime area for criminal activity."

"Is there any reason one of the flights can't be scheduled around 10:00 p.m.? This will be very positive press for the police department."

After I described the entire event in detail, including its purpose, he became enthusiastic and relented.

He gave me a hand-held two-way radio to use and instructed the helicopter pilot to fly over and check the lot on my command. They hovered a block away over Farrington Field while they waited for my command. (It didn't hurt that, coincidently, the pilot worked security for the concert hall when he was off-duty and had a good relationship with me and the musicians.)

The evening was an amazing success. People even drove down the street honking their horns after they left the lot, continuing to perform "Parking Lot" for I don't know how long. The result was another front-page article with a large photo of the finale that showed the cars flashing their lights, turning on their windshield wipers, the cheerleaders with sparklers, and the helicopter employing its searchlight!

Music critics

The qualifications for music critics have evolved greatly. Music critics in the past were important composers, performers, and musicologists. Their remarks were heeded. The list includes Claude Debussy, Robert Schumann, Richard Wagner, Hector Berlioz, Paul Hindemith, and Paul Dukas. When a musician of this stature reviews you, you seriously consider the evaluation.

Lili Kraus played the Mozart Concerto in A Major, K414 on the Fort Worth Chamber Orchestra series at TCU. That concerto can be problematic because the orchestration is sparse and extremely transparent. The orchestra only plays a few tutti sections in between solo sections that are underscored with simple backgrounds.

Lili had a memory slip during one of the solo sections during which the strings play simple sustained notes. She stopped, looked at me, and said, "Let us start over again at the last full orchestra tutti." We did; she repeated her entrance and made the same memory slip. We started at the same place once more, came to the same spot, and she made the same slip again.

Lili rose from the audience side of her "throne" and with a dramatic gesture, threw the long train of her elegant gown over her right arm. She strode around the piano bench throne, head thrown back, to my podium with the air of royalty. She stood on it close to me, pointed to my score while facing the audience, and whispered from the side of her mouth, "Where the hell are we?" We started again at the same place, this time with success, and there were no more mishaps throughout the rest of the concerto.

The next day's review in the *Star-Telegram* read:

"At one point in the first movement, the regal Madame Kraus was forced to stop and elegantly rise from her throne to show the young conductor, who obviously was lost, where they were."

Music critics can be positive and supportive. They also can be inaccurate and mean-spirited.

We had just played our first concert with the full thirty-five-piece chamber orchestra, the major orchestral piece was Mozart, Symphony no. 35. We all were extremely pleased with the performance, especially considering it was the full chamber orchestra's debut. The local reviewer should have been supportive of this historic event. Instead, at the reception following the concert in Martha Hyder's home, he approached me and said, "John, I'm so sorry the symphony was so bad."

I was taken aback and angry. "What? Surely you are joking," I said. "First, the performance was superb. I have no idea what you were listening for, but you are completely wrong. This was a historic performance, the first by an orchestra I intend to develop into one of the finest in the world. We need your support, not your damaging negativity. You might have created a difficult barrier to overcome. Many believe what they read in print."

He apologized and explained that he thought a negative review would attract more attention to the orchestra and thus have a positive impact on its popularity. I do not understand that line of reasoning.

A negative review of the FWSO's first performance of the Mahler First Symphony presented another example of irresponsibility and dishonesty from music critics. The performance was better than I expected it to be. The orchestra was excited and poured its heart and soul into the performance.

Luiz de Moura Castro, a piano professor at TCU, called me the day the review appeared. He asked, "John, have you read the paper? I have something important to tell you. The reviewer didn't attend last night's concert but panned it. Something must be done."

"What? I haven't read it yet, but he panned a concert he hadn't attended?

"Yes, when I read the review I called him and asked him how he could possibly give that wonderful performance a bad review. He said 'The Mahler wasn't very good at all.' So I responded, 'It was great; you must have been at a different concert than I was. Where were you sitting?' 'In my usual seat,' he said. 'No, you weren't. Your seat is in the row directly in front of mine. You weren't there, were you? How dare you review a concert you didn't hear?'"

Sheepishly the reviewer answered, "No I wasn't, but I wrote the review before the concert because I didn't think the orchestra was capable of playing Mahler."

That critic eventually became a champion of the orchestra and was highly instrumental in helping to promote our activities.

Ruidoso Festival

In 1980 one of our patrons, Roy Browning, proposed that we establish a music festival in Ruidoso, New Mexico. A festival would give extra employment to our musicians and develop a new audience for the Chamber Orchestra. Many Fort Worthians either have permanent residences or own vacation homes in Ruidoso. Many race their quarter horses at Ruidoso Downs.

Leon Brachman was president of the FWSO Board at the time. He offered to fly Ann Koonsman and me to Ruidoso in his private plane to begin the process of establishing the festival and initiate a fund-raising campaign to underwrite the project. The Ruidoso airport was in a valley between two mountain peaks, making it extremely difficult for landing and takeoff.

Leon's plane, while in good mechanical condition, was not cosmetically very well taken care of. For example, it didn't have a headliner in the cabin and wires hung from the ceiling almost touching passenger's heads. When he received clearance for takeoff at Fort Worth's Meacham Field, he still was closing his door, which was difficult to latch, as he taxied down the runway, and barely closed it before takeoff. The landing in Ruidoso was harrowing because of the necessary fast descent to the very short runway in a valley between two mountain peaks. Leon was an excellent pilot and made a perfect landing (so I was told . . . my eyes were closed).

The meeting with the potential supporters in Ruidoso was successful. They were enthusiastic and pledged their support. We established a Summer Festival that initially took place in one of the horse barns at the racetrack. The festival was successful and continued for several years. We scheduled weekly concerts by the Fort Worth Chamber Orchestra, classical concerts by the FWSO with many major artists, Pops concerts featuring stars like Dionne Warwick, Phyllis Diller, Victor Borge, Al Hirt, Doc Severinsen, and park concerts. All concerts were presented "cabaret style" with audiences seated at round tables. Drinks and food were served prior to the concerts and during intermissions.

A Serendipitous Substitution Caused by the Birth of Gina Crisanti

Jan and Andy Crisanti, our principal flutist and principal clarinetist, were expecting a baby during one of the festivals. Jan went into labor the day of a performance and the Crisantis decided to return to Fort Worth for the birth. They immediately left the festival and began the drive to El Paso for a flight to DFW. (There were no commercial flights to Ruidoso at the time.) Jan and Andy didn't reach El Paso in time. Gina Crisanti was born in a small town halfway between Ruidoso and El Paso.

We had to fill two major voids at the last moment, and it was impossible to find qualified replacements who could arrive in Ruidoso in time for the evening's concert.

However, Lee Gibson, the clarinet professor at the University of North Texas, and Jean Larson Garver, the principal flutist with the Dallas Symphony, were in Ruidoso on vacation with their spouses, who played in the FWSO. Lee's wife, Ruth, was one of our violists, and Jeannie's husband was Loren Larson, our principal hornist. They stepped in at the last moment and saved what potentially could have been a disaster. I often wondered what the odds were that two superb artists who played the exact instruments we needed happened to be in Ruidoso.

Al Hirt Tragedy After Ruidoso Festival

During one of our Pops concerts we presented Al Hirt and his jazz band. Al's pianist, Freddy Crane, was one of the foremost jazz pianists in the US. His improvisational skills were legendary. I had known Freddy for several years and played with him in several recording sessions and other occasions in Dallas. His solos were particularly extraordinary that evening, leaving all on stage awestruck.

After the concert Al, his band members, Al's close friend Don Thomas (our first trumpeter), and I were planning to have dinner at a restaurant that had agreed to remain open for us. Don and I waited outside the band's dressing room for the group to change clothes. Freddy was the last musician to leave the dressing room. I embraced him and said, "Freddy, you were amazing tonight; I've never heard you play better!"

He said, "Thank you, man." Then he collapsed into my arms. He had suffered a fatal heart attack.

The Spencer Theater's Creation in Ruidoso

Jackie Spencer, the festival's major supporter, detested the concert venues. They either were in the Ruidoso Downs horse barns or at the Mescalero Apache "Inn of the Mountain Gods." She wanted to build a proper concert hall. One day Jackie invited Ann Koonsman, Robert Davidovici, our concertmaster, and me to join her to reconnoiter some of the area around Ruidoso and identify a location on which a first-class venue for concerts could be built. One of the areas that was being developed was in Alto, a plateau located close to the Ruidoso city limits in the foothills of the El Capitan mountain range. Much of Alto's prairie land was owned by Jackie.

Ann and Jackie were walking across a field in an area that Jackie was considering for the building. Robert and I were walking several yards behind them. I saw an object half buried in the rocky terrain that caught my attention because of its odd shape. I picked it up and brushed off the dirt. It was a tin template that luthiers use in making violins! Robert explained that it probably was a tool pioneer "fiddle makers" used while traveling west on wagon trains, and this one probably was lost while crossing the prairie. Pioneers often made their own musical instruments, and "fiddles" were the basic instrument used in their Celtic-derived music. (It was fun to speculate that it might have fallen out of a wagon during a pioneer family's frantic attempt to outrun attackers.)

We showed the template to Jackie. She became very excited and said, "This is an omen! I will build the new concert hall on this spot!"

A few years later she built the Spencer Theater on that location. It has become an important performance venue in the entire region. Ann kept the template in her office bookshelf for several years. When Spencer Theater was built, the FWCO played the premier concert. After the concert Ann and I presented the template to the manager of the theater and explained its significance. He lost it!

The Ruidoso Festival was an important component in the artistic development of the orchestra and further enhanced the public's awareness of the FWSO by extending performances to another part of the country.

Menotti and Miracles

In 1977 the Texas Boys Choir was conducting a search for a new director. I recommended Jack Noble White. Jack was a talented organist, composer, educator, and administrator. It was a perfect fit. The choir flourished under Jack's expert guidance and continued its artistic growth and international reputation.

One of Jack's important accomplishments at the helm of the TBC was to convince philanthropists Mary D. and F. Howard Walsh to commission Gian Carlo Menotti to compose a work for the TBC and the Texas Little Symphony. When Jack suggested a commission for a boys choir and chamber orchestra to me, we discussed at length whom we should ask. Gian Carlo Menotti was our first choice because of the lyrical romanticism of his compositions and the beauty of his vocal/orchestral works.

Menotti had a reputation for being late in delivering his commissions. We decided to take a chance because we were confident that with continuous coaxing, he would create the work on schedule.

Jack and I met with Menotti in New York in January 1977 to make the proposal, and he accepted the commission. Concerned with Menotti's propensity for not delivering a work on time, we insisted that a deadline of December 1, 1977, be a major part of the contract. Since the premier was scheduled for April 1978, five months after the contracted delivery date, we assumed that we had scheduled a long enough buffer period. The title of the work was *Miracles*, based on a series of settings of poems written by children as part of the UNICEF program. Transitional orchestral sections were to be interspersed throughout the forty-minute piece.

Menotti ignored the December deadline. The choir parts arrived six days before the April premiere. Menotti arrived in Fort Worth three days before the first rehearsal with only a partially completed full score. We rented a suite for him in a local hotel and set up an assembly line to complete the work in time for the premiere. He finished the piano scores of the compositions and passed them to me. I arranged and orchestrated them and in turn passed them to three professional copyists whom we had engaged for the "emergency." They extracted the individual instrumental parts from my scores by hand. We worked around the clock and finished one day before the performance.

Several weeks later I was browsing in a record store in New York and thumbed through the Gian Carlo Menotti section, where I discovered a recording of our performance. It is forbidden by the Musician's Union to record anything without permission from all parties involved and negotiating a fee for the musicians. This obviously was a black market recording, secretly made by someone in the audience with a small, high-quality handheld recorder. The program notes were excellent, and the recording is quite acceptable. It was acclaimed as "A live recording of one of the finest works by Gian Carlo Menotti." To my knowledge, no artistic participant or the composer received any remuneration of any kind from that record.

Stradivarius Violins

The Davis Strad

In 1981 Norwood Dixon, an active board member, led an instrument acquisition program that we established to secure instruments for the orchestra. One of the most important elements that contributes immeasurably to the quality of a symphony orchestra is the addition to the string section of fine instruments.

Our concertmaster, Robert Davidovici, informed me that Jacques Francais, a legendary New York broker of rare string instruments, had gained possession of a Stradivarius violin made in 1710, part of Stradivarius's "Golden Age." Robert asked me if it might be possible to find someone to purchase it and loan it to the

ABOVE
FWCO performing Saint-Saens' Carnival of the Animals *at a park concert in the Ruidoso, New Mexico festival.* Author Collection.

FWSO for use by the concertmaster.

I contacted Norwood, and we devised a strategy to find a patron who might purchase it for the orchestra. Mitzi and Bill Davis were close friends of ours, major supporters of the FWSO, and had the means with which to purchase the instrument. They also had several friends with the same capability. I called Mitzi, explained the circumstance to her, and asked if she had any suggestions of who might be interested in buying the violin for our use. She offered to host a recital at which Robert would play the Strad in their home and invite several of their friends.

Robert borrowed the instrument from Francais and performed at the Davis home. Following the performance, I addressed the group and explained the importance of having instruments of the highest quality in the orchestra. Norwood explained the acquisition program and pleaded for a patron to come to the fore.

After the superb performance by Robert, and when the guests had left, Mitzi turned to Bill. "We are going to buy it, aren't we?" she asked.

Bill enthusiastically agreed, and it was one of the most important milestones in the development of the FWSO.

The MacKenzie

Shortly after that serendipitous event, the gesture by Bill and Mitzi Davis inspired Genie MacKenzie Guynn, another dedicated patron, and she convinced her family to follow suit. They purchased another wonderful Strad made in 1685 and placed it on loan to the orchestra.

Where's Emile?

In 1980, the Fort Worth Press Club presented me with the 1979 "Newsmaker Award in Arts and Humanities." At the ceremony an elder statesman of Fort Worth, Emile (pronounced Eh-meal) who was more than eighty years old, was being recognized for his outstanding contributions to Fort Worth. He was not able to receive the honor for health reasons, and Jim Rosenthal, a young man in his early thirties, was asked to receive the award in Emile's absence. Jim and his wife Cathy were supporters of the Fort Worth Symphony.

When Jim stepped off the stage after receiving Emile's award, I said, "Congratulations Emile; you look spectacular for your age. As a matter of fact, you could very well be in your early thirties!" Jim and I enjoyed the repartee. Subsequently, every time I saw him I addressed him as "Emile."

A few months later, Cathy and Jim hosted a reception in their home after a Fort Worth Symphony concert. Often I cannot eat anything before a concert and usually am hungry after the performance. The FWSO management normally requested that the post-concert reception hosts prepare a snack for me. Cathy (not aware of my referring to Jim as "Emile") was busy in her kitchen preparing an after-concert dinner.

I arrived at the Rosenthal's several minutes after the guests, and declared loudly, "Cathy, I'm here! Where is Emile?" Except she thought I said, "Where's my meal?"

"Please be patient. You will just have to wait a moment for food. I'm doing the best I can!"

I never referred to Jim as Emile again.

Brownwood Concert—Brahms's Second Symphony

We performed a myriad of concerts throughout Texas, and it was rewarding to meet so many classical music lovers everywhere we performed.

We annually performed a series of concerts in Brownwood that were always well attended. We played the masterworks of such great composers as Beethoven, Brahms, and Tchaikovsky, and frequently featured guest artists from our classical series in Fort Worth.

On one of the concerts we performed Brahms's Second Symphony. After the concert a gentleman, dressed in soiled jeans, cowboy boots covered in dried mud, and a cowboy hat, appeared backstage.

"Maestro, I want to tell you how much I enjoyed the symphony tonight. Please excuse my appearance," he said.

"Don't be concerned about that," I replied. "The important thing is that you're here."

"Thank you for your understanding, but I must tell you the reason why I'm dressed so inappropriately for a symphony concert."

"I was in one of the fields of my ranch, repairing a fence close to the road. My neighbors happened to drive by and stopped to say hello. They asked if I were going to the symphony tonight. It already was six o'clock, too late to go home and get ready. I asked him what you were playing. When they told me it was Brahms's Second Symphony I had to come no matter what I looked like because it's my favorite piece of music. I didn't have time to go home and change so I got in their car and came with them."

ABOVE
Discussing the score of "Miracles," the work for the Chamber Orchestra and the Texas Boys Choir with the composer Gian Carlo Menotti and Jack Noble White, director of the Texas Boys Choir. Author Collection.

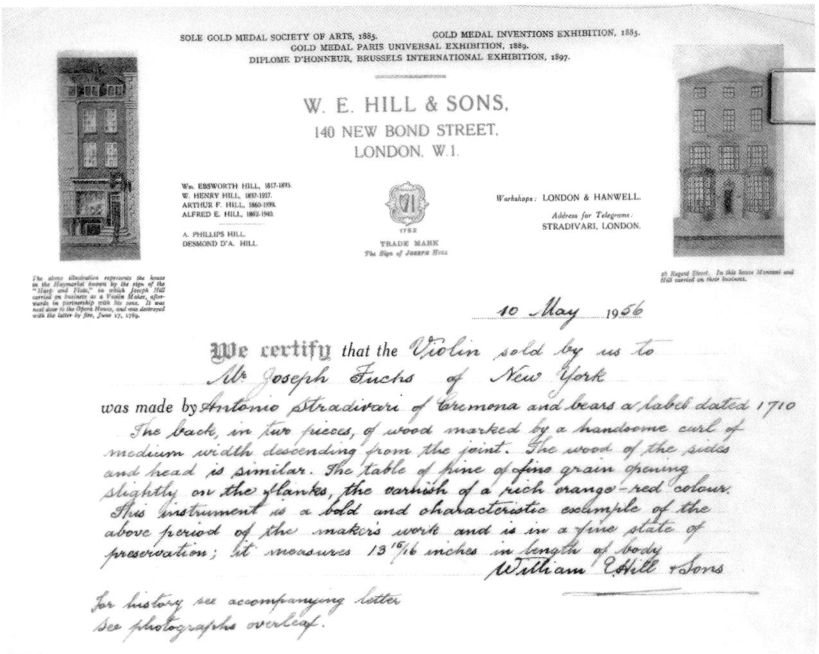

SOLE GOLD MEDAL SOCIETY OF ARTS, 1885. GOLD MEDAL INVENTIONS EXHIBITION, 1885.
GOLD MEDAL PARIS UNIVERSAL EXHIBITION, 1889.
DIPLOME D'HONNEUR, BRUSSELS INTERNATIONAL EXHIBITION, 1897.

W. E. HILL & SONS,
140 NEW BOND STREET,
LONDON, W.1.

Wm. EBSWORTH HILL, 1817-1895.
W. HENRY HILL, 1857-1927.
ARTHUR F. HILL, 1860-1939.
ALFRED E. HILL, 1862-1940.

A. PHILLIPS HILL.
DESMOND D'A. HILL.

1762
TRADE MARK
The Sign of Joseph Hill

Workshops: LONDON & HANWELL.
Address for Telegrams:
STRADIVARI, LONDON.

The above illustration represents the house in the Haymarket known by the sign of the "Harp and Flute," in which Joseph Hill carried on business as a Violin Maker, afterwards in partnership with his sons. It was next door to the Opera House, and was destroyed with the latter by fire, June 17, 1789.

10 May 1956

We certify that the Violin sold by us to
Mr Joseph Fuchs of New York
was made by Antonio Stradivari of Cremona and bears a label dated 1710
The back, in two pieces, of wood marked by a handsome curl of medium width descending from the joint. The wood of the sides and head is similar. The table of fine of fine grain opening slightly on the flanks, the varnish of a rich orange-red colour. This instrument is a bold and characteristic example of the above period of the maker's work and is in a fine state of preservation; it measures 13 15/16 inches in length of body
William E Hill & Sons

For history see accompanying letter
See photographs overleaf.

ABOVE
Robert Davidovici playing the Davis Stradivarius on its dedication concert. Courtesy of the FWSO.

ABOVE (TOP)
The Davis Stradivarious violin certificate of authenticity. Author Collection.

The Chamber Orchestra's Holiday Concerts

The FWCO toured annually throughout the state during the holiday season. We performed standard symphonic music appropriate for the season on the first half and popular Christmas music, including a sing-along, on the second.

We printed a program insert with the lyrics of the songs. One of the songs in the sing-along was "Winter Wonderland." Before the inserts were printed, one of our younger staff members who was not familiar with the words to "Winter Wonderland" called and asked me to dictate them to her on the phone. I neglected to proofread the insert.

During the concerts I noticed that every time the audience sang "Winter Wonderland" several snickers were heard and orchestra members noticed some angry expressions. The words to the bridge (middle section) of the song are: "In the meadow we can build a snowman. We'll pretend that he is Parson Brown." The lyrics that we distributed read: "In the meadow we can build a snowman. We'll pretend that he is parched and brown."

Celebration of Peace

In 1986, I had a crazy idea that it would be fun and a good publicity stunt for the FWSO if I conducted the entire city of Fort Worth. Then, after that was successful, I could follow it by conducting the state of Texas, the US, and eventually the world!

We had recently recorded a Christmas album underwritten by RadioShack that was distributed in their stores throughout the US. The beautiful arrangements were written by composer/arranger Phil Kelly. The recording, issued on 33 1/3 records and cassette tape, sold out in one day.

My concept was to organize the city into

segments that would turn on their Christmas lights on my cue as I conducted the city from a helicopter. My concept for the grand finale consisted of:

1. Activating all the lights that outlined the downtown buildings, including the Tandy Towers light that displayed Merry Xmas;

2. Launching a fireworks display from the top of a downtown building;

3. Ringing of all the church bells in the city; and

4. Acquiring lasers and klieg lights and getting approval for their usage.

Creating the project depended on the cooperation of several components:

1. Convincing KERA radio station to cooperate and broadcast our Christmas album;

2. Dividing the city into designated neighborhoods;

3. Devising a way to advertise and inform everyone in the city of the project;

4. Convincing the city to turn the lights on my command, obtaining funding for fireworks;

5. Acquiring laser lights and klieg lights, convincing churches to ring their bells; and

6. Arranging for the use of a helicopter from which I could view the city and give the cues.

I proposed the idea to Katie Sherrod, a popular columnist with the *Star-Telegram*, who not only was receptive to the idea but also wanted to expand the concept. She convinced the newspaper's publisher, Richard Conner, to help.

The public radio station, KERA, agreed to broadcast the event. We enlisted the assistance from city leaders to permit us to turn on the spectacular holiday downtown city light display, including the RadioShack Tower's lighting display of "Merry Xmas," at my cue. We also obtained the use of a police helicopter from which I could give the cues.

Everyone agreed to participate; it had the potential of crystallizing relationships between the various segments of the city and be a unique and spectacular contribution to the holiday season. The *Star-Telegram* published several front-page articles advertising the event, and KERA followed suit with promo radio spots.

We divided the city into neighborhood segments and assigned numbers to each, included diagrams for the division of the neighborhoods, and published them daily beginning a week before of the event. We identified several high-ground areas from which the public could view it.

The project grew beyond our expectations, and many requested to participate, including: Jim Wright, Speaker of the US House of Representatives, Mayor Pro-Tem Bert Williams, Fort Worth City Manager Douglas Harmon, the police department, the fire department, Richard Conner, publisher of the *Star-Telegram*, the City Council, the Council of Churches, represented by Barry Bailey, pastor of the First Methodist Church, the Texas Boys Choir, directed by Jack Noble White, and Schola Cantorum, directed by Gary Ebensberger.

One of the city leaders, Carol Hendrix, chaired the event and coordinated the organizational details.

The appointed day arrived. The event began on the lawn in front of the Amon Carter Museum with a brief concert by the Texas Boys Choir and Schola Cantorum. After they sang their last piece, the police helicopter, with Santa aboard, landed on the lawn. Santa deplaned and distributed candy. I took his vacated seat. The helicopter took off, our Christmas album broadcast on KERA started as planned, and "Celebration of Peace" began.

ABOVE
Narrating "The Night Before Christmas" at a Corpus Christi Symphony Orchestra (CCSO) concert. Author's Corpus Christi Symphony Orchestra (CCSO) Collection.

It worked! Everyone responded to my cues, some neighborhoods remarkably in sync. I cued the neighborhood lights followed by the laser show, the klieg light display, then the city's lights, church bells, and fireworks:

"Neighborhood number ONE: turn your lights on NOW! Neighborhood number TWO: turn your lights on NOW," etc. through the entire sequence.

They were responding perfectly! Then it was time for the climax. We surprisingly also pulled it off like clockwork.

"CUE KLIEG LIGHTS—FORT WORTH—TURN THE CITY LIGHTS ON NOW! CHURCHES—RING YOUR BELLS—START THE FIREWORKS!"

Everything was taking place as planned but we hadn't prepared for a potential danger. The helicopter was in the middle of the fireworks display, they were exploding all around us! The pilot shouted, "OH MY GOD!- I HAVEN'T GONE THROUGH ANYTHING LIKE THIS SINCE VIETNAM! WE'RE GETTING OUT OF HERE FAST!"

The event was a success, and everyone who participated had great fun. The helicopter pilot and I, however, were the only ones who had a perfect view of the entire event.

Claude Frank, Giordano Piano Piece - October 1991

Claude Frank performed Mozart's Piano Concerto in D Minor, K. 466 with the FWCO during the 1991-92 season. When possible, I rehearsed alone with guest artists before the first orchestra rehearsal to familiarize myself with their interpretation; it saves valuable time in orchestra rehearsals.

When I arrived for the solo rehearsal with Claude, he was practicing in the concert hall. He told me that he recently discovered a new piece and asked me to identify the composer. He played it for me.

"Do you know who wrote this?" he asked.

"I have no idea, but it sounds like a cross between bad Strauss and bad Rachmaninov."

"Wrong. Of course you know it, it's Giordano."

"That's impossible. Umberto Giordano never wrote anything like that; he was a good opera composer and that's a mediocre piece."

"No, not that Giordano. *You*—You wrote it!"

"That's ridiculous; I never wrote anything like that."

"Yes, you did, I found it on Susan Tilley's piano. You wrote it as a birthday present for her."

Susan was chairman of the Cliburn Board of Directors. A few years earlier I composed the piece for her birthday party, and Buddy Bray performed it. Claude had been practicing on the piano in Susan's home and the piece was placed on the piano's music rack. I had completely forgotten about it and couldn't imagine that a pianist of Claude's stature would take the time to memorize such an insignificant piece.

Van Cliburn Performs Three Concertos in One Evening

In 1991 Van played an historic concert with the FWSO, performing three concertos in the same evening, a tour de force rarely attempted. In the first half he played Liszt's E-Flat Concerto no. 1 (eighteen minutes long), followed by Beethoven's Concerto no. 5 in E-Flat (thirty-five minutes long). We took a fifteen-minute intermission, and he played Tchaikovsky's Concerto no. 1 (thirty-five minutes long).

Van always was extremely nervous before a concert. He arrived at a venue one or two minutes before his performance, walked directly onto the stage, acknowledged the applause, sat at the piano, and began to play.

Knowing the program was long, and to avoid going into costly overtime, I programmed the Mozart "Marriage of Figaro" Overture, a sparkling three-minute piece. Van had not appeared at the time the concert was to begin. I made my entrance and conducted the Mozart. Van still hadn't arrived. Several minutes passed, and he still hadn't appeared. Ann Koonsman was nervously pacing backstage, constantly looking at her watch, becoming more and more anxious.

Van arrived at least five minutes late, said nothing, and strode directly to the piano. I followed him, stepped onto the podium, gave a downbeat, and the concert began. Van had been driving around the block waiting to make his last-second entrance. There was a traffic problem that caused him to be especially late.

It was an amazing experience. His performance of every concerto was spectacular. Each is extremely difficult, and pianists normally have the stamina to play only one. He played all three effortlessly. We went into overtime, but the concert was so successful that there were no complaints.

Killeen Tragedy

On October 16, 1991, there was a massacre in Killeen, Texas. Twenty-two people, including several local schoolteachers and soldiers from nearby Fort Hood, died.

The FWCO played a series of concerts annually in Killeen, and we had developed a close relationship with many of our patrons there. Many were either victims or relatives of victims.

When the orchestra learned of the massacre, they immediately offered to play a memorial service with no fee. The bus company that we used on tour learned of the orchestra's offer and participated by supplying free transportation.

The concert was a memorable, heartfelt, and emotional experience. We continued to receive notes from grateful patrons for several years telling us how much they appreciated the performance and the healing power they received from classical music.

Big Spring Restroom Prison

We frequently joined forces with local choirs for performances of the Messiah during the holiday season and rehearsed with them on the day of the performance.

The most memorable performance took place in Big Spring, Texas. After the break in the rehearsal with the Big Spring massed choir, our principal violist, Dave Herman, had not returned to the orchestra. It was puzzling because it was a Sunday afternoon, and nothing was open in Big Spring near the concert hall, a historical converted movie theater. He was nowhere to be found, and none of the orchestra or choir members had seen him since the first half of the rehearsal.

The entire company was assembled on stage and with the limited rehearsal time it was necessary to continue without him. As I prepared to give a downbeat we heard a faint cry: "Help, help!" We couldn't determine the location of the plea, but we recognized Dave's voice. His cries continued until one of the choir members in the back of the stage shouted, "I think he is locked in the men's room!"

The door to the restroom was made of solid

RIGHT
Van performing three concertos with the FWSO. Author Collection.

oak with a steel frame. The lock had broken, and the door couldn't be opened from either side. We called the fire department after several futile attempts to rescue Dave. They arrived, experienced the same dilemma, and finally used a skill saw to cut a hole in the door large enough for Dave to crawl through.

At the end of the concert that evening, the orchestra and choir presented an arrangement of flowers in an old toilet bowl to Dave.

There is a federal prison in Big Spring, but it's more difficult to break out of the men's bathroom in the theater.

Poison the Conductor

I returned to my dressing room after a run-out concert with the full FWSO in the Brownwood Convention Center to find a plate of food under a napkin on my dressing room table. It contained a filet mignon, mashed potatoes, vegetables, and a dessert. On top of the plate was a handwritten note on an elegant note card. "Dear Maestro, we know how hungry you are after performances. Please enjoy this meal especially prepared for you."

Delighted in learning that our sponsor would be so thoughtful, I picked up the knife and fork and began to slice into the steak. Everything on the plate was disgustingly moldy!

There was a knock on the door. One of the musicians, very distraught, glanced at the plate and noticed that the steak had been cut into:

"Oh, My God Maestro! You haven't eaten any of that, have you? If so we must call for an ambulance immediately. I'm so sorry; it was a prank. We found the plate of rancid food that was left over from a function that obviously took place some time ago. We never thought that you would actually eat it but I panicked and worried that you might have unknowingly eaten part of it so I tried to warn you!"

I laughed and said, "Well that was a rather extreme way to get rid of me!"

A Dialogue with Beethoven

A touring concert in San Antonio in 1982 featured the current 1981 Cliburn Competition Gold Medalist André-Michel Schub performing the Beethoven Fourth Piano Concerto. The concert took place in Beethoven Hall, a historic rock building with a tin roof.

The second movement of the Beethoven is a brief dialogue between orchestra and piano that makes a dramatic transition to the third movement. The format of the movement consists of short phrases exchanged between the solo piano and orchestra. The orchestra makes several strong fortissimo brief statements interspersed by very soft passages played by the piano. There is a theory that Beethoven was representing a conversation of a pleading sinner being admonished by the Almighty.

As we played the opening powerful statement a sudden violent thunderstorm began with torrential rain, creating deafening sounds on the tin roof. It was as if Beethoven were saying: "You are destroying my masterpiece!" The piano was pleading for forgiveness to no avail. The storm became even more violent, the roof began to leak, and rain started to drip on André-Michel's head. We stubbornly continued until water began to fall on the piano. We stopped, André-Michel and I pushed the piano out from under the area that was leaking, and we resumed performing. As the movement began to diminish, the storm diminished in unison with it and stopped completely as the third movement began. I guess Beethoven forgave us.

Frank Almond—horse, pig

Our new concertmaster, Frank Almond, was from San Diego, and it was the first time he had spent any time in Texas. During the period of his tenure the FWCO was playing several touring concerts per year.

In 1992, we were returning from a concert in West Texas, driving on a two-lane state highway. Frank was driving alone in his own car. Associate conductor James Miller, my assistant Sylvia, and I were in another car, and James was driving. Before we left the concert venue we agreed to stay in contact with Frank because the drive is primarily through desolate unpopulated country, pastures, and farms.

Frank was a mile ahead of us. In the distance we saw his car stopped by the side of the road with his emergency lights flashing. Suddenly a horse appeared on the highway running toward our car. James, a superb driver, braked, the horse jumped over our car, so close that his hooves barely missed the windshield. Our car went into a tailspin but James was able to control it, and we somehow ended up in a farm's driveway. Frank had seen the horse running down the road and was trying to warn us.

The next day Frank was sitting on the patio of his rental house in the middle of a quiet Fort Worth residential neighborhood. He heard a strange grunting sound coming from the neighbor's garden. He stood on a chair and looked over the fence dividing the properties. He discovered a pig rooting in the neighbor's yard. (It was a pet Vietnamese Pot-bellied pig.)

He called me the next day and said, "I know that I'm really in Texas. One night I see a horse running down a highway and the next day I discover a pig in my neighbor's yard!"

A Real Conductor

There are several "Opry Houses" throughout the Western states that date back to the "Wild West" during the late 1800s, in which myriad types of entertainment were presented. A number have been restored and are presenting programs again.

We performed in several of these venues. This concert took place at a renovated Opry House in West Texas.

Railroad tracks ran close to the back of the building. As I was giving a downbeat to begin the concert, a train passed and sounded its loud whistle. I couldn't resist. I stopped, turned to the audience, and said, "I've always wanted to be a real conductor!"

Union Strike

Union contract negotiations took place during the time that the orchestra board and administration were having an annual fundraising event. FWSO gala evenings included a performance by the orchestra with a major artist as soloist. This season the soloist was Itzhak Perlman, who was to play Brahms's Violin Concerto.

The negotiations had broken down, and the orchestra decided to strike for the rehearsal but still perform the concerto.

The morning of the scheduled rehearsal, Itzhak called me.

"John, I understand the orchestra is going to strike for the rehearsal. Is that true?"

"Unfortunately yes, but the concert will go on as planned, I hope it will be okay with you."

"I don't care, I hate to rehearse. I know the piece, you know the piece, the orchestra knows the piece, everything will be fine."

Itzhak was right, it was a superb concert.

Several years later, Itzhak performed Beethoven's Violin Concerto with me and the Corpus Christi Symphony.

Corpus Christi Symphony

In 2002, I was offered the position of music director of the Corpus Christi Symphony Orchestra. I remained in this position until my retirement in 2016. The CCSO is a regional orchestra comprising musicians from San Antonio, Austin, Fort Worth, and Houston, in addition to those residing in Corpus. It is a high-quality orchestra. Several former musicians from the CCSO have won positions with major symphonies throughout the US and abroad. Several also previously held top positions with major orchestras including San Antonio, Houston, and the National Symphony in Washington, DC.

In 2005, we performed the inaugural concert for the new Performing Arts Center on the Texas A&M University campus in Corpus Christi with Van Cliburn as soloist. During my tenure, we presented many other internationally acclaimed soloists such as Efim Bronfman, Joshua Bell, André Watts, Frederica von Stada, Pepe Romero, Itzhak Perlman, Robert McDuffie, Joseph Kalichstein, David Finkel, Barry Douglas, Stephen Hough, Daniel Binelli, Edgar Meyer, Evelyn Glennie, and the Eroica Trio.

Itzhak Perlman

Many of the musicians, especially the younger members, had never performed with the likes of Itzhak Perlman, and a majority of them were somewhat awestruck during the rehearsal when he performed Beethoven's Violin Concerto with us.

Beethoven structured the work to have the orchestra play the entire long exposition (first section) before the soloist enters. Inspired by Perlman's presence, the orchestra played magnificently, and Itzhak was smiling and enjoying their performance. When Itzhak began to play, however, the orchestra suddenly stopped. He leaned over to me:

"What is going on? Why did they stop?"

"They're intimidated by playing with you."

He turned to the orchestra.

"Come on guys, play! I'm just a simple fiddle player."

That broke the ice, the orchestra relaxed and played with passion as never before.

Isaac Stern

The magnificent violinist Isaac Stern performed a concerto with the FWSO in 1997. During the rehearsal, after I accompanied him accurately in a notoriously difficult passage, he pulled out his wallet and handed me a one-dollar bill. He autographed it for me after the rehearsal. It's a treasured possession.

Mstislav Rostropovich

Rostropovich was one of the greatest cellists of all time. His performance of Dvorak's Concerto with us in 1981 was one of my most memorable musical experiences. He played very freely, especially in slower rhapsodic sections, very seldom in a steady tempo. The Dvorak is replete with those passages. That made it extremely difficult to accompany him precisely. After the rehearsal, he paid a meaningful compliment to me, "Very, very good. Rostropovich very difficult."

He had a tiny dog that always stayed with

him. He carried the dog in a valise and even during rehearsals placed the valise next to his chair on stage. Union regulations require that a break be taken precisely after one hour and fifteen minutes. In the rehearsal, precisely after one hour and fifteen minutes, the dog stood up in the valise and barked loudly.

The Van Cliburn International Piano Competition

During my long affiliation with the Van Cliburn Competition I was afforded many unique experiences in my relationships with Van, the Cliburn administration, board, competitors, and jurors.

Alberto Ginastera

While Ian Hobson, a pianist with extraordinary technique, was performing difficult transcriptions of orchestral works in the preliminary round of the 1977 competition, Ginastera became furious and indignant because Hobson was playing transcriptions. He stomped his feet loudly on the platform on which the jurors were seated and shouted (fortunately in French):

"This is complete merde! How dare he play this merde at an important international competition! It is an insult to this important jury! Does he not know any music written for the piano?"

Moura Lympani

During a conversation with fellow juror Cécile Ousset, whose husband's name was Pierre, Ousset said to Moura Lympani at the end of the last session of the day, "I'm tired and not feeling very well."

Lympani responded, "I'm also tired but at least you can go back to the hotel and sleep with Philippe!"

Philippe Entremont was another juror.

Lympani also whispered to me during a competitor's performance, "My God, what is that odd noise?"

"He's singing," I said.

"Oh yes, it's beginning to get on my nerves!"

Lympani said, after reading this Russell Sherman recommendation for a competitor:

"Gifted with a radiant intimacy of sound and regal grace, she nevertheless has the power and brilliance of a descendant of Ghengis Khan. The combination is as splendid as it is rare. It also extends to her stage character, which is both magisterial and sylph-like. The bonus is that she is that species who never surrenders, who fights for the precious grail of aesthetic values with every ounce of fiber and being, nor is there one more generous or charitable. Nobody has it all, as they say, but she offers a wonderful facsimile of the total package and yet of all her gifts, a compassionate musical eloquence is the flagship."

BELOW
Daniel Binelli performing with the CCSO. Author's CCSO Collection.

ABOVE
After the CCSO concert with the blind pianist Nobuyuki Tsujii, 2009 Cliburn gold medalist. Author Collection.

LEFT (TOP)
The Romero family guitar quartet with the CCSO. Author's CCSO Collection.

LEFT (CENTER)
Barry Douglas, winner of the Bronze medal in the 1985 Cliburn and the gold medal in the 1986 Tchaikovsky Competition. Author's CCSO Collection.

LEFT
Joshua Bell with the CCSO. Author's CCSO Collection.

Lympani, before that competitor's performance, said, "She can't be as good as all that!"

And after the performance, said, "I was right!"

After learning of another juror's dislike of a competitor's performance, Lympani said, "He wishes he could play that well!"

Alexis Weissenberg

Alexis Weissenberg, upon his arrival at a jury meeting, introduced himself to another juror who spoke very little English and opened the conversation with: "I'm Weissenberg, I need Alka Selzer."

The non-English speaking juror responded: "I'm sorry, she's not here, she must have gone out!"

Opening of The Ballpark in Arlington

In April 1994, the FWSO with Van Cliburn as soloist performed at the opening of The Ballpark in Arlington.

Prior to his becoming president, George W. Bush formed a consortium with several business leaders in the DFW Metroplex and purchased the Texas Rangers baseball team. They built a state-of-the-art stadium in Arlington.

Owners Tom Schieffer, a member of the consortium, George W. Bush, and Norm Lyons, the team's director of operations, requested that I meet with them. They wanted to have a unique event at the first game in the stadium to celebrate the ballpark's opening and asked if I had any suggestions. I realized that this could be a great opportunity to bring the FWSO to the forefront and recalled that Van played the National Anthem at many national events and for several presidents. His interpretation was beautiful and inspirational.

I suggested that we ask Van Cliburn to play the National Anthem on the field with the Fort Worth Symphony Orchestra. George Bush said

OPPOSITE
Itzhak Perlman performing the Beethoven concerto with the CCSO. Author's CCSO Collection.

OPPOSITE
Isaac Stern's signed dollar bill gifted to me in appreciation for my accompaniment in a FWSO concert. Author Collection.

OPPOSITE
Sharing a humorous moment with Fort Worth mayor Kenneth Barr and Wes Turner, publisher of the Fort Worth Star-Telegram, *during a Fort Worth Symphony Gala.* Author Collection.

that Van never would consent. I told him that Van would if he knew that the request came from him because Van loved the Bush family and was a close friend of his father, President George H.W. Bush. When I asked Van, he agreed without hesitation.

Ann Koonsman was enthusiastic about the event because of the positive exposure it would give to the FWSO. Since the stadium was intended to serve the entire metroplex, we felt it would be appropriate to ask the Dallas Symphony if they would like to participate. The DSO's musicians learned of the event and enthusiastically offered to unofficially participate.

I composed a fanfare-like introduction to the anthem, followed by Van playing the anthem accompanied by the orchestra. I composed a modulation that led into a key comfortable for group singing after Van's performance and repeated the anthem so everyone could join the orchestra. I asked Van to improvise an accompaniment.

We rehearsed in the player's locker room immediately prior to the game.

The Rangers staff, under the supervision of Norm Lyons, constructed a platform on the pitcher's mound on which they placed Van's grand piano. We dressed in tails; Van and I wore a white tie and the orchestra wore tails over a Rangers' tee shirt and donned Texas Rangers baseball caps. I stood on a podium made for the occasion, and the orchestra was placed in their normal stage configuration in front of me.

Van and I made the usual concert entrance, cheered by some 49,000 excited fans. We began. The orchestra played the fanfare introduction as rehearsed, Van played his beautiful and inspired patriotic version the first time through as planned, followed by the transition to the orchestra's performance. But Van, surprising us all, instead of playing with the orchestra, stood in front of the microphone and led the entire stadium singing the piece with gusto.

It was one of the most thrilling experiences of my life, standing on the diamond, surrounded by thousands of patriotic fans enthusiastically singing the National Anthem. To this day, President and Mrs. George W. Bush, all the Rangers players and staff, and all the performers say that it was a unique experience and one that will remain indelible in their minds.

Coincidence, Carol Leone, 1999

I've experienced several unusual coincidences. One took place at a jury orientation dinner for the first Cliburn Amateur Competition.

I was seated at one end of a long table. Richard Rodzinski sat on the other end, and Carol Leone, chairman of the piano division at SMU and a new juror, sat next to him. I overheard the following conversation:

Richard said, "Where are you from Carol?"

"Fredonia, New York," she answered.

I interrupted and said, "Excuse me, where did you say you were from Carol?"

"Fredonia."

"What? I don't believe it. That's where I was born and lived there as an infant in my grandparents' home!"

"What a coincidence! Do you remember the street?"

"I believe it was Prospect Avenue."

"That was the street we lived on. I'm going to ask my mother this evening if she remembers your grandparents."

When I saw her the next day at the competition's first session she said, "I asked my mother about your grandparents, and you won't believe it but my parents rented the second floor of your grandparents' home and I was born there!"

"That's not possible!"

"Not only that but my mother babysat for you when you were an infant and my father dated your mother in high school."

"This is surreal! We both were born in Fredonia, New York, lived in the same house, both studied music, and both ended up living in the

DFW Metroplex? And now both on the Cliburn jury? That is bizarre! I'm going to ask my mother if she remembers that."

My mother substantiated the story:

"Of course I remember the Leones; they rented the second story of Gramma and Grampa Giordano's house. In fact, they had a child who was born there. Gramma and Grampa had a large two-story home and always rented the second floor."

The next day the coincidence became even more bizarre. Carol took me aside. She said,

"There is more. I learned from my mother that my grandparents and yours were from the same small town in Sicily, Valledolmo, and were close friends. The town has a population of about five hundred and has remained the same size. My mother explained that your grandparents came to this country first and convinced my parents to join them and settle in Fredonia. They invited my parents to stay with them while they were getting settled. They needed somewhere to stay until they could find a home of their own, so they rented the second floor of your grandparent's home. During those days housing was difficult to find."

Carol since has made several pilgrimages to Valledolmo and even has become acquainted with some Giordanos.

My sister, Carol, and I recently visited Valledolmo and discovered the record of the Giordano side of the family in the city record ledger of 1870.

Andrew Litton/ André Watts Tornado

In 1999 André Watts played a recital in Ed Landreth Auditorium at TCU to a capacity audience. The parking lot across the street from the building was filled. My car was in the lot facing the street. Conductor of the Dallas Symphony Andrew Litton's car also was parked facing the street with one car between us.

LEFT
With President George W. Bush.
Author Collection.

The concert was suddenly interrupted by a calm but firm announcement:

"Ladies and Gentlemen, we have just been informed that a tornado is heading in our direction. We must take immediate cover. Please follow the ushers in a calm, orderly fashion to the basement and remain there until further notice."

The tornado struck but only touched down in the parking lot. It created havoc there, but nothing else in the area was disturbed. Most of the vehicles were severely damaged. Those that didn't sustain any damage were strewn around and placed in weird configurations. The car in the lane behind me was placed in the street and suffered no damage. The one next to it was moved into the street sideways and wasn't damaged. However, the car between Litton's and mine was lifted in the air and slammed upside down on the roof of his, completely totaling both vehicles. My car was not touched by the storm.

A few years later, Andrew Litton and I were attending another André Watts recital in Bass Hall. When we recounted the tornado incident that we jointly experienced, Litton said, "I wish

ABOVE
The FWSO performance of the National Anthem with Van Cliburn at the opening of the Ballpark in Arlington in 1994. Author Collection.

ABOVE (TOP)
Rehearsing with Van and the FWSO at the Ballpark in Arlington in the Rangers locker room. Author Collection.

I had known what happened to our cars—that yours wasn't touched and mine was destroyed. We missed a golden opportunity! Can you imagine what the headlines would have read the next day?"

Radu Lupu

Radu Lupu was a Cliburn Gold Medalist in 1966 who has established himself as one of the most prominent pianists of the twentieth century. We became close friends after our first collaboration. The FWSO engaged him as often as possible because of his brilliant artistry and his popularity in Fort Worth. During one of his visits to Fort Worth in winter, he was a guest in our home one day, along with Robert Davidovici, our concertmaster, and Martha Hyder. Radu, in addition to his piano virtuosity, was a very good table tennis player and a skilled bridge player.

Robert and Radu were playing a table tennis match in our den when a rare and sudden snow and sleet storm hit the area. It was such a violent storm that we couldn't leave the house for several hours.

Knowing of Radu's love of bridge, Mary Alice, a life master bridge player, organized a game while we waited for the storm to subside. After the game, Robert convinced Radu to play some works for piano and violin with him. When they ran out of printed music Radu suggested they play violin concertos. Robert said he didn't have any more printed violin/piano music. Radu told him that he probably could fake his way through a "couple" of violin concerto orchestra accompaniments.

Playing full orchestra accompaniments on piano is difficult. Playing them by memory is rare. They played several by memory!

During one of the concertos the electric power went out, leaving us in total darkness. They continued as if nothing had happened.

One time Mary Alice, Radu Lupu, Karel

Husa, and I went to dinner after a concert in which Radu played Beethoven's First Piano Concerto and the orchestra performed Husa's "Music for Prague 1968," a work in memory of the 1968 Soviet invasion of Prague.

During the dinner Karel related a humorous story about an event that occurred shortly after the Husas had moved to Ithaca, New York, where Karel had accepted a professorial position at Cornell University. Mrs. Husa spoke very little English.

They were inundated with congratulatory phone calls from magazine sales people explaining they had been selected to receive a prize if they registered for a subscription to that magazine. Excited about the prospect of receiving a "prize" Mrs. Husa bought subscriptions to several magazines. Karel wasn't aware of her purchases until they began to receive a plethora of magazines in the mail. He admonished her never to accept any more prizes.

The next day she received a call when Karel wasn't home: "Is Dr. Husa there? "No, he is not." "I am calling to tell him that he has won the Pulitzer Prize." She responded: "We don't want any prizes," and hung up.

One season Radu played Beethoven's First Piano Concerto with us. We had only one rehearsal scheduled for the concerto. When it was time to rehearse the concerto, Radu quietly walked on stage, greeting no one, and sat at the piano. I hadn't even noticed that he was there until he played the A for the orchestra to tune. He nodded to me, and we played the entire thirty-five-minute piece without stopping.

I asked, "Radu would you like to go over anything?"

With almost every soloist it's normal to adjust tempos, work on tricky entrances, and check the balance between the piano and orchestra at several spots. Radu is one of the rare soloists who projects exactly what he wants without stopping or saying anything. Nevertheless, every concerto has tricky spots where playing them a few times gives everyone more

ABOVE
André Watts performing the Brahms Second Piano Concerto with the CCSO. Author's CCSO Collection.

security. Not with him!

"No! It will be fine."

"Do you want to play through the cadenza so we can make certain the orchestra entrance will be accurate?"

"No. It's not necessary."

"Which cadenza are you playing?" (There are two cadenzas for Beethoven I.)

"The short one of course. I don't like the long one."

That constituted the rehearsal.

I arrived about a half hour before the concert. Mary Alice was helping me carry my things into my dressing room. Radu was there, obviously upset and nervous, and he was pacing the floor.

Radu is one of the greatest pianists of our time and, in a few minutes, we had to perform a major concerto to a sold-out audience, so I couldn't have my soloist having a breakdown backstage.

Mary Alice came to the rescue and said: "Radu, John has to go on stage in five minutes and conduct the overture. People have come to hear you because they love your music making and admire you."

Her admonition worked; he laughed, relaxed, and delivered an inspired performance.

Claudio Arrau

The season following the 1985 Cliburn Piano Competition we engaged one of the most revered pianists in the world, Claudio Arrau. We were fortunate to book him for this season because it was his final tour. He agreed to play Beethoven's Fourth Piano Concerto in G Major.

One of the unique features of this competition was the collection of pianos offered to the competitors from which they could choose for their participation. They were offered a choice between: an American Steinway, a Hamburg Steinway, a Bosendorfer, a Baldwin, a Yamaha, and a Kawai. This garnered much publicity in that no other international competition offered their competitors such an extraordinary array of instruments.

Maestro Arrau's New York management telephoned our executive director, Ann Koonsman, and insisted that he be given the opportunity to choose a piano. It was expensive to move the instruments to the stage of the Convention Center and tune them. However, his management insisted and threatened to cancel Maestro Arrau's appearance if he were not given that opportunity. Ann reluctantly agreed, and we placed six nine-foot concert grand pianos end to end, extending from one side of the proscenium to the other.

I drove Maestro Arrau to the hall because he wanted to practice and become familiar with the piano. When he opened the stage door and saw the six pianos lined up across the stage, he exclaimed, "Oh my God! What is that?"

I said: "Maestro, your management informed us that you wanted to choose which of these pianos you want to use."

He responded, "Why? I can only play on one at a time! Oh well, let's have a look."

He walked across the stage, paused at each instrument, and played a G major arpeggio. He returned to the Steinway that we had placed in front of the podium and said, "I'll take this one!"

Beethoven's Fourth Piano Concerto presents several challenging moments for the conductor. Many solo piano passages contain fast runs which are rhythmically free and notoriously difficult for the conductor to precisely cue the orchestra entrances. I was perfect in the rehearsal—not missing one entrance. Arrau was very complimentary and told me that it was rare for a conductor to direct those entrances so precisely.

In the concert I miscued almost every entrance. As we left the stage together after the final bow, I apologized, "Maestro, I'm so sorry!"

He smiled and said, "Don't feel bad, John, Szell missed them too!"

Kathy Battle

My first performance with the soprano diva Kathy Battle was at the beginning of her career. Prior to her remarkable success as a performer she was a music teacher in Western Ohio. We engaged her to perform the soprano solo for our performance of Orff's "Carmina Burana." Her final solo passage near the end of Carmina that begins with a soft octave leap to a high B on the word "Dul-cis-si-me" was breathtaking and a wonderful experience for all on stage. The entire passage is "Dulcissime, totam tibi subdo me." (Sweetest of men I give myself to you wholly.)

Kathy performed several times with the FWSO during my tenure, and each performance was superb. As her career progressed, Kathy garnered a reputation for being difficult to work with; however my relationship with her always was enjoyable. I have often wondered if she earned that reputation because she always strove for perfection and was frequently misunderstood.

Because she was such a fine artist and collaborator, I requested that we engage her as a soloist in my final season with the FWSO. She agreed to sing Mozart's *Exultate Jubulate*, a wonderful work for soprano and orchestra, which she performed magnificently.

I scheduled a piano rehearsal prior to the first orchestra rehearsal with her, the orchestra's pianist and keyboardist, Shields Collins (Buddy) Bray, and me. Piano rehearsals with the soloist prior to the orchestra rehearsals save time because they give the conductor the opportunity to become familiar with the artist's interpretation prior to the rehearsal with the orchestra. Kathy was charming and accommodating during the rehearsal.

Exultate Jubilate has two major sections connected by a brief melismatic solo accompanied by a sustained organ chord, which was played by Buddy in this concert. Kathy found Buddy before dress rehearsal and sat right next to him on the organ bench. Kathy wanted Buddy to help her "paint" the words. She was very specific about what she wanted and when she wanted it. Kathy had it all very well-thought out and she was impressive, but Buddy couldn't keep up with her rapid-fire instructions. When Buddy managed to stop Kathy's rapid-fire at one point, he asked her to repeat some of the instructions she had just given. *That* was the wrong thing to ask.

Kathy said, "I just *told* you what I wanted; don't make me use my voice unnecessarily!"

And with that, she hopped off the bench and was gone.

Despite this encounter, Kathy was gracious and performed superbly in the concert. During the reception dinner at Mr. and Mrs. Sid Bass's home, Kathy stood and gave a toast.

"Here's to John," she said. "You must appoint him Music Director Emeritus for everything he has done for the Fort Worth Symphony."

FIVE

Guest Conducting

BRAZIL

Rio

I accepted several guest conducting engagements when I could schedule them between FWSO concerts and Cliburn activities.

My first engagement in Brazil was in Rio de Janeiro. I had been used to dealing with orchestras in the US, Europe, and Asia. Symphony orchestras in the US are members of the American Federation of Musicians, and contractually the union demands that rehearsals, performances, intermissions, and meetings begin and end on time.

The engagement was with the National Symphony Orchestra of Brazil. I arrived forty-five minutes before the first rehearsal to meet the music director and familiarize myself with the routine for rehearsals. The orchestra's music director, Maestro Silva Pereira, invited me to his office, where he had arranged for coffee and hors d'oeuvres. We had a pleasant conversation in French because it was our only common language. When it was time for the rehearsal to begin, I was anxious and reminded the Maestro of the time. He said, "It is not a problem, they can wait!"

We continued our conversation for at least another fifteen minutes. Abruptly, he stood up and said it was time for the rehearsal (fifteen minutes late!). When we entered the rehearsal hall, the orchestra stood.

Maestro Pereira introduced me to the orchestra. He then introduced me to the concertmaster, who was French, told him that I spoke French, and asked him to help me. He excused himself, explained that he had a flight to catch, and quickly left. As soon as Pereira left the room, the concertmaster quietly addressed me, "Je m'excuse Maestro, mais je suis un peu malade aujourd'hui. Puis je simple observe le repetition pour quelques minutes y pas jouet?" ("I feel a bit ill. May I only observe the rehearsal for a few minutes and not play?").

After a few minutes, he said he felt much better and could play. He obviously was auditioning me to decide whether or not he would play the concert.

After we had rehearsed for about an hour, the concertmaster interrupted me when I stopped the orchestra to correct something, and told me that it was time for a break. All the musicians immediately stood, left the building, and were gone for about half an hour. The rehearsal was scheduled from 2:00 p.m. until 5:00 p.m. We started one half hour late, rehearsed for only an hour, and had a thirty-minute break. At 4:00 p.m. the concertmaster said, "Maestro, the traffic is very bad here in Rio and our conductors always dismiss us early to help us avoid the traffic."

I thought, *I guess that's the way things work here*, and ended the rehearsal. We only rehearsed less than two of three hours. That explained why they schedule twelve rehearsals for the concert in contrast to the usual four in the US.

On the way to the hotel after rehearsal I accidently left my briefcase in the taxi, containing all the scores for the concert, my batons, and several documents. No music store in Rio had conductor scores for the concert; subsequently I had to conduct the remaining rehearsals by memory. I frequently conduct concerts by memory but never rehearse by memory.

There were different players in the wind and percussion sections at every rehearsal. That forced me to go over the same problematic passages and repeat the same instructions every day. I later learned that for orchestra musicians to earn a living in Rio it was necessary for them to accept additional engagements to supplement their income (another reason twelve rehearsals were necessary). I was not pleased with the progress of the rehearsals and was anxious that the concert would not go well. Every day after rehearsal the concertmaster would console me: "Don't worry, Maestro. This is Rio and we always have a miracle at the concert!"

I eventually decided to become a Brazilian and just didn't worry about anything.

Lili Kraus happened to be in Rio to perform a recital. One day we were having lunch in Copa Cabana, which is at least a half hour drive across the entire city to the rehearsal site, depending on the amount of traffic congestion. At 1:00 p.m. she reminded me that I had a 2:00 p.m. rehearsal and probably would be late to the rehearsal if I didn't leave immediately.

I said, "It doesn't matter Lili, I always arrive thirty minutes late; they expect it."

The day of the concert arrived. It was scheduled to begin at 8:00 p.m. When I arrived at the hall that evening, at 7:30, the building was completely dark, the marquis lights were off, and no one was anywhere to be seen. I banged loudly on the stage door . . . no response. Finally, the custodian heard me and opened it. I asked him, using pigeon Portuguese and sign language, if I were at the right concert hall. He assured me I was but I had arrived too early and nobody else had arrived yet. He escorted me to my dressing room after persuading me with sign language and pointing to the poster advertising the concert that this was the right night, time, and place for the concert. I couldn't believe that there would be an audience.

At 8:15 the musicians began to arrive for the 8:00 performance. At 8:30 the concertmaster asked if I would like to join him and some of the musicians for a pre-concert coffee. The concert eventually started about 9:00 p.m.; the audience filled the hall; the orchestra played magnificently; and, as the concertmaster told me several times, it was a "miracle."

I was paid in cruzeiros. (Brazilian currency now is the real.) I went to a bank to exchange them for dollars and asked a Brazilian friend to accompany me to translate. The teller explained that it was illegal to exchange cruzeiros for dollars. So there I stood, with a check for 150,000 cruzieros. I thought, *This might make attractive wall paper*! My friend, unbeknownst to me, happened to be a buyer for H. Stern and generously sold emeralds to me that he had purchased many years prior. There was no US import tax on gems that had been cut in Brazil. He provided me with official documents from H. Stern certifying the stones were cut in Brazil. I sold the emeralds to a jeweler at home for a profit.

São Paulo

A few months after the concert in Rio I was invited to conduct the Mahler Third Symphony with the São Paulo Symphony. It is ninety minutes long and requires an extremely large orchestra, women's choir, and boys' choir.

During the first rehearsal's intermission, a member of the boys' choir, which had been prepared by its music director, Elias de Sylva, approached me. De Sylva translated for him. The boys do not sing until the end of the last movement, about an hour and a half into the piece. This boy had not heard the symphony before and said, "Maestro, this really is a very long 'song.' I don't mind waiting to sing for over an hour during the rehearsals, but I think the people will like the song much better if we start where our part begins!"

São Paulo was crime ridden and not very safe for a foreigner to shop or sight-see. It was unsafe to carry large amounts of money. The orchestra paid artist fees by check, which was difficult for US citizens because you couldn't change cruzeiros to dollars or cash it in the US. However, an orchestra staff member who had been helping me during my stay came to my rescue. He offered to arrange to have the check cashed at a local bank and changed to US dollars on the black market.

He escorted me to the bank the afternoon of the concert. We were accompanied by a uniformed armed guard carrying an automatic rifle. My escort had instructed me to bring an empty attaché case.

We arrived at the bank and were directed to one of the bank's officers whose desk was in the lobby area. Our guard stood directly behind us. The staffer leaned over to me and quietly instructed me to sign the check, hand it to the bank officer who spoke English fluently, and place my empty attaché case alongside his desk. The bank officer made a quick phone call. An assistant arrived immediately, greeted us, picked up my empty attaché case, and left.

The bank officer and I continued to chat about my experiences in São Paulo for a few minutes. The assistant reappeared and returned the attaché case to its former position next to the officer's desk. The orchestra staffer addressed me nervously, "Do you want to count it Maestro? I suggest not, it might be dangerous for anyone to see that much money. They are very honest here in the bank."

"No, that won't be necessary," I said.

I picked up the attaché case and we quickly walked to our car parked in front of the bank and were driven to the hotel.

We entered the hotel lobby and met a man dressed in a baggy, navy blue pinstriped suit, who was waiting for us.

When you checked into São Paulo hotels you were issued an official hotel identification card complete with your photograph. It had to be shown everywhere: the elevator to the rooms, guest shop, restaurant, pool area, etc. The guard at the elevator checked my photo ID and stared suspiciously at my guests. I vouched for them and we went to my suite.

We sat in the living room area. The orchestra staffer translated and instructed me to lay my attaché case on the coffee table and open it. It was like a movie scene in which the ransom money is in an attaché case filled with $100 bills. My attaché case was filled with bundles of crisp, new 1,000 cruzeiro notes placed in neat rows (about 140,000 cruzeiros is equivalent to $7,000).

The black-market agent had a money belt that contained new fifty- and hundred-dollar bills. We both counted and verified the exchange. He filled his pockets, money belt, and every part of his attire that could accommodate the Brazilian currency. (His baggy suit was ill fitting to accommodate the cash.) We all shook hands, and I said "muito obrigado" (many thanks). They responded, "de nada, boa viagem, Maestro" (you are welcome, bon voyage). We bid each other "ciao" and they left.

Brussels (Jochum in Amsterdam)

In 1978 I was invited to conduct the National Symphony of Belgium. The major work on the program was the Brahms Fourth Symphony. Steven De Groote, the 1977 Cliburn gold medalist, was the soloist.

I was seated in the first-class section of a 747 and planned to stop in Amsterdam to meet with my European manager, Mme. Johanne Beck of Inter Artists, before continuing to Brussels.

On the flight to Amsterdam I was marking bowing directions for the string sections. I asked my flight attendant if I could change to an empty seat in the upper first-class section to have more privacy and work uninterrupted. She told me that that section was empty and I could make the move. After the dinner service, she joined me in the upper level, noticed what I was doing, and asked if she could help. I thanked her and explained that I was marking music and it required a musician who had technical knowledge of string instrument bowing technique.

She said, "I think I can help. I majored in violin at Indiana University!"

After my meeting with Mme. Beck, I attended a performance of the Concertgebouw Orchestra that evening, conducted by Eugen Jochum. The major work was the Brahms Fourth Symphony. The concert was particularly interesting to me because the Concertgebouw is one of the world's great orchestras; Jochum was one of the finest interpreters of Brahms; and the work was the same I would be conducting in Brussels.

After the concert, I went backstage to visit with Jochum. He was extremely cordial and when he learned that I was going to conduct the Brahms in Brussels, offered to give me a coaching session. It was a rare opportunity.

The next morning I took the early train to Brussels. That afternoon when I entered the hall for the first rehearsal, I had a pleasant surprise. One of my best friends and former classmate at the Royal Conservatory, Jerry Rubenstein, was concertmaster of the orchestra. Jerry is a superb violinist, has a great sense of humor, and was responsible for many unforgettable experiences when we both studied at the Conservatory. Jerry never has lived anywhere except Manhattan and Brussels. After graduation from the Royal Conservatory, he served as the concertmaster of the Monet Opera Orchestra and subsequently for the National Symphony.

Jerry has a unique ability to relieve tense moments during rehearsals, especially when conflicts occur between orchestra members. During one incident at the first rehearsal, a violinist, violist, and cellist got into a heated discussion concerning their differences of opinion for the bowing direction of a passage. The principal violist asked if he might change a bow direction that I had indicated. The argument began when I gave him permission to do so. One of the violinists resisted the change, insisted that it was fine the way it was marked, and a heated disagreement began. A cellist chimed in. It became so heated I was concerned that the disagreement would get completely out of hand and result in a fist fight. Jerry, always under control, rose and demanded everyone's attention. He settled everyone down by saying, "Ladies and gentlemen, let's all remain calm. Thank goodness we only have two choices—up and down—otherwise we never would finish playing anything!"

That broke the tension, everyone laughed, and we continued rehearing with no more incidents.

The performance was well attended and very successful. The major critic in the Brussels review was the most knowledgeable, sensitive, and illuminating I have ever encountered. (Most reviews, positive or negative, frequently are incorrect.) Most of his critique was favorable. However, the review made me realize that some of my interpretation needed to be improved, and I adopted some of his suggestions in future performances of the Brahms.

"The young conductor gave an inspired performance," the review read. "However, he demanded so much excitement from the orchestra that the climax occurred before the end of the fourth movement. This symphony should be approached as if it were one long crescendo from the first note of the first movement to the last of the fourth."

Jerry's Great Day

I stayed in Brussels for a few days after the concert to schedule meetings relating to the Cliburn with officials from the Queen Elizabeth Competition and to meet with some potential jurors. Jerry invited me to stay with him. He also invited me to accompany him to a rehearsal for the next concert they were performing with a very young conductor who was being touted in Europe as the next superstar.

Some of the musicians were not behaving respectfully to the conductor, mocking his flamboyant gestures, laughing, and talking loudly. At one point Jerry stood up when the conductor stopped to correct something, "Ladies and gentlemen, you are behaving like little children," he said. "Will I have to spank all of you?"

They chuckled and behaved properly after his admonition. They tuned haphazardly after the break in the rehearsal and again Jerry chastised them, "Ladies and gentlemen, please tune carefully. If you want to play out of tune, please do so at home."

The young conductor's gestures were very flamboyant and difficult to follow. That upset Jerry. I was standing next to him as he was putting his violin in the case after the rehearsal. He asked me to accompany him backstage because he wanted to speak with the conductor and thought I would enjoy the conversation. When we arrived at the conductor's dressing room, Jerry asked me to wait outside the door and eavesdrop. He knocked on the door. When the conductor opened it Jerry said, smiling, "Maestro, may I speak with you?" He entered the room and left the door ajar.

In a soft and pleasant manner Jerry said, "Maestro, welcome to Brussels. I know that you are young and inexperienced. When you become famous you can do whatever you like, but you are not Leonard Bernstein yet and we need a downbeat!"

The conductor was stunned and didn't even respond.

Jerry continued, "Have a pleasant evening Maestro, I'm looking forward to tomorrow's rehearsal."

He turned left the dressing room and closed the door.

As we were driving home Jerry said, "I've had a great day! I was able to reprimand the orchestra twice and lecture the conductor."

Hong Kong Philharmonic

Conducting Their First Pops Concert

My guest conducting in Hong Kong led to an affiliation with the Chinese people that eventually resulted in the participation of Chinese pianists and jurors in the Cliburn Competition and the Fort Worth Chamber Orchestra's tour of the People's Republic of China. The initial concert was with the Pan Asian Symphony. (Mary Alice joined me for that concert, after which we had a brief tour of Japan.)

The result of that initial engagement led to several performances with the Hong Kong Philharmonic, a very good orchestra comprising Chinese, British, and American musicians. These concerts subsequently led to my association with the PRC.

One of the performances was presented in the Hong Kong Coliseum, which could seat several thousand concertgoers. It was the first Pops concert by the Hong Kong Philharmonic. The theme was "A Space Odyssey" and included the music from Holst's *The Planets*; *Star Wars*; *2001, A Space Odyssey*; *Star Trek*; and *Superman*. For *2001, A Space Odyssey*; *Planets*; and *Star Wars* I designed lighting effects, lasers (graphic and beams), pyro techniques, and other sound effects. For *Superman* the only prop or stage effect that we used was a red telephone booth set on stage right. I made my stage entrance for the opening of the second half from the booth. Neither the orchestra nor I wore any special costumes, and I conducted the entire concert wearing a black tuxedo.

The Associated Press published a flattering international review. Here is an excerpt of the review that referred to the suite from *Superman*:

"Maestro John Giordano made his entrance for the second half of the concert by stepping out of a phone booth as if he were a mild-mannered conductor, magically changing to a super conductor and led a reading of the music from Superman with great energy."

Two weeks later I received a notice from the legal department of MGM that they were filing a lawsuit against me for impersonating Superman. The same evening Mary Alice and I attended a dinner at the Kimbell Art Museum. Stanley Marcus (Neiman Marcus), a marketing master, was seated at our table. One of the other guests at our table had read the Associated Press review and teased me. I protested, "I did not wear a costume."

One of our tablemates chimed in, "Right! We all know you and wouldn't put it past you to do that!"

"You're not the only one who thinks so," I told them. "I received a letter today from MGM suing me for impersonating Superman. I didn't do it, but I know that it will cause a lot of problems."

Stanley Marcus interjected, "I only have one question: did they spell your name right?"

Phillippines (Manila)

I was invited to conduct the Philippines Philharmonic in Manila on January 19, 1982. The date immediately followed a performance I had with the Hong Kong Philharmonic. I was scheduled to be in Manila for one week, with rehearsals beginning the day after I arrived. I was fortunate to get a flight to Manila the next morning after my last concert in Hong Kong.

On the flight I became acquainted with the passenger seated next to me, a very nice Philippine physician. We chatted, and he seemed to be impressed when he learned that I had been invited to conduct the Hong Kong Philharmonic by Mrs. Marcos.

As we were beginning our descent to Manila, the flight attendant announced that prior to deplaning we should collect all our documents including the visa that was supposed to have been issued prior to the flight. I didn't have a visa and was anxious. I had no idea how I would handle the situation. The doctor comforted me. "Don't worry, you are the guest of the First Lady and I am certain that everything has been taken care of for your visit."

We landed and the plane taxied to the gate. A black limo pulled up to the foot of the plane's stairs. The limo driver and my host from the Philippines cultural department met me there, had my luggage removed from the cart before it entered the baggage area, and placed it in the trunk of the limo.

After leaving the airport we passed through the Cultural Center reclaimed from the sea by Marcos's executive order in 1966. Imelda Marcos, the First Lady, was the primary force behind the project. During the drive to the hotel we passed the site of the new Manila Film Center currently under construction and adjacent to the hotel. It was the location for the First Manila International Film Festival. (The center's construction was controversial, because the building collapsed at one point, killing scores of Philippines laborers who were working in twenty-four-hour shifts frantically trying to complete it in time for the festival.) As we passed the center, I observed thousands of laborers on scaffolding. My host informed me that the First Lady invited me to attend the opening. I declined explaining that I couldn't stay in Manila that long because I had to return to Fort Worth immediately after my concert. He explained, "You will be able to attend the opening because it will take place the evening before your concert."

"That's not possible, the construction is not finished and the concert is this Saturday."

"It will be ready," he insisted.

My invitation to the opening ceremony was waiting for me in my room. The dress code required women to wear long formal gowns and men to wear a barong Tagalog, formal shirts similar to Mexican wedding shirts. The only shop where one could purchase them was in our hotel's boutique, owned by Marcos.

The next morning, I went to buy my barong in the hotel shop and found myself standing in a long line consisting of film producers, directors, and actors from all over the world including

Franco Nero, Ben Kingsley, and Robert Duvall. I happened to be standing behind Gregory Peck, director of the Academy Awards, who was representing the US in the festival. We struck up a conversation regarding the event's dress code and concurred that it was a good source of income for Marcos, as the shirts were quite expensive.

My hotel room had a window overlooking the center's construction site. Every day dramatic progress took place. The building was completed in time for the Friday evening event with full landscaping, exotic flowers, and fully grown trees. I sat on one side of the First Lady and George Hamilton III, her frequent companion, on the other.

My concert and reception was the following evening. President and Mrs. Marcos were in attendance.

The morning after the concert I was picked up at the hotel by the same host and limo and taken to the airport. The limo drove directly on the tarmac to the plane's boarding stairs.

The entire experience was surreal. I have no official proof that I was in the Philippines: no passport stamp, no airplane ticket, nothing except my barong Tagalog, my invitation to the Film Festival opening, and the concert's program.

Italy

Milan

The Milan Chamber Orchestra is a leading chamber orchestra in Europe. I had the opportunity to conduct it a few times. I arrived in Milan for one of the engagements and was met by the orchestra's president of the board, a handsome, dashing gentleman elegantly dressed in beautifully custom-tailored clothes. He informed me that I had a couple of days unexpectedly free because the weekend rehearsals had been cancelled due to a public transportation strike. He invited me to spend the weekend at his home on Lake Como, one of the most beautiful areas in the world. Having only briefly visited Lake Como, it was an exciting opportunity for me to spend more time there, and I accepted his invitation.

He drove me to his home in his new Maserati. His home was one of the grandest villas in the hills surrounding the lake. He drove up his circular driveway and his uniformed butler met us at the front door.

During dinner, I asked, "I hope I'm not being rude, but what business are you in?"

"Not at all, I'm the publisher of the Communist newspaper in Milan."

Reggio Emelia, Teatro Municipale

Some of my conducting experiences in Reggio Emelia were ones to forget. The concert's venue was the historic Teatro Municipale. The legendary Arturo Toscanini was the music director of the Emelia-Romagna Orchestra for many years and brought the orchestra to international prominence.

There was a rock and roll concert the evening of my first rehearsal.

After the rehearsal, I absentmindedly left my scores on my music stand. As I was leaving the theater I realized what I had done and returned to the stage to retrieve them. The stage hands were removing the orchestra's chairs and music stands in preparation of setting the stage for the evening's performance. They hadn't removed mine yet.

There were very large speakers that were to be used for that evening placed across the front of the stage. I stepped over one of them, and as I did an enormously loud feedback emitted from it and knocked me unconscious. When I awoke, I was in the hospital with cotton in my ears to stop the flow of blood. It took a few hours before I regained my normal hearing. I was treated like a king during the rest of my time. A limousine transported me everywhere, including to the Milan airport for my flight to the US. They provided sumptuous meals for me and put fresh flowers daily in my dressing and hotel rooms.

My recommendation to all conductors: Don't step over large rock and roll speakers on stage but if you do, do it in Reggio Amelia.

El Salvador

José Serebrier, who had become a good friend after his stint as a juror in the 1977 Cliburn Competition, called and asked if I were available to guest conduct his orchestra in San Salvador, El Salvador. He said that the only stipulation was that the program and the soloist had been determined and printed and I would not be able to make any changes.

LEFT
Rehearsing with Lilian Rivas.
Author Collection.

The program included Bernstein's Candide Overture, Chopin's First Piano Concerto, and Beethoven's First Symphony, and concluded with Wagner's Prelude to Meistersinger. Fortunately, I knew all of the works well, and the soloist was one of the country's favorite pianists, Lilian Rivas, so I accepted the engagement.

El Salvador was in a period of extreme strife and there were daily armed demonstrations against the government. It was a dangerous time for tourists. Lilian and I were staying in the International Hilton, a five-star hotel protected by armed guards stationed around its perimeter. The property was enclosed by concertina wire and resembled a WWII prison camp. We were issued photo IDs that were checked at the gate of the hotel, lobby, and at all elevators. Armed guards were assigned to accompany Lilian and me wherever we went.

The concert hall in San Salvador is a beautiful, renovated nineteenth-century theater with superb acoustics. The only problem is there are no backstage dressing rooms for the orchestra and only one dressing room that must be shared by the conductor and soloist, making it necessary to don my tuxedo in my hotel room.

On the evening of the concert the orchestra's manager, the limo driver, and our armed guard arrived to pick us up at the hotel.

When Lilian and I arrived at the theater before the concert we went directly to our shared dressing room and opened the door. The room was filled with floral arrangements, including several sprays over six feet high. There were so many flowers in the room we couldn't enter. I asked the stage manager to remove them. Lilian was adored everywhere and had an enormous fan base in San Salvador. The plethora of flowers reflected their adoration.

Before making my first entrance to conduct the overture I heard the orchestra onstage laughing boisterously. When the stage manager opened the door for my entrance I saw that the stagehands had placed the flowers they removed from the dressing room across the entire stage in front of the orchestra. There were so many tall arrangements the audience could not see the orchestra, soloist, or conductor. I stopped, closed the door, and asked the stagehands to move the flowers to each side of the stage.

When I finally made my entrance the orchestra members traditionally stood continuously giggling. Instead of placing the flowers on each side of the stage they had placed them behind the orchestra. They completely covered the area but made a lovely backdrop. The orchestra performed the overture well and received an enthusiastic response.

Chopin's Piano Concerto in E minor is a difficult work to conduct, because soloists play it very freely, and the conductor must be flexible to precisely match the pianist's rhapsodic performance. Every phrase of the solo part demands great virtuosity, but after the opening orchestral section there is little for the orchestra to play except for sustained notes in the strings.

During one of the slow sections in which the strings play long sustained notes, I noticed that at least half of the string players were paying no attention whatsoever and, in fact, many seemed to be asleep. I became extremely anxious because a section that called for precision was imminent. I decided that I had to do something dramatic and not in character of that passage to get their attention, so I made a huge, upbeat gesture hoping that my exaggerated movement would get their attention. As I brought my right arm up in a large sweeping movement, the tip of my baton caught on the edge of the music rack and sailed at least fifteen feet into the air. The entire orchestra observed the baton's skyward flight, curious as to the location of its landing. However, as it came down I grabbed it and gave the downbeat precisely at the right time. The orchestra applauded by shuffling their feet in unison as they continued to play.

Lilian's performance was beautiful as usual and received an immediate standing ovation. The public demanded she play several encores.

After intermission, the program included Beethoven's First Symphony and ended with Wagner's Prelude to Meistersinger.

The orchestra was in great form, playing enthusiastically and precisely throughout the Beethoven first movement. Feeling comfortable and confident, I started the second movement. After a few measures I noticed that members of the orchestra were distracted and looking at the audience. They continued to play but were constantly glancing in that direction. It was disconcerting, and I imagined several things that could have been happening: someone in the audience becoming ill or revolutionary demonstrators entering the building. Several other things crossed my mind, but I continued to conduct.

Whatever was happening became so distracting that I couldn't resist looking over my right shoulder. There, behind the audience stood a man, unkempt and wearing filthy coveralls. He had opened one of the lobby doors and was backlit by the lobby lights. He closed the door and proceeded to walk down the outside aisle in plain view of the entire audience. He continued to walk down the aisle and ascended the stairs onto the stage. By this time, he had garnered the full attention of the entire audience as well as the musicians. Everyone in the hall was restless.

He stopped at the bass section, nodded, waved to them, and shook hands with the principal. He repeated that routine throughout most of the string section and seemed to be completely oblivious to the fact that we were performing. He continued, casually strolling through the cello and viola sections, greeting individuals and shaking hands. The orchestra continued to play as if he were not there. He made his way to the stage door behind the orchestra, opened it, gave one last wave, and left.

Everything settled back to normal until we began playing the return of the principal theme, close to the end of the movement. The stage door opened, the same man reappeared and reversed his actions. He strolled back through the orchestra waving goodbye to them and left the stage, then casually walked up an aisle to the lobby. We completed the symphony with no further incident and performed the Wagner.

The performance was a great success. During the after-concert reception, not an orchestra member, stagehand, staff person, or audience member explained the man's presence, revealed who he was, or even mentioned the incident. To this day I still have no idea who he was or what he was doing there.

Spain

Bilbao

Bilbao is the capitol of the Spanish Basque region, which citizens consider to be a separate country. The flight from Madrid to Bilbao is an international flight, and it's necessary to go through customs. Even though residents of the region all speak Spanish, Basque is the only language spoken everywhere, including in movie theaters and on TV. Basque is completely different from the other languages of Europe. In fact, it's not related to any other known language. (There is a legend that Noah's Ark landed in the mountains of the Basque country; his descendants settled there; and Basque was their language.)

It was raining nonstop when I arrived in Bilbao. I had an all-weather trench coat but no hat, so I bought a Spanish beret. When I met the Bilbao Symphony Executive Director, he strongly suggested that I not wear the beret because it was a symbol of the Basque terrorists who were active at the time, and I might be mistaken for one. It was either take the risk of wearing it, be mistaken for a terrorist, and get shot by the police, or not wear it and end up in the hospital with the flu. I chose to wear the beret and somehow managed to evade being shot by the police.

The language barrier made it difficult to conduct rehearsals. However, several members of the wind section and the concertmaster spoke English and several others spoke French, including one of the violinists, so between speaking English and French I could make myself understood.

The concerts in Bilbao took place on Tuesdays and there were no rehearsals on weekends. There was nothing to do with one's spare time, neither going to movies nor watching TV: they were in the Basque language with no subtitles.

Bilbao is one of the sailing centers of Europe. One of the America's Cup winners is moored there. During my first visit, a French-speaking violinist approached me at a break and said that he had heard that I liked to sail. He told me that he had a physician friend who crewed on a large sailboat. He had informed him that I enjoyed sailing and had the weekend free. When the sailboat owner learned of my interest, he invited me to join the crew on Saturday. The violinist further explained that a major regatta was taking place on Saturday and might be enjoyable for me to see it. In describing the activity, he said it would be interesting because his friend's group was going "to watch" the regatta from their vessel. He used the wrong verb, regarde, when he should have said *participer* (to participate), in a regatta. He said that his friend, who didn't speak English, would pick me up at 6:00 Saturday morning and instructed me to wear warm clothing and suitable shoes. He explained that there was foul weather gear on the boat in case of rain.

Saturday arrived, the violinist's physician friend picked me up at the hotel at 6:00 a.m., and we drove to the marina. A group of about eight men were gathered at the docks, all wearing matching jackets with *Portu* embroidered on the back. They were conversing in Basque and politely interrupted their conversation to introduce themselves to me. I still didn't have a clue as to exactly what was happening.

Eventually Pelo Bursurco, the yacht's owner, arrived. The yacht was named *Portu* after his steel pipe manufacturing company in Bilbao. He introduced himself in perfect English: "I am Pelo Bursurco. It is a pleasure to have you join us as my guest." He turned to the group, greeted them and said, "Good morning everyone! It's time to go before the tide goes out!" (The tide is extreme in that part of the world and can vary by several feet. The larger sailboats must be moored at least fifty yards from the docks making it necessary to take a skiff to reach them.) We boarded the skiff and motored to *Portu*, a beautiful eighty-foot, cutter-rigged vessel. Pelo said, "I'm very happy you can join us today. I understand that you are a superb sailor and we are short a crew member. I'd like for you to work the foredeck."

(The foredeck crew, among other duties, mans the spinnaker. Its pole on a boat that large is very difficult and unwieldy to set, raise, and lower.)

"That's an exaggeration. I'm an okay sailor but never have crewed on a boat this large before, especially the foredeck, and I don't speak the language at all!"

"You are being modest. Just watch me. When my thumb points up, you raise the spinnaker; when down, lower it. Besides there will be two others with you, so simply follow their lead."

"I am very excited to be able to watch a major regatta from the vantage point of the sea."

"What? Watch the race? We are in the race! I hope you are aware that it is an overnight race, and we won't be back until Sunday evening. There is foul weather gear below. Find some that fits. It's cold this time of year. Wear it when you are on deck."

Though that came as quite a shock, I was thrilled to be a part of a crew on a large yacht. It was truly a once-in-a-lifetime experience. The comradery among the crew was amazing. It was composed of intelligent professionals from all walks of life.

After we left the harbor and were a few miles at sea, Pelo requested "Pedro, vino por favor!" (In Spanish, I'm certain for my benefit, assuming I spoke it. In any case "vino" is universally understood!) Pedro descended into the cabin, returned with bottles of a good Spanish red wine, and distributed it among the crew. "Pedro, musica por favor." Again, Pedro descended into the cabin and in a few moments the soothing sounds of the boat moving through the sea was accompanied by Mozart's Piano Concerto in A Major. I turned to Pelo and said, "This is great! I love it! But why did you play Mozart?"

"Only the purity of Mozart's music fits perfectly with the beauty of the sea," he answered.

"Do you know what I am doing here in Bilbao?" I asked him.

"I don't. I was told that a friend of Dr. Aduriz would be joining us."

"I'm conducting the Bilbao Symphony Orchestra on next week's concert."

"What? I don't believe it! I will be there; I am on the board of directors."

The experience was almost surreal. We raced to the beautiful city of San Sabastian and docked in the harbor. We won the race, and the other large yachts rafted up with us. We then enjoyed a progressive meal. Tapas and wine were served on one boat, the first course on another, the main course on *Portu*, and dessert on another. After dinner we felt a thump.

Pelo: "Friends—we must set sail immediately; the tide is going out!"

The evening sail back to Bilbao was magical: stars twinkling in the crystal-clear evening sky, lights from houses glistening throughout the mountains, the phosphorescence of our wake, the sound of the yacht gliding through the waves, and the refrains of Mozart. It was unbelievably beautiful.

I was fortunate to have conducted the Bilbao Symphony frequently and every time tried to arrange my schedule to add a few days to join Pelo and the crew of *Portu*.

Valladolid Train

I frequently conducted the Valladolid Symphony Orchestra. Each time, someone from the administration picked me up at the airport. The drive between Valladolid and the Madrid airport is more than one hundred miles and passes through several small towns. It was inconvenient for the orchestra's staff to make the trip if there was an alternative.

I learned that there was a direct nonstop train service from the Madrid airport to Valladolid, so I offered to take the train on my next engagement. They agreed and said that taking the train from the airport was easy and the trip was much faster. They cautioned me to be certain that when I purchased the ticket at the station in Madrid I buy a first-class ticket on the Express train (RENFE) and not the Direct line. One takes one hour, the other, several hours.

I bought the wrong ticket. Not only was the

ticket not for the Express Train, but it didn't even go to Valladolid at all. When I boarded the train, I asked the conductor if it stopped in Valladolid. He confirmed that it did. Perhaps it did, but it also was scheduled a stop at every village in Spain!

Several hours after the time I was supposed to have been met at the Valladolid station, the train came to a halt in some remote village in the mountains. It was late in the evening. Everyone, including the official personnel deboarded, the lights were turned off, and the doors locked. The small platform next to the tracks only contained a couple of benches and a dim street light; there was no station. I stopped several people as they were leaving the train, hoping to glean any information that might help, but none spoke English. Those who understood my questions replied very fast and unintelligibly. I decided to wait until the next train arrived and get off at the first place that looked like a city, no matter where it was. I had to try to call the Valladolid Orchestra.

A train finally arrived after what seemed to be an eternity. I asked the conductor if it stopped in Valladolid. He replied yes and told me it made several other stops as well. I boarded and anxiously looked at every sign indicating the town in which the train stopped. It eventually arrived in Valladolid. A man from the orchestra's office was waiting for me on the platform. He told me that members of the staff had been taking turns over several hours and met every train from the Madrid airport. Also, the orchestra had started an investigation tracking me since my flight from DFW. They didn't know if I had forgotten the engagement, the flight had been cancelled, I had been kidnapped, or some other dire possibility had occurred.

From then on, they insisted on meeting me at the airport.

East Texas Symphony Orchestra

I agreed to act as a temporary music director of the East Texas Symphony during the 1984-85 season to help them find a new conductor. I recommended that they hold a fund-raising Pops concert gala during the season and persuaded Doc Severinsen, a close friend, to perform as the guest artist at a reduced fee.

I was visiting with one of their patrons, a wealthy bank owner, during the intermission of Doc's rehearsal with the orchestra. The president of the association and chairman of the Gala passed by our table. She appeared to be very anxious. "You seem to be very upset, Betty, what's the matter?" I asked. "I don't know what to do. The Mazda dealer has donated a Miata for our raffle and we've only sold a couple of tickets." "How much are they?" I asked. "$100 apiece." I turned to the banker: "I really need a new car and always wanted a Miata. If you will buy twenty tickets, I'll buy one, and together we will have almost all of the tickets. We can't lose, so when we win I'll reimburse your $2,000. I'll have a new car and you won't be out a penny." "Sure, that's a great idea," he said. I called Mary Alice, explained everything, and told her that I would be driving home in a new Miata.

They held the raffle at the Gala dinner following the concert. Between the banker and me we had twenty-three out of twenty-five tickets. When it was time to draw the ticket for the car the banker turned to me and told me to be ready to pick up my new car. The card was pulled out of the bowl. True to form—a gentleman who had purchased one ticket won!

Prairie Portrait

We had performed several times with Don Edwards, a cowboy balladeer who had garnered much acclaim throughout the US singing ballads principally derived from Celtic songs. He even had a cameo singing role in the film *The Horse Whisperer.* During one concert we featured Don and cowboy poet Waddie Mitchell. It was extremely successful, and subsequently the recording company, EMC, decided that a recording of it should be made. The recording featured Don and Waddie's narration of several of his poems and several orchestral works, some of which Phil Kelly arranged.

The Cowboy Hall of Fame selected the recording as that year's best recording of Cowboy music. We titled the recording "Prairie Portrait," a movement of one of my compositions originally composed for a documentary film *Milepost 407: A West Texas Story*. We placed it as the last cut on the CD, and the theme was inserted as background music to several of Waddie's poems.

The CD received great reviews. One particularly complimentary review from EMC said:

> *I love cowboy music and orchestral music, but the concept of putting these very different styles together was beyond my comprehension. I'm so glad I bought it and I find myself listening often. The haunting words, the beautiful sounds from the orchestra, Don's voice and Waddie's wistful recitations all come together beautifully in this collection. I recommend this to anyone who enjoys taking a bit of a chance in exploring something different. . . . It's a wonderful production in every way.*

ABOVE
With Kareem Abdul-Jabbar at the Western Heritage Awards in 2001. The FWCO won the award for Outstanding Traditional Western Album.
Author Collection.

SIX

Bass Hall

The Bass Hall Seed is Planted

My early musical development during the 1950s included learning to play jazz. It had an important influence on the creation of Fort Worth's Bass Performance Hall twenty years later.

When I was in high school I wanted to improve my jazz playing. I often played in jam sessions in the Zanzibar Club, an after-hours jazz club on East Rosedale. That's where I met Ornette Coleman, a young jazz saxophonist who also was developing his playing. As two young saxophonists with the same goal we became friends. I veered from that goal after a few years, unlike Ornette, who eventually had a major impact on the world of avant-garde jazz. We rekindled our friendship twenty years later in a rather bizarre situation. That event had an impact on the creation of Bass Hall.

In the 1970s many people were experimenting with countercultures such as Werner Erhard's EST, the Alexander Technique, etc. Tony Vann, an active figure in Fort Worth arts and a proponent of the counterculture movement, arranged for a tour of the Fort Worth Chamber Orchestra in Puerto Vallarta. He was an interesting man who embraced a wide scope of creative activities.

Tony invited me to attend a gathering of several interesting, creative, and intelligent people at the Blackstone Hotel in downtown Fort Worth. The group consisted of avant-garde proponents in various disciplines including Buckminster Fuller, John Allen, Edward Bass, and my old friend Ornette Coleman.

John Allen assembled the group to discuss future projects. He was the founder and CEO of an organization called Global Ecotechnics Corporation. Under his direction Ecotecnics built a Hotel in Katmandu, conducted a project to experiment with developing natural grasslands in Australia on which to raise cattle, and conducted a scientific study of the Amazon River in a converted Chinese junk. The topics of this meeting were his two future projects: the construction of Caravan of Dreams in Fort Worth and the creation of Biosphere II.

Biosphere II was named *Biosphere II* because it was meant to be the second fully self-sufficient biosphere after the Earth itself. Securing funding for the project came primarily from the venture's financial partner, Ed Bass, who many years later successfully led the fundraising campaign for the creation of Bass Hall.

During the evening, it became clear that Ed was a brilliant visionary. He and I had a conversation in which he revealed his plans for the revitalization of downtown Fort Worth. It included the construction of a major hotel and the Caravan of Dreams, a jazz club, and a small performing arts center.

I told him of our desperate need for a first-rate concert hall and how it could be the crowning jewel of the transformation of downtown Fort Worth.

ABOVE
Waiting to enter the stage before a FWSO concert in the Tarrant County College theater. Author Collection.

I explained how a fine concert hall could serve the FWSO, the Van Cliburn International Piano Competition, the opera, and the ballet, and would attract major artists and musical entities of every style. An architecturally significant building could stand alongside a world-famous structure like the Kimbell Art Museum as a symbol of the importance of Fort Worth's performing arts, comparable to its already internationally famous venues for the visual arts.

Ed Bass engaged the Fort Worth Symphony to perform Ornette Coleman's original version of "Skies of America," featuring his band Prime Time, to celebrate its grand opening. The unattractive ambiance and poor acoustics of the JFK Theater were evident in that performance. Thus the seed for Bass Hall was planted.

The performance of "Skies of America" in the Tarrant County Convention Center was received with very mixed reaction; some thought that it was a work of genius but most in attendance declared that it was loud and ugly.

The FWSO performance was the second; the first was with the London Symphony in 1972. Since Ornette was not a trained musician, his notation was impossible to decipher unless one understood free jazz and was familiar with his style. I made the piece work because I have been familiar with Ornette's theory since I was a high school student and understood what he was trying to accomplish. I explained how the piece worked to the orchestra and even sang and created gestures to dictate entrances of the orchestra's various sections.

Soon after its construction I had an electronic music studio in Caravan of Dreams and developed a closer friendship with Ed. I brought up the subject of a need for a proper performing arts venue in the city as frequently as possible, and emphasized how important it would be in the development of downtown Fort Worth. I pointed out the impact that prominent theaters and concert halls had on their cities and countries, like Carnegie Hall and Lincoln Center in New York, Musikverein in Vienna, Concertgebouw in Amsterdam, and Palacio de Bellas Artes in Mexico City. He agreed that we needed a proper performing facility, but I don't know how convinced he was of its importance. He put aside the notion of a concert hall to join his family in the development of the downtown area.

Skies of America

After the performance of "Skies" in the Tarrant County Convention Center, I told Ornette that "Skies" could be an exciting work for symphony orchestra performances if it were arranged and notated in a traditional manner, thus making it practical to play without requiring a conductor who understood his abstract philosophy of Harmolodics. Ornette was extremely creative and forward thinking, and I thought that the concept of "Skies" was brilliant and had great possibilities. He agreed and asked me to orchestrate and arrange it to make it playable with a minimal amount of rehearsal time.

I created a new version by working closely with Ornette for more than a year.

This is a transcription of my explanation of our procedure during a BBC radio interview:

"For the most part the notation is traditional. But I also used aleatoric techniques including hand signals, to help the piece reflect Ornette's free style of improvisation. I familiarized myself with his concept of melody, counterpoint, and freedom of rhythm, and then transformed it to traditional notation. It still is Ornette's composition though, in every sense.

"Ornette would say something like: 'I want this section to sound like a thunderstorm over the Grand Canyon.' Or: 'This should be a pastoral setting of the skies over the grasslands of Texas.'

"I then would write the section using standard notation of his thematic material, make a synthesized midi version, and either play it on the phone for him or in person during one of my visits to NYC. Together we fine-tuned the sections to reflect his concepts."

The premier performance took place at the Verona, Italy, Jazz Festival and was an overwhelming success. That performance led to others in several European cities including Reggio Emilia, Zurich, and London.

The work received the Duke Ellington Award in Washington, DC, for most creative composition of the season. A few years later the New York Philharmonic played the piece in a NYC jazz festival. "Skies" was an enjoyable and artistically fulfilling experience.

The Evolution of Bass Hall

Sid Richardson Foundation and Val Wilkie

A major factor of the Fort Worth Symphony's success was the support we received from foundations based in Fort Worth. The Richardson Foundation provided key support and was instrumental in paving the way for other foundations. Val Wilkie was its director during my tenure with the symphony.

Val was steadfast in his belief that the appreciation of classical music is mandatory for a complete and well-rounded education. He understood that a fine symphony orchestra is critical to the fabric of any community and encouraged others to appreciate its value. His significant presence and respect from everyone had an important impact on our success.

The First Attempt

In 1974, Anne and Robert Bass had just returned to Fort Worth after Robert had graduated from the Stanford Graduate School of Business. They attended a FWSO concert and came backstage afterwards. Bob was extremely effusive with his compliments to the orchestra. However, he detested the cosmetic stage and awful acoustics, and said that something had to be done to correct the situation. Soon afterward he and I met again to discuss the possibility of finding a better venue for concerts. One of the facilities we considered was the historic Will Rogers Auditorium, located in the Arts District near the Kimbell and

BELOW
Rehearsal of my version of "Skies of America" with the Verona, Italy Jazz Festival, Symphony Orchestra, and Ornette Coleman. Author Collection.

Amon Carter Museums, the Museum of Science and History, and Casa Mañana Theater. Bob subsequently funded a study by Jaffe Holden Acoustics to ascertain if any of the facilities in the city could be renovated to have proper acoustics and provide an environment for symphonic music and the other performing arts. The results of the study revealed that, other than building a new facility, Will Rogers Auditorium had the best potential. They determined that the current venue was hopeless but could be modestly improved with their unique sound reinforcement system.

Bob hired the Martin Growald architectural firm to create a preliminary design for renovation of Will Rogers and construct a scale model. We decided that the existing historical Art Deco façade should not be changed.

Bob's concept for the success of the project was that the Growald design could be used to help convince the city to float a bond issue for partial city funding. He also thought that matching private funding could be raised to supplement public funds.

When Bob presented the idea to his family, they rejected the concept and stated that any new performance facility should be in the downtown area.

The Second Attempt

Anne Hendricks Bass, the former Mrs. Sid R. Bass, was a major supporter of the Fort Worth Ballet as well as the Symphony. We knew that the only way we could build a superb ballet company and orchestra was to employ dancers and musicians on a full-time basis, rehearsing and performing daily. That is the only way great and precise performances can be developed. We formulated a plan in which the Fort Worth Chamber Orchestra, supplemented by musicians on an as-needed basis, could perform for the ballet as well as serve the community in a multitude of ways—educational opportunities, audience development, and just bringing great music to every segment of the community.

The need for an appropriate performing venue for both organizations became even more critical. Anne, with Val Wilkie's support, convinced the Bass family of the need for a proper performance facility. They formed a committee led by Woody Woodward, a former executive with American Airlines who recently had been hired by the Bass company, and charged him to chair a committee and investigate several multipurpose performing venues throughout the United States and some in Europe to determine if an appropriate theater could reasonably be built.

They decided that I would work closely with the committee and report to them which concert halls where I conducted would be good patterns for our hall. That included venues like the pre-renovated Carnegie Hall and Concertgebouw in Amsterdam.

I conducted the Colorado Springs Symphony and was extremely impressed with the quality of their new hall's acoustical properties and outstanding architectural design. Russell Johnson, the founder of Artec Consultants, the company that designed the McDermott Concert Hall, Meyerson Symphony Center, in Dallas, designed it. I reported my observations to Woody. The Bass family subsequently engaged Johnson to conduct a study to determine location, size, and cost of the project. He submitted a two-hundred-million-dollar proposal that included a two-thousand-seat concert hall, an eight-hundred-seat concert hall, a theater, and an opera house. When the Basses explained to him that they were thinking more in the thirty million range for one multipurpose facility, he said that he would not be interested in such a small project because the anticipated growth and potential future demographics of Fort Worth called for a Lincoln Center-type facility. They dropped the matter.

The Third Attempt

The third attempt was to win another bond election to help fund renovations of the Will Rogers

Auditorium. It almost succeeded, but there was steep opposition because its detractors ridiculously claimed that it would eliminate another bill on the docket: granting firemen and police a raise. Of course they deserved higher salaries, but that issue would have had no effect on our project. The detractors' campaign emphasized the notion that the arts were frivolous and not necessary or critical to our society.

Ann Koonsman was instrumental in promoting the project, including the Bond Issue. She and I were extremely disappointed with the results. We waited for the voting results in front of Will Rogers with a group of supporters, listening to the progress on the radio, and were certain that the issue would be successful. We lost by a very small margin.

Success! The Nancy Lee and Perry R. Bass Hall

The credit for the existence of Bass Hall goes to Ed Bass. Ed is a rare individual who has dedicated his life to the development of Fort Worth. He is brilliant and would be successful in any endeavor he decided to undertake. He is a sensitive gentleman who understands the value of the arts in our society and has done everything in his power to see that Fort Worth is recognized throughout the world as a city that embraces the fine arts and proudly includes it in the fabric of the community.

Ann Koonsman and I, and the many others who had fought for a suitable performance venue for the FWSO and for all the performing arts in Fort Worth, were finally rewarded in 1989, when Ed attended a concert performance of the Cliburn finalists with the FWSO, which took place in the architecturally, acoustically terrible JFK Theater. As with every Cliburn's final phase since it was established in 1962, dignitaries from around the globe were in attendance, including heads of state, royalty, leading musicians, New York managers, major business leaders in the US, Europe, and Asia, major political leaders, celebrities, etc.

Ed was acquainted with most of the dignitaries in attendance. They all were highly complimentary of the competition, but many questioned the quality of the theater and were puzzled that there was nothing better in Fort Worth to highlight an international event of the competition's caliber and stature.

This convinced Ed of the importance of having a major arts venue of the highest quality possible, and he was dedicated to see that Bass Hall came to fruition.

Ed insisted that every aspect of Bass Hall be functional and properly accommodate everyone who used the hall: stagehands, technicians, and opera and ballet directors.

I had input when it came to musicians' areas, dressing rooms, and design. Ed requested that I design the musicians' lounge areas and locker sizes. I suggested that the musicians be included in the planning of all areas that pertained to their usage. He concurred, and the lounge area was designed and constructed as the musicians requested.

In a similar incident, Ed called one day and asked if I had any suggestions regarding the design of the dressing rooms. I suggested that a few "star" dressing rooms have double doors allowing easy access for moving grand pianos in and out of the rooms without disassembling the pianos. The double doors have proved to be invaluable and have saved labor and piano tuning costs. (When a piano is disassembled for moving it requires tuning.) During the Cliburn Competition, the warm-up pianos are placed in the dressing rooms to give the competitors an opportunity to warm up on a concert instrument similar to that on which they will perform. Also, FWSO guest artists and recitalists would have a warm-up grand piano in their dressing rooms.

One of Ed's more unique requests proved to be a difficult challenge. He asked me to create

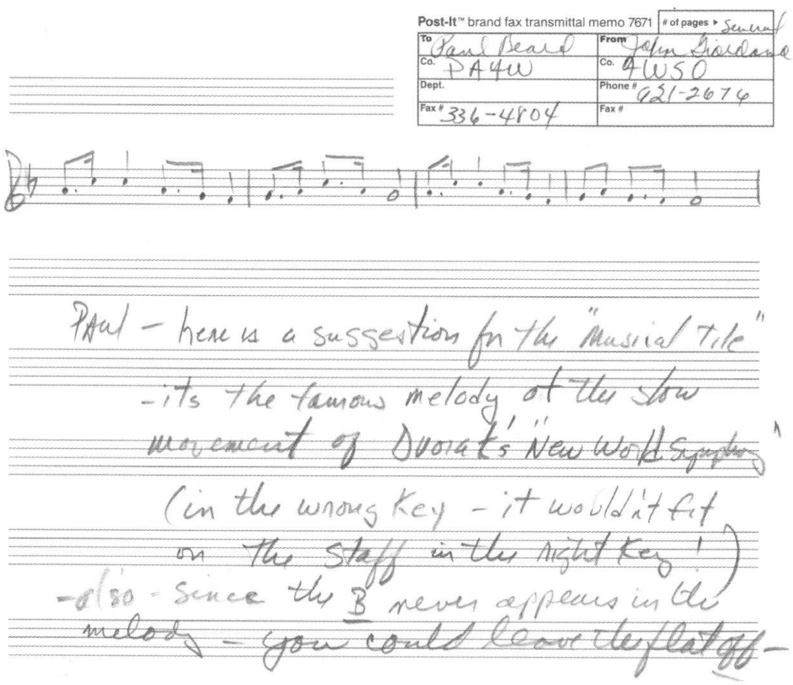

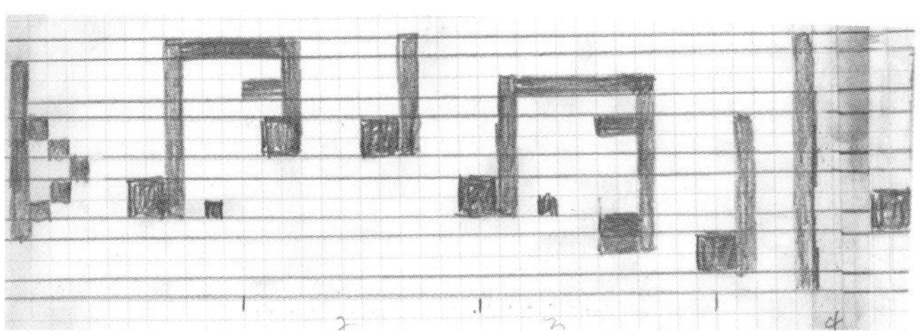

ABOVE (TOP)
Traditional music manuscript for the murals. Author Collection.

ABOVE
Bass Hall restroom murals on graph paper. Author Collection.

décor for the restroom walls from traditional musical notation. Ed wanted something whimsical and unique.

I asked if it would be a mural. He explained that it would not and my design had to be made from one-inch black and white porcelain tiles that would be used on the walls.

Lines and spaces of treble and bass clefs were simple to create with one-inch black and white tile, but creating a design that would work for the notes was a different issue. I used graph paper and drafted several designs. I decided that an extant recognizable melody would be much more interesting than a decorative and random meaningless placement of notes. It was challenging because accidentals (sharps and flats) would almost be impossible to create out of one-inch tiles. I thought that it would be fun to use a melody that would be recognizable by anyone who could read music and still be an attractive musical design for anyone who didn't. After much research and reflection on the design, I chose the melody from the slow movement of the Dvorak New World Symphony, which Dvorak took from the Negro spiritual "Goin' Home." It fit the bill perfectly: it didn't have any accidentals, was a famous folk song, and was the melody of a symphonic masterpiece.

Ed loved the idea and instructed the contractors to use my charted "tile music" design of the piece in treble clef in the ladies' restrooms and in bass clef in the men's. A few months after I retired from the FWSO, a docent was conducting a tour of Bass Hall and when showing the restrooms, she said, "There is an interesting story regarding the music on the walls. The former Maestro of the Fort Worth Symphony, John Giordano, made the design. Do any of you who read music recognize the melody?"

One lady responded: "I do. That is the Negro spiritual 'Goin' Home'! Did he choose that song because he was going to retire?"

During a planning meeting to determine the programming and concerts to celebrate the hall's opening, Ed suggested, "Why don't you play the

ABOVE (LEFT)
Frederica von Stade performing with the FWSO in the dedication concert for the opening of Bass Hall. Author Collection.

ABOVE (TOP)
Conducting Carmina Burana with the FWSO for the opening season of Bass Hall. Author Collection.

ABOVE
Ribbon cutting ceremony for the John Giordano piano wing in the Walsh Performing Arts Center, Ed Bass and Mary Dee Walsh. Author Collection.

LEFT
First rehearsal in Bass Hall. © Fort Worth Star-Telegram, 2000. Author Collection.

music that's on the restroom walls? The New World Symphony?"

Perhaps the most recognizable feature of Bass Hall is the angels adorning the front of the building. Ed requested that I meet with him and Márton Váró, the sculptor of the angels.

"John, you can be a lot of help," Ed said. "The angels will be playing herald trumpets, and I want them to be authentic. Do you know anything about ancient brass instruments?"

"A little," I said. "I'd be happy to research ancient trumpets, but since it is a work of art why not let Márton use his imagination?"

"It must be authentic, because a hundred years from now, if a musicologist looks at the trumpets, I want him to recognize that they're accurate."

Ed asked that I bring some photos of ancient herald trumpets to the meeting. We met, and I showed several to Márton and Ed. Márton was pleased that a reproduction like the one he envisioned was included, and his original sketch could be revised to use it. Ed insisted that the trumpets must be accurately proportionate as if they could be played. I found a treatise that included the proportions of the original instruments, and those are the ones Márton used.

A few days later Ed called again. "John, I need some more help on the trumpets. I found pictures of trumpet mouthpieces for Márton but he doesn't want to duplicate them for the sculptures because he is afraid that they will cover the angels' lips. The lips are extremely important to him because they represent the sensuality of music."

I replied, "Ed, as I suggested before, why not let Márton use his imagination?"

"No, I want them to be authentic," he insisted.

I explained that many different styles of brass instrument mouthpieces existed. I called a trumpet professor at the University of North Texas, Keith Johnson, whose doctoral dissertation was on ancient brass instruments. Keith let Márton borrow several brass mouthpieces, and Márton selected one that did not obscure the angels' lips.

As a result of this careful time and planning, the trumpets are so authentically reproduced to scale out of proper metal they could be played by a forty-eight-foot tall trumpeter. Perhaps that is why they are so notable today.

Van Faints at the Opening of Bass Hall

One of the concerts celebrating the opening of Bass Hall took place on May 16, 1998. Van was scheduled to perform Rachmaninov's Second Piano Concerto. Van had performed a solo recital as part of the celebration the night before. He also had attended every social function relating to the opening and was under a great deal of stress because of all the activities.

The rehearsal went extraordinarily well; Van was in top form and everything was splendid. The ensemble was precise, and the entrances were perfectly coordinated with the orchestra that was also in top form. We all eagerly awaited the historic performance that evening. In addition, Mrs. Mercedes Bass had organized an elegant reception to take place on stage immediately following the performance. The concert was a sellout, everyone eager to hear Van play Rach no. 2; his recording is the quintessential recording of the work.

We began the first movement, and when Van played the first three chords of his entrance, displaying the extraordinarily beautiful tone quality that was unique to him, the entire hall, orchestra and audience alike, could feel that something special was going to take place. The first movement was breathtaking: precise, emotional, and wonderfully expressive. The beautiful second movement was so moving that everyone on stage and in the audience were emotionally spent. I had relaxed to the point that I wasn't even looking at the score and hadn't turned several pages. The silent transition to the third movement set up its momentum perfectly.

Then everything fell apart. Van began to make errors in places where he never had before. I knew that he might be in trouble and began frantically turning pages to find a place to bring the orchestra in if the piece broke down. Suddenly there was a series of atonal descending crashes coming from the piano keyboard. Many members of the orchestra stopped playing and gasped. I turned and saw Van lying face down on the floor next to the bass side of the piano.

I immediately stopped the orchestra, turned, stepped off the podium, and knelt at his side. I reached down and put pressure on the side of his neck to ascertain if he had a pulse, fearing that he might have suffered a heart attack. Before I could even rise to my feet, the stage was filled with physicians who had come from the audience, led by Bobby Brown, one of the most well-known heart specialists in Fort Worth.

After assessing Van, Bobby looked up at me and said, "He did not have a heart attack, he fainted."

An ambulance had already been summoned, and within a few minutes, it arrived and workers carried Van out to the vehicle to race him to the emergency ward of Harris Hospital, which was only a few minutes away. As soon as Bobby told me that Van was going to be all right, I stepped to the front of the stage and announced: "Ladies and gentlemen, Van is going to be fine. The doctors told me that he fainted from stress along with heat exhaustion.

"You have just experienced the best performance you will ever hear of the first two movements of Rachmaninov's Second Piano Concerto, and I guarantee that you always will remember the opening concert of Bass Hall. Please give us a few moments to clear the stage and set up the tables for the reception."

During the reception that followed the concert we officially learned that Van had collapsed because of exhaustion and stress. After a couple of hours of observation, he was released and taken home.

As soon as the reception finished, around midnight, Mary Alice and I drove to Van's home to check on him. The security guard met us at the gate to his property. He told us that Van was home and invited us to go inside. We declined, explaining that we didn't want to disturb Van's rest from the ordeal. We called him from the car.

"Van, we are concerned about you. How are you?"

"I'm fine. I'm so embarrassed. I guess you will never ask me to perform with you again."

"Of course I will Van, as long as you begin with the last movement of Rach no. 2."

Dinner with Van and Mrs. George W. Bush, January 2013

Shortly before Van's death on February 27, 2013, he invited Mary Alice and me to join him for dinner at his home. His other guests for the evening were supposed to be President George W. Bush and his wife, Laura; however, President Bush had to decline at the last moment and was replaced by Mrs. Bush's best friend.

I sat between Mrs. Bush and her friend. It was a very poignant and memorable evening. Van related many memories of his close relationship with the Bush family, dating back to Mrs. and President George H. W. Bush, and recounted several stories about his experiences with world leaders such as every US president since 1958 and leaders from the Soviet Union and Russia like Nikita Khrushchev, Mikhail Gorbachev, and Vladimir Putin.

During dinner I asked Mrs. Bush if she would share her stressful and dramatic personal experience during and immediately after 9/11. She obliged and shared that she was with Senator Ted Kennedy in his office just prior to her scheduled address to the Senate Education Committee that morning. Days later at the Crawford Ranch with her immediate family, the secret service security received a warning of a possible impending attack on the ranch. Listening to her relate the dramatic story of that event was an extraordinarily unique experience.

Thank You, Cliburn Competition

In 2015 the Cliburn Competition gave a special concert and reception in my honor at Bass Hall to celebrate my association with the competition since 1973. The concert featured several prize-winning musicians during my tenure: Vladimir Viardo, André-Michel Schub, Simoni Pedroni, Jon Nakamatsu, Stanislav Ioudenitch, Joyce Yang, and Haochen Zhang. It was an extremely memorable and emotional event for me because of the many friends I was fortunate to have met through the Cliburn, especially the competitors, brilliant jurors, chairmen, and administrators with whom I worked. They all are very special to me. They all are people dedicated to helping young artists and promoting classical music throughout the world. My most inspirational affiliation was that with Van Cliburn. He was a magnificent artist and, most importantly, a wonderful individual who dedicated his life to bringing great music and love to us all.

Thank You, Fort Worth Symphony

The most humbling and fulfilling events that took place during my retirement in 2000 from the FWSO occurred during the send-off I received. They made me realize that my twenty-eight-year tenure was appreciated much more than I could have fathomed in my wildest imagination. The Tandy buildings were lit with the words "Bravo, John" and the gala held in my honor was overwhelming.

Mary Alice and our children were proud of the evident appreciation everyone had for me, and I was overcome with emotion, internally reminiscing about the special twenty-eight years of my affiliation with the FWSO. However, none of my accomplishments would have been possible without the support and understanding of the demands on my time from my wife and our children, especially from Mary Alice, who truly is the unsung hero.

Fort Worth is a unique and magnificent city. I doubt there is another city anywhere that embraces every aspect of the community as Fort Worth does. The city gives so much support to the superb visual and performing arts that are an integral part of its fabric. It was serendipitous that I happened to be at the right place at the right time to have an unforeseen and magical marriage with the Fort Worth Symphony. The number of people who made its success possible was astonishing. It would not have been possible without the working relationship I enjoyed with Ann Koonsman. We were a special team, both dedicated to achieving the same purpose.

The number of patrons who supported our efforts are too numerous to list, for fear of excluding someone. It includes the dedicated musicians, board of directors, patrons, and, most importantly, the citizens of this community who embrace, support, and are an indispensable part of the orchestra's success.

AFTERWORD

Music is a moral law. It gives a soul to the Universe, wings to the mind, flight to the imagination, a charm to sadness, and life to everything. It is the essence of order, and leads to all that is good and just and beautiful.

—PLATO

In 1966 I was preparing a paper for a graduate music history course on the value of great music and discovered this quote by Plato. It had a profound effect on me. I realized that the path I had chosen to follow is a truth known and understood for thousands of years. If I had any doubt that I had erred in dedicating my life to music and recreating some of man's most significant contributions, those fears were alleviated.

It was serendipitous that my family moved to Fort Worth, Texas, while I still was searching for a path to follow for my education and vocation. I always loved good music of many styles, and fortunately I grew up having been exposed to the finest classical and jazz artists. The quality of music in Fort Worth and Dallas is at an extraordinarily high level.

How fortunate that I met and performed with some of the most skilled and inspiring musicians in both classical music and jazz at a very young age. I had the opportunity to hear and perform with great artists in both disciplines. Exposure to their superb music making inspired me to work as hard as possible to attain their level. I was motivated by hearing classical artists like Van Cliburn and Isaac Stern in person and performing with jazz icons like Ella Fitzgerald and Stan Kenton.

Classical music became my priority when I was completely immersed in it during my developmental years as an undergraduate at TCU. Even after returning to the USA from having been exposed to the greatest music making in Europe, I had no idea that I would be fortunate enough to be affiliated with the Van Cliburn International Piano Competition so intimately for forty years and would fall in love and dedicate my life to the Fort Worth Symphony. Also, I attribute my transition into the world of conducting to the Fort Worth Youth Orchestra. It opened those doors to me, and for that I am eternally grateful.

This journal was conceived primarily to archive the development of the Fort Worth Symphony and Van Cliburn International Piano Competition during my tenure with those magnificent organizations.

ACKNOWLEDGMENTS

My tenure in Fort Worth with the Fort Worth Symphony, Van Cliburn International Piano Competition, the Youth Orchestra, and TCU was serendipitous. My family and I fell in love with a fabulous city, one replete with kind, generous, and caring citizens who love and support its extraordinary arts. We were received amazingly well by everyone along our magnificent journey.

I was encouraged by several friends and colleagues to document the growth of the organizations included in this manuscript, which I hope I achieved with what is an anecdotal history. This book barely touches the surface of my experiences with these critically significant organizations, not to mention my personal ones.

My gratitude initially goes to my mother and father, who supported all of my musical aspirations and first encouraged me to appreciate many varieties of high-quality music, including opera and symphonic music. My cousin and godfather, Dominic Guzzetta, who played jazz saxophone to fund his education through his PhD studies, inspired me to follow his example and pursue higher education utilizing music to realize those goals.

I am grateful to my Birdville High School band director, William Bohannon, who gave me the opportunity to be his assistant director and organize the school's first jazz ensemble, and to the talented high school musicians, Ronnie Martin and Charlie Pearson, who convinced me to attend TCU and encouraged me to major in music and continue to develop my love and appreciation for great music of all styles. The composer-arranger Lew Gillis convinced me to begin my formal education at TCU. His compelling recruitment was an important element in my decision-making.

My gratitude includes the "Big Bands" of Ted Weems, Hal McIntyre, and Stan Kenton. They presented opportunities for me to work with the superb musicians in their ensembles and perform with important artists such as Ella Fitzgerald, Mel Tormé, Tony Bennett, the Four Freshmen, and the High-Lows. These led to opportunities for me to play in "jam sessions" with such sensational jazz artists as Al Hirt, Cannonball Adderly, Ellis Marcellis, Bobby "Butter" Burgess, and Bud Shank. My experiences with those outstanding musicians proved to be critically important to my career in conducting because of the example they set through their brilliant artistry, dedication to improving their musical skills, and their professionalism. These components are applicable to all styles and positions in music

My education at TCU was unique. The faculty and music administration were dedicated to supporting every student's musical development and doing all they could to help them succeed. I am appreciative for having had the privilege to study with TCU's talented and dedicated faculty, especially Dr. Ralph Guenther and Dr. Michael Winesanker. Director of Bands James "Prof" Jacobsen afforded me the rare opportunity to organize and lead the TCU Jazz Band and conduct the concert band. In graduate school Prof supported all of my efforts in performing, conducting, composition, and arranging.

The faculty of the Royal Conservatory of Music in Brussels, Belgium, demanded a resolute work ethic, and my private saxophone professor, François Daneels, was an exceptional teacher and a performer of the highest rank. He was inspirational and conveyed a rare insight into the meaning and structure of classical music, not limited to the saxophone repertory. He also was a fine orchestra conductor and insisted that his students adhere to the comprehensive musical analysis necessary for conducting.

Ezra Rachlin gave me the first opportunity to conduct a symphony orchestra, the Youth Orchestra of Greater Fort Worth. His conducting lessons were inspirational and impressed upon me the importance of learning every aspect of the music I would conduct. I am grateful to Betty Utter for having led the group of dedicated music lovers who established the Youth

Orchestra, and for her collaboration as its executive director with me. The founders motivated the creation of a performing entity that always has been composed of brilliant and talented young musicians. The YO board of directors and support groups have worked tirelessly since its inception to assure its continuous success and financial support

A symphony orchestra is the heartbeat of the performing musical arts in a community. It was serendipitous that my appointment as music director of the FWSO was made when the community was on the brink of developing an appreciation of symphonic music. It was a unique period in Fort Worth's history, one during which some of its most influential and hardworking leaders emerged. They supported my artistic aspirations and were willing to provide Ann Koonsman, the orchestra's remarkable executive director, with the financial support she needed to establish the administrative environment necessary for our success. Her guidance, leadership, and willingness to collaborate with me were exceptional. We were blessed with having boards of directors led by chairmen who worked tirelessly for untold number of hours to help us realize our goals. My deep gratitude goes to Mercedes Bass, with whom I had the pleasure to work and who is the current chairman of the board, for her tireless support. Her love of classical music and determination to propel the FWSO to take its place among the legendary orchestras of the world is incomparable.

I am fortunate to have been given the opportunity to work with the extraordinary musicians of the FWSO. Their artistry, service, passion for great music, enthusiasm, devotion to the orchestra, and their determination to produce the highest level of music making possible is remarkable. They were the foundation of the success we enjoyed.

The Van Cliburn International Piano Competition has always strived to create an organization that encourages and promotes the careers of young artists. Since its inception, the competition has been a major force in the development of some of the finest pianists in the world, and always has reflected the passion and integrity of its namesake, Van Cliburn. In addition to pursuing its primary goal of supporting young artists, it has promoted classical music locally, nationally, and internationally. Working with Martha Hyder was a unique experience. She set the tone for the competition to become the most important piano competition in the world. I am grateful to her for her faithfulness and support in all of my artistic endeavors. Every board chairman with whom I worked was passionate about advancing and reaching the Cliburn's goals.

The superb performers, teachers, impresarios, critics, and composers in the annals of classical music who served on the juries I chaired were exceptionally cooperative and helpful. I especially appreciate the opportunity to have worked since 2001 with Veda Kaplinsky, one of the Cliburn's most qualified and brilliant jurors. Veda is one of the world's premier piano professors with whom I share the same philosophy of music making. She offered superb advice and her suggestions, including engaging jurors of knowledge and integrity and recruiting the competitors, was critical. I had the good fortune to collaborate with superb executive directors and presidents, especially Andrew Rayburn, Alann Sampson, and Richard Rodzinski. Richard, one of the most brilliant, musically astute, and creative individuals I have known, worked tirelessly with me. He led the development of the Cliburn to great heights and implemented new technology that helped realize the Cliburn's lofty goals while heeding the noble value of great classical music represented by our namesake, Van Cliburn.

My twelve-year affiliation with the Corpus Christi Symphony Orchestra also was an artistically rewarding experience. The orchestra musicians recreated great music on an exceptionally high level and were devoted to delivering meaningful and exciting performances. I appreciate the support and determination of the orchestra's board of directors, led by outstanding presidents who assured the community that symphonic music would flourish. I want to thank Raymond Rodriguez for his support and assistance in engaging internationally important artists. My special recognition goes to the intelligent, efficient, and hardworking Debi Miller, who continuously supported my efforts and successfully led the board of directors to assure that classical symphonic music continued to thrive in Corpus Christi.

Many have helped in the creation of this manuscript. Especially Molly Spain for her expert advice in its editing, along with the staff of the TCU Press. Maggie Estes, director of communication for the Van Cliburn Competition, was invaluable in helping me select many photographs pertaining to the Van Cliburn Competition and in her meticulous reading of this manuscript.

Shield Collins (Buddy) Bray, a brilliant, articulate, efficient, creative, ethical, and outstanding individual, has remained a great friend and supporter since his affiliation with the FWSO in 1986 and the Cliburn Competition for over fifteen years. He assisted me in the selection of photographs for the book and served as an expert reader of the manuscript.

My special gratitude goes to Richard Gipson for his friendship, advice, encouragement, and sharing his knowledge and expertise. Richard also served as an expert reader of the manuscript.

I am grateful to the Fort Worth Symphony Orchestra, Van Cliburn Foundation, Fort Worth Youth Orchestra, Corpus Christi Symphony Orchestra, TCU, and the *Fort Worth Star-Telegram* for the generous permission to use their material in this manuscript.

My deepest gratitude goes to my family. None has been more important in my life than my wife of sixty years, Mary Alice. She has stayed the course throughout our lives and supported my every endeavor, never complaining through any adversity we faced. She reared three wonderful children, assuring that they are honest, have high moral values, love and support each other, and strive to contribute as significantly as possible to society. Anne Lasko, Ellen Austin, and John, our children, received Mary Alice's guidance. They, in conjunction with their spouses, Steve Lasko, Stewart Austin, and Veronica Barron, are disseminating those values to their exceptional children. Anne and Steve's daughter, Natalie; Ellen and Stewart's daughters, Sarah and Elizabeth; and Veronica and John's son, John Charles and their daughter, Mia all embody the same critically important values.

INDEX